I LOVE YOU A THOUSAND WAYS

THE LEFTY FRIZZELL STORY

DAVID FRIZZELL

FOREWORD BY
MERLE HAGGARD

SANTA MONICA PRESS

LEFTY

PRAISE FOR
I LOVE YOU A THOUSAND WAYS

"I can't think of anyone better to tell the story of my friend, Lefty Frizzell, than his little brother, David, who is also one of the best country singers in his own right. The first song that I learned to sing when I started singing was 'Mom and Dad's Waltz.' He will always be one of the greatest country singers that ever lived. David, I love you and thank you for telling Lefty's story."
— LORETTA LYNN, country music legend

"*I Love You a Thousand Ways* is an extraordinary personal account of one of the most historic eras in country music. It's both a fascinating and detailed recollection of heartbreak and success, and a look at what it took to come from having nothing to having it all. The Lefty Frizzell influence can still be heard in today's music. Well done, David Frizzell! Movies are made of great stories such as this one." — CHARLIE CHASE, national television and radio host, *Crook & Chase*

"I'm reading your book, *I Love You a Thousand Ways*, and can honestly say that I can't put it down! I have never read a book based on the life of one of our entertainers that is stronger or more enjoyable than this. Sure, it has its super-sad moments, but that's what adds to the value! It's honest, and it's real! If I can help in any way in promoting this work of art, just let me know. You have my full endorsement and support. It will be an honor." — BILL MACK, Country Music Hall of Fame DJ and XM and SIRIUS radio host, *Willie's Place*

"A 'must-read' for true traditional country music fans—or for anyone who seeks a good read. David has offered up a warm and compelling tribute to his brother, Lefty. And it is a tribute to my good friend David for capturing the voice of simpler times, and for doing such a superlative job in putting into words a 'snapshot' of yesteryear. My dad and Lefty, in the days David so creatively reconstructs, were at the top of their respective games. They toured together, they traveled together, they ate together, they drank together, they lived together and, between them, at one point they dominated the charts together. This book is as close as you will ever get to being a fly on the wall of our earliest superstars when they didn't know they were, and when their everyday existence permeated their music, their lives, and their creative muses. You're gonna love it!"　　**—JETT WILLIAMS,**
country music star and daughter of Hank Williams, Sr.

"Thanks for the bio on Lefty. It reads well, David—and tells it like it really was. I enjoy talking about Lefty. He was a real good buddy. I just loved him so much. He's the kind of feller you'd want in your foxhole. You'd know you could count on him when the bullets started flying. We had many great times together."
—MEL TILLIS, country music legend

"The Frizzell family name is one of the most revered in the history of country music. David Frizzell has given us a glimpse into the family circle, and it's an honored place to be."
—MARTY STUART, country music star

Published by: Santa Monica Press LLC
P.O. Box 850
Solana Beach, CA 92075
1-800-784-9553
www.santamonicapress.com
books@santamonicapress.com

Printed in the United States

Santa Monica Press books are available at special quantity discounts when purchased in bulk by corporations, organizations, or groups. Please call our Special Sales department at 1-800-784-9553.

ISBN-13 978-1-59580-058-9

Library of Congress Cataloging-in-Publication Data

Frizzell, David.
 I love you a thousand ways : the Lefty Frizzell story / by David Frizzell ; foreword by Merle Haggard.
    p. cm.
Includes index.
ISBN 978-1-59580-058-9
1. Frizzell, Lefty, 1928-1975. 2. Country musicians—United States—Biography.
I. Title.
ML420.F86F75 2011
782.421642092—dc22
[B]
                                    2011003277

Cover and interior design and production by Future Studio

Mixed Sources
Product group from well-managed forests and other controlled sources
www.fsc.org Cert no. SW-COC-002
© 1996 Forest Stewardship Council
FSC

CONTENTS

DEDICATION

There are many people to whom this book could be dedicated. Each is worthy of that honor. I could dedicate this book to Lefty for living such an extraordinary life, for giving me a story to write; however, there is one person who stands head and shoulders above everyone. One with the most amazing personality and devotion to family, one with a sense of humor that helped us to literally laugh our way through the hardest of times. This book is dedicated to our mom, AD Frizzell.

ACKNOWLEDGMENTS

Lefty told us many times, "Your world is only as big as you make it. You can be and do anything. Don't be afraid to reach out because nothing is impossible." I want to thank him for that inspiration and for teaching me to believe in myself. He told me many times, "David, you can, you can." He didn't tell me even once that I couldn't. In addition, I had him as an example.

I want to thank Brothers Bill and Allen, and Sisters Betty and Mae for opening their hearts and sharing their memories of our older brother, Sonny. I would like to thank Lefty's children, Lois Aleta (deceased), Rickey, and Marlon for making Lefty's life more complete.

Thanks to my many friends in and out of the music industry who always have a story about Lefty, most of which are about having fun, writing songs, or just "carrying on," as Lefty put it.

Thanks to some special friends who in their own way are helping to keep his legend alive: Merle Haggard, Mel Tillis, Bill Mack, Whitey Shafer, Loretta Lynn, Jay Jackson, Yvonne Conner, Merle Kilgore (deceased), Carol Lee Cooper, and Jean Armitage. For their invaluable assistance and friendship: Keith Adkinson, Jett Williams, Judy Baker (deceased), Summer Harmon, Earl Owens, Gordy Collins, Jerry Adams, Jimmy Frizzell, Dorothy Lambur, and Junior Cox; from Roswell, New Mexico, Chaves County Sheriff Rob Coon and Deputy Sheriff Pat Garrett, and others too numerous to mention here. Thanks also to those who read the manuscript and gave us feedback: Marty Stuart, Charlie Chase, Lorianne Crook, Jimmy Fortune, "Little" Jimmy Dickens,

Jeannie Seeley, Helen Cornelius, Larry Stewart, Leroy Van Dyke, Ronny McDowell, Shelly West, Elwood Reid, and Patrick Markey. If I have inadvertently omitted someone, please forgive me and know that I appreciate you all.

Special thanks to David Jácome and Peer International Corporation, and Jason Wilburn and Sure Fire Music for their help and courtesy in permitting us to use excerpts of several songs in this book.

A special thank you to Viola Ebert for helping me put all these words in the right places.

A very heartfelt thanks to my wife, Jo, for her undying patience and support in putting this book together.

Last but not least, thanks to Jeffrey Goldman at Santa Monica Press for his support and patience while we made the final adjustments to the book.

FOREWORD

by Merle Haggard

Although my name is Haggard, I have felt for years like I was a part of the Frizzell family and, through God's music, I am sure that Lefty and I are closely related.

The great Lefty Frizzell was one of a kind, an original; no one could handle a song like Lefty. He would hold on to each word until he finally decided to drop it and pick up the next one. Most of us learned to sing listening to him. There is a little bit of Lefty left in a lot of the country singers out there, all the way from me to Tim McGraw. Early on in my recording career there were times when I would think, *I wonder how Lefty would sing this part or that one,* and it would always help me to make the song the best it could be.

When people first heard Lefty on the radio in 1950 singing his number one song, *If You've Got the Money, I've Got the Time,* they became instant fans. All across the country people were singing along with this curly haired, curly voiced boy from Corsicana, Texas.

The impact Lefty had on country music is not even measurable. When I saw Lefty in concert for the first time all dressed in white—*heroes usually are*—he sang *Mom and Dad's Waltz,* which he said he wrote for his parents and that they would receive all the royalties from sales. Lefty, right then, made a friend for life and he hadn't even met me yet. That song was later the inspiration for my own song, *Momma Tried.*

Once while touring Texas I went by Lefty's hometown and stopped to see his life-sized bronze statue. I will never forget standing there with Lefty wishing I could just take him with me.

One of my most prized possessions is the J200 Gibson guitar that Lefty owned and played throughout his career. I keep it right by my chair at home.

When Lefty passed on I sent a beautiful flower arrangement to the funeral with a card reading: *Life's Like Poetry and thank yous are Always Late; we'll miss you Forever and Always.* That is how I truly feel. I've always thought Lefty hung the moon; I'm still not sure he didn't.

FAMILY CHART

NAAMON ORVILLE FRIZZELL BIRTH FAMILY

William Monroe Frizzell — Velma (Unknown)
↓
Lawrence ↓ Naamon ↓ Thaddus ↓ Sister ↓ Carra Mae ↓ Theola

AD COX BIRTH FAMILY

John Cox — RT Burton
↓
Jennie ↓ Johnnie ↓ RA ↓ Eller ↓ Ethel ↓ Sally ↓ OV ↓ AD ↓ LB ↓ LZ

LEFTY FRIZZELL BIRTH FAMILY

Naamon Orville Frizzell — AD Cox
↓
William Orville ↓ Billy Edgar ↓ Lawrence Lesley ↓ Betty Jo ↓ Johnnie Lee
↓ ↓ ↓ ↓
Ola Mae, Loui David, Billy Ray, Allen Doyle

LEFTY FRIZZELL MARRIAGE FAMILY

William Orville Frizzell — Alice Lee Harper
↓
Lois Aleta ↓ Rickey Rodgers ↓ Marlon Jaray

INTRODUCTION

The idea to write the real life story of my brother, Lefty Frizzell, one of the greatest personalities in country music, came from all the things that have been written and said about him since his death in 1975. Almost everything previously written about him, other than the documented facts, most of which are presented in this book, is either untrue or simply distorted depending on who is doing the telling. Most of those writers did not know Lefty. They have obtained their information from someone else who either did not know Lefty or told their story from their personal perception and point of view. This memoir/biography is told from Lefty's point of view, right or wrong, as I knew it. If Lefty said it or if Lefty believed it, that's what matters.

The facts show Lefty had four songs on the *Billboard* national charts at the same time. That's a great accomplishment to write about, but isn't it even better to know how Lefty felt about having four songs on the *Billboard* national charts at the same time? That's how this book is written.

The facts about Lefty were relatively easy to find, facts like all the hit records he's had and all the great shows he's done. This book gives names of other stars who knew him well. It tells the location where you can find his star on the Walkway of Stars in Hollywood, California.

The titles, times, and dates of his first hit record, his second hit record, and so on are given here. The date he was inducted into the Country Music Hall of Fame is included. This book is filled with facts about a career unparalleled in country music.

Dialogue has been reconstructed based on what contributors remember as the gist of the particular conversation. Language used, such as profanity, manner of speech, or grammar, is patterned after that known to be used by the individual speaker. Other quotes are taken from written material such as letters or documents.

It is well known that Lefty Frizzell has directly or indirectly influenced just about every artist singing today. His many accomplishments are all in this book. The story in and around those accomplishments comes from my knowledge of and relationship with him as his brother and his friend. This book flowed from my many years of working with Lefty, partying with Lefty; driving the long, hard, lonely, tiring roads with Lefty; talking with him, laughing, and sometimes crying with him. I opened his shows and was his road manager from 1956 to 1960.

This story came about with the help of the Frizzell family who each opened their hearts and memories to tell their own stories of Lefty. Special friends like Freddie Hart, Whitey Schafer, Merle Haggard, Bill Mack, Johnny Rodriquez, and many more all shared their memories of the great man.

I will tell you also how it all started. You are going to hear about the boy who wanted to sing more than anything else in the world. You will read about our momma who took young Sonny, as the family called him, to the radio stations and the dances around the country so he could sing. You will learn of the hardships he had to overcome. There were plenty.

This is a true story of rags to riches, a tale of one of the most loved, respected, and imitated singer/songwriters in the history of country music, a man whose music touched the lives of everyone. Even today, thirty some years after his death, his presence in country music is still felt. This is our story of William Orville Frizzell, known to the world of country music as Lefty, and known to our family as Sonny, the oldest of nine children.

This is the Frizzell family's story. This is also my story but, first and foremost, this is Lefty's story.

DAVID FRIZZELL

PROLOGUE

Our father, Naamon Orville Frizzell, was a hard working, hard living man who started working in the oil fields at the young age of thirteen. He worked in the lumber camps, did a little moonshining, sold a little whiskey, and hung out in a few pool halls drinking, and playing cards and dominos. Daddy liked men things; he believed in working eight to ten hours a day; he didn't even like anyone who didn't work hard. He would always say, "Do a good job for 'the man' and you'll never feel guilty about taking his money."

Daddy never understood music though; he didn't understand how it worked. He couldn't figure out how Lefty made a living. Getting up on a stage and playing a few songs was not work to Daddy. Sitting around the house trying to write a song was a waste of time to him. He knew about working up a sweat, getting oily and dirty, and picking up a paycheck at the end of the week. This he understood, but music, no!

Every man who ever worked with Daddy said he was the best. He could do every job in and around an oil derrick. He drilled thousands of feet for oil in his lifetime. Daddy was the kind of man who felt if he could hit it with a hammer, rope it, chain it down, run into it, or kick it into place, well then, that worked for him. Where Daddy had problems was in saying, "I love you," giving you a hug or kiss, or maybe simply holding your hand. Although, several years before his death in 1993, at the age of eighty-four, he learned to do all of those things very well.

Our mother, AD, on the other hand was the most loving person in the world. She had a personality second to none; she would stand beside you, hell or high water. Her children were always right no matter how wrong they were. She was a natural comedian; she could find the humor in any situation. Many times, when we had no food in the house, and that was most of the time, she would gather all us kids around and start telling stories. She would have us laughing so hard we'd forget the hunger in our bellies. She was also our best friend, our pal. You could tell her anything and she would help you with it, stand by you on it, or simply help you get over it by laughing about it. Like Lefty, she was one of a kind.

Lefty and our mother both had the ability to make you laugh, cry, jump up and down, scream with delight, or just sit for hours listening to them tell stories. Momma would tell about her growing up, things that happened with her brothers and sisters. She was always telling us about what Daddy had done or was doing. Sometimes, whether he was there or not, she'd whisper some little tidbit about him as if she didn't want him to hear. All the kids would gather around a little closer and she always had everyone's complete attention.

Lefty, on the other hand, had a way of telling stories that got you involved. He would tell of things you'd be able to do one of these days. He made all us kids feel so important. He would say maybe Sister Betty was going to be a big movie star because she was so tall and pretty, and Betty felt sure this was really going to happen. One time Lefty told me how tough I was, how big my muscles were. He had me so pumped up I suddenly reached over and slugged Sister Mae. Boy, the fight was on. Lefty would just stand there laughing at us.

Although Momma never sang or performed professionally, she had the most perfect voice. She would sing and play chords on the piano. Even today, after all these years, if I close my eyes and listen really hard, I can still hear her sweet voice.

CHAPTER ONE

MOM AND DAD'S WALTZ

Red switched the big diesel engine to idle, hooked the end of the chain to the brake handle, and shouted to the other roughnecks, "Break time. Damn, it's hot." He waved to the man at the top of the derrick to come on down.

The men followed Red to the tool shack laughing, pushing and joking with each other. Red liked working hard, and he liked working with hard men. They were all dirty, oily and sweaty, but they were used to it, it didn't bother them at all.

Around eight o' clock in the evening, Red heard someone calling his name.

"Red, Red, where are you? AD's in labor."

Red came out of the shack at a run, calling back over his shoulder to a fellow by the name of Gene to take his place running the big engine.

"Gotta go home and look in on AD. I may be back and may not, depending on how she's doing. We're gonna have a baby." Red jumped into the old truck beside his friend saying, "How's she doing, is she having the baby now?"

"Don't know," his friend said. "My wife is with her. She just said to come and get you. I think she just started, though if she did this might take a while." They roared through the oil camp known as Tuckertown and slid to a stop in front of the little shotgun house where Red had lived for only a few months. He hit the ground running.

"AD, AD, I'm home. Where are ya?" He entered the bedroom and saw AD lying on the bed.

"The first pain was about two hours ago," AD gasped, breathing heavily, "It comes and goes."

Red, still oily, dirty and sweaty, leaned against the door jam, looked over at his wife of two years and said, "Okay, well just take it easy, lay there and rest. I'm here, so let me know when and I'll fetch the doctor."

AD felt another pain coming on. "Six or seven minutes apart," she gasped. "Bring me a wet wash rag, Naamon." She clasped her hands underneath her swollen belly, looked up at Red and added, "We're gonna…have…a…very big baby I think."

The doctor came out of the bedroom and closed the door behind him. He walked to the front door of the little shotgun house, opened the screen door and said, "It's been a pretty good night, hasn't it. I think it's gonna be a nice day, Mr. Frizzell. You have a fine, big baby boy. Your wife and baby are both doing great, but she's gonna need plenty of rest."

Red grinned, walked over and gave the doctor a firm handshake, "Thanks, Doc, for coming all the way out here. I don't have much money, but I want to do what's right."

The doctor walked over to the far side of the porch and took out a pen and pad from his pocket. He said, "We'll get to that in a minute. First, let me get some information for the birth certificate. Okay, let's see. Name of child?"

Red grinned at the doctor. "William Orville Frizzell after me and my dad."

After a few more questions, the doctor wrote:

Full Name of Child: William Orville Frizzell
Place of Birth: Corsicana, Texas
(Because Tuckertown was only an oil camp and not a real town)

County: Navarro
Date of Birth: March 31, 1928
Father of Child: Naamon Orville Frizzell
Color or Race: White
Father's Age at Time of Birth: 19
Father's Birthplace: Chidester, Arkansas
Occupation: Driller
Business: Oil Field Worker
Mother of Child: AD Cox
Color or Race: White
Mother's Age at Time of Birth: 19
Mother's Birthplace: Sulphur Springs, Texas
Occupation: Housewife

Red and the doctor agreed on a payment. Red thanked the doctor, and then walked to the bedroom to see little William. However, AD and Red never called their son William. He was always called Sonny by his parents, brothers and sisters, but he was to be known later by millions of country music fans as "Lefty Frizzell," and . . .

The Legend Was Born.

Our father, Naamon Orville Frizzell, was born on November 11, 1908, in Chidester, Arkansas. He started working with his dad in the lumber camps by the time he was ten. Hard working "Red," as everyone called him, took up oil field work at the age of thirteen, starting out as a roust-a-bout doing a man's work, earning a man's wage, and trying to complete the eighth grade at the same time. He would work after school and during the summer, and then bring all his money home to his parents. At the age of nineteen, Red worked the big rigs as a "Cat Head Man." A Cat Head Man ran the big engine that powered the drill. Red was considered one of the best. All the other roughnecks looked up to the young man with the red hair. Daddy quit school and started following the oil field work, traveling from one rough boomtown to the next. Among the booming oil towns in southeast Texas was a place called Tuckertown, just outside of Corsicana and about an hour south of Dallas. That is where this story begins.

Our mother's maiden name was AD Cox. She was born one of ten children on January 14, 1909, in Sulphur Springs, Texas. Momma wasn't given a full name. She was named with initials like her mother, and some of her sisters and brothers.

Although a few of the older kids had some schooling, Momma was not as fortunate. She could neither read nor write; however, she could sign her own name. Our mother had something a lot of people don't have, and that is common sense and a tremendous personality. There wasn't one of her brothers or sisters who didn't have a great sense of humor. All of them could keep you laughing, especially Momma. She had the uncanny ability to find the funny side to almost any situation. Even though her life was filled with hardship, tragedy and pain, somehow she would find the strength to smile and keep on going. Momma never lost that ability. She never lost the child within herself. Finding humor within tragedy was her strength and her survival.

Not much is known about Momma's father, John Cox. She said that he had some mental problems and that sometimes he was mean to them. It all ended out in the barn one day when he took his strait razor and cut his throat from ear to ear. Momma, who was around seven years old, was playing on the front porch with her older sister, OV, when she saw her daddy trying to walk back up the hill to the house. She could see him stumbling and, when he got closer, she saw the blood pouring down the front of his shirt from the slit in his neck. Both girls started screaming.

Their mother, RT, came running out of the house and

grabbed him before he fell to the ground. She helped him into the house, threw everything from the kitchen table, and laid her husband down. He was barely alive. While she cleaned the wound, she sent her oldest son, Johnnie, to fetch the doctor. John had severed his windpipe. RT cleaned out a piece of sugar cane and, cutting it to size, placed one end into his throat. Then, very calmly and patiently she kept her husband alive until the doctor arrived. He died a short time later, while Momma and OV looked on from a distance.

Our grandma had to find a way to support her kids after granddaddy's death. She was a very stern and strict lady, no stranger to hard work and adversity. Momma would say of her mother, "She never had over two dresses at any given time in her life and they were always black. She had no sense of humor at all, which is strange because all of us kids do."

Momma and her brothers and sisters loved to sing and dance, but her mother wouldn't allow the girls to go to any parties unless they were dressed right. Dresses had to button around the neck and cover down to the girls' ankles.

Grandma was known as a mid-wife around the county; people would call on her to deliver babies and help expectant mothers. She was also known as a medium and a healer. She had the ability to stop blood. If someone cut themselves or was hurt in an accident and the bleeding wouldn't stop, they'd send for RT Cox. Because Momma and some of the other kids were small, they would go with their mother and watch her perform her miracles.

Momma described one such scene: "One day this man came to our house and asked Momma to come over and help with his wife. Her time of the month had come and gone, but she wouldn't stop bleeding. Momma and we four kids went to the man's house. Momma put her hands on the lady's belly and closed her eyes. I could see Momma was saying something, but it wasn't loud enough for anyone to hear. Within minutes the bleeding stopped."

Later on before her death, Grandma passed the gift on to Momma who used this amazing healing power many times in her own life.

Our mother and baby Sonny followed the oil field work all over Texas and parts of Arkansas with Daddy. Momma's mother, RT, lived in Soper, Oklahoma, right outside of Hugo. Sonny was almost a year old and RT had not seen her grandson. Momma was excited about seeing her mother and couldn't wait to show off her big boy. Grandma RT was sitting on her front porch when they drove up, and even though she didn't get up from her chair she did give them a little grin. She still didn't like our father, Naamon, and wouldn't pretend she did. Momma got out of the car carrying Sonny. She walked over and offered to let Grandma RT hold the baby. Grandma took Sonny from Momma's hands.

"Mighty big boy you got here, AD, good looking too. How much does he weigh?"

"When he was born he weighed nine pounds and six ounces," Momma told her. "Now he is probably closer to twenty-five pounds or better."

Grandma RT had taken the blanket off Sonny so she could get a better look. "You have a precious little guy here." She ran her hand along the right side of Sonny's face and down onto his neck. "AD, this is quite a birthmark here. Look!" She traced the birthmark with her fingers up onto Sonny's chubby little cheek, back to his ear, down to his chin and onto his neck. The color was a light pinkish brown and had a rough textured feel to it. She asked Momma, "When you were pregnant did something happen to you, anything out of the ordinary, other than being married to him?" She glanced over at Daddy then turned her attention back to the baby.

Daddy stepped up on the porch without saying a word. He knew Grandma RT would never pay him any attention anyway. She never said "hi" or "bye" to him. He didn't exist as far as she was concerned. When Momma and Daddy married, they did so without her mother's knowledge. Consequently, Grandma RT never liked that red-haired man.

Our mother answered, "Momma, something did happen one day when I was around seven months pregnant. I think it was last January, and it was real cold. Naamon and some guys he worked with were down in the barn. I hollered to Naamon to bring some firewood in, but he couldn't hear me so I left the house and was walking down to where they were. I had on my coat and was pulling my wool cap down over my ears. When I came around the corner of the barn, all of a sudden I saw Naamon cut the throat of a pig. A loud and chilling scream came from that pig. It startled me and scared me so bad I couldn't move. When I finally realized what was going on, I remember my right hand was on my cheek but moved down around my throat."

Grandma RT looked up at her. "You've marked this child. This boy's birthmark is light now, but as he gets older it will darken. When he gets to be a man it will lighten up again, but he will always have it, it'll never go away." She looked over at Daddy. "Might of known you were the cause of it."

Throughout Momma's life she believed that she was the cause of Sonny's birthmark, and no one could convince her differently.

Daddy moved our family back to El Dorado, Arkansas, when Sonny was about a year and a half old. El Dorado had been a rough lumber town, but with the discovery of oil people from everywhere were moving there. It had gone from a town of about eight or nine thousand to well over twenty thousand.

William Monroe Frizzell, like his son, Naamon, was a hard worker and hard drinker. He was a carpenter by trade but, now and then, he worked alongside his son and his brother, Troy, falling timber in the woods.

One evening before dark Daddy and his father were drinking with some other men down by the railroad tracks. Bets were being made to see who was the strongest. The bet was over who could lift one of the old rusty train rims lying over by a tin shed. It wasn't long before the damnedest fight broke out; blood and teeth were flying all over the place. The father and son team were getting the best of the fight. When the police showed up men scattered every which way. Some got away, but the Frizzell team didn't escape the arm of the law. However, they did break one of the arms of the law, bent a few more, and broke a nose or two before seven police officers finally got them to jail.

For some reason they let Grandpa William go, probably because he made bail, but they wouldn't release Daddy. Later that night three of them came into his cell and beat him up. They beat him so brutally that they caused a rupture in his lower abdomen.

Momma would come to visit Daddy. She often said how bad he looked and how sick he seemed to be. He was sentenced to six months on the road gang. It's not known how he escaped, but he did.

The police showed up at the house one night. When Momma opened the door, one of the officers said, "We've come for Red, tell him to come on out."

Momma was standing in the door holding Sonny. "Red? Red who? I don't know any Red. You've got the wrong house!"

The policeman was getting a little irritated, "Lady we've come for Red, your husband. Now get out of the way 'cause he's going back to jail."

The police didn't find Daddy that night. He was at that very moment out in back of the house hiding in the tall grass.

After the police left Daddy said, "AD, I've got to leave tonight. Give me whatever money you have and pack me a few clothes. When I get settled somewhere, I'll send for you and the boy."

By the time Daddy sent for them, Momma and Sonny were staying with one of her sisters in Oklahoma. OV had come down to El Dorado and taken them back with her.

Daddy made his way over to east Texas. He worked some in Marshall and Longview, but it was in Kilgore that he thought he'd found a pretty good job. After working a few months on a big oil drilling rig, he had earned enough money to buy an old four-door Chevy sedan, and he sent Momma money to take a train from Hugo, Oklahoma, to Longview.

Daddy was waiting at the train station when our eight and a half month pregnant mother and three-year-old Sonny got off the train. Momma was holding a barefoot Sonny's hand. Someone had tossed a lit cigarette down and Sonny stepped right on it. He cried out in pain. Some men sitting close by started laughing.

Daddy saw all of this while trying to get to his wife and child. He picked up Sonny and turned to the men. He said, "I see nothing funny about my boy being in pain. Does this cigarette butt belong to any of you?" The fire in his eyes was enough to light each of them a cigarette. He handed Sonny over to Momma and stood facing the men.

One of the men said, "You're right, man, there's nothing funny here."

Daddy turned, took back his son, who had stopped crying, and led Momma over to the sedan. They didn't have a house. They didn't have an apartment or even a room, but it was plenty big enough inside that sedan.

The year was 1931, the time of the Great Depression.

Daddy's workplace was about five miles out of town. Every day that he went to work, he would see a black farmer working the stretch of land that the workers always had to cross to get to the rig. One morning Daddy had an idea.

"Hello, hey, hold up a minute," Daddy was hollering and waving his arms trying to get the attention of this middle-aged black man driving a mule and wagon team down that old dirt road. "Hey, hold on, stop, I want to talk to you." The wagon stopped, the black man turned to watch the red-haired, stocky young man running toward him.

"Hi, my name is Naamon but everyone calls me Red."

The black man said, "Well, hello to you, Red, and you can call me Ira. What you want?"

Daddy smiled. "Ira, I've got me an idea that might make you some money. Think you want to hear me out?" Daddy put his hand out and shook Ira's hand.

"Well, I always need money," Ira smiled. "What's your idea, Red?"

Daddy cleared his throat. "I work over yonder on that oil rig, and every day going to work we have to cross right over this land. Some of the guys said that you owned it, do you?" He paused, waiting for a reply.

"Yes," Ira said. "This fifty odd acres once belonged to my daddy and his daddy before him. It's been mine now for a long time."

"I was just thinking, the only way to get to that rig is right through your property. My idea is to charge those boys a toll."

Ira was quiet for a moment. "I don't think I could get away with it. I doubt anyone would pay me any mind much less pay to cross my land. Anyways, I don't want no trouble. You know what I mean."

Daddy just smiled again. "Oh yeah, I know, but I'm not talking about you charging a toll. I'm talking about me charging a toll, and enforcing it. I'll put up a little shack about half way down your road, and I'll put up a two-by-four barrier and, believe me, they'll pay. Whatever I get, we'll split it, what do ya think? Money, I believe, that is rightfully yours anyway, half of what I take in."

Ira didn't say anything.

Daddy added, "Ira, right now one of two things is gonna happen. I got a family to feed and my wife is expecting our second child any day now, so I'm either gonna go to work over there or I'm gonna go over there and quit. I ain't got no more time to talk about it."

"Now wait a minute, Red, you say that you'll do all the collecting. I won't have to and we'll split all money right down the middle, and..."

Daddy interrupted, "Right, Ira, you won't have to do nothing but stay out of the way and make your money. I'll handle everything."

Momma, waiting patiently in the car, tried to feed Sonny. When Daddy got back, he slid in behind the wheel and headed back toward town. "We've got to pick up some lumber. We're going into business!"

Daddy built a little shack and put a two-by-four barrier across the rutted road that went straight through the lower part of Ira Johnson's property. Daddy charged the oil workers two bits to come in and out. Momma cooked stew on an open fire, made sandwiches and had soft drinks for sale. Daddy parked the sedan close to a big oak tree, tied a quilt from the car to the tree, and spread another one on the ground. This was their home when Billy Edgar Frizzell was born on July 6, 1931.

Daddy made two bits for every vehicle crossing the property. He also made a few nickels and dimes selling stew, sandwiches and soft drinks, but where Daddy made his real money was selling bootleg whiskey to the men driving past his toll gate. He sold whiskey to them coming and going and, you know what, nobody knew about it except the seller and the buyers. Momma didn't know and Ira Johnson didn't know either. The men would drive up, pay the toll, and buy a sandwich or something. Then Daddy would sell them a bottle of hooch on the side. He would raise the barrier and they would be on their way.

Sometimes even the best laid plans will screw up. Somehow the police got wind of Daddy's selling bootleg whiskey out on old Ira Johnson's place. One day a police cruiser pulled up to the toll gate. Daddy walked up to the car.

One of the officers said, "I understand a man can buy whiskey here."

Daddy just stared at him. "Not from me. There's no whiskey here; only me, my wife and boys, but you're welcome to look for yourself."

Daddy stepped back as the officer and his partner got out of the car and started looking around. One of the officers walked over to the sedan where our mother was keeping the boys and asked if she had any whiskey. Momma told him she had never seen any and paid no more attention to him. Those two officers looked everywhere, in and around the toll shack, and in and out of the sedan. There was just no whiskey to be found and nowhere else to look. They got back into their car and told Daddy they better not hear anymore about any whiskey being sold.

Daddy waved and smiled as the officers backed down the rutted road to the main highway. They drove back toward the town of Kilgore without knowing that Daddy's whiskey was hidden beside the toll house, in the center mound between the ruts, right under their cruiser.

Men were working around the clock drilling for oil at the other end of Daddy's dirt road. He knew exactly when one shift would start and the other would end. He would be ready to collect. Things were going well, so well in fact that Daddy hired two guys to build a room onto his toll shack. They built one large room complete with a door and a window. Momma finally had a home. Daddy and Momma bought a bed and a table with two chairs. The boys slept on a pallet beside the bed. Yes, things were going well.

One night, Daddy was sleeping soundly because he had been drinking his own whiskey, but he had to be up by eleven thirty for the shift change at midnight. Around ten o'clock, when everything was quiet, Momma was holding Baby Billy while Sonny was playing on the floor. She heard something outside and looked over at the window. She thought she saw the face of a man. Momma intended to wake up Daddy, but the face disappeared. She stood up from the chair, put Billy on his pallet, and walked a little closer to the window. Still, she could see nothing. Suddenly there was a knock on the door; Momma nearly fainted. There was another knock.

"Who is it, what do you want?"

A man's voice came from the other side of the door. "Ma'am, I need to see Red. I wants to buy a bottle of whiskey and I knows he's got some."

Momma stood there in the middle of the room scared to death. "Red ain't got no whiskey. 'Sides, he don't do business this time of night. Go away."

"Lady, is Red in there? If he is, tell him to open the damn door, I want to see him now."

Momma stood staring at the door. She was so scared she didn't hear Daddy get out of bed. She didn't see him grab the shotgun leaning against the wall, but she did hear him say, as he pushed her out of the way, "Red is here all right, you son-of-a-bitch. When I open this door, I'm gonna shoot the first thing I see." Daddy kicked the door open and fired. He walked out the door and saw someone running toward the road, running fast. He let go another round and the man disappeared into the dark.

The next day Daddy and Momma packed what little belongings they had, put the boys in the car, and settled up and said their goodbyes to Ira. Then they headed back to El Dorado.

The Frizzells were travelers, never staying in one place very long. Something would happen and Daddy would pack up his family and move them without a second thought. Sometimes he didn't even know what direction they would go, but when they moved back to El Dorado this time they stayed long enough for two more children to be born: Lawrence Lesley on November 1, 1933, and Betty Jo on March 29, 1935. Daddy followed the oil trail into Baton Rouge, Louisiana, where Johnnie Lee was born on December 12, 1936, and back up through Cooper, Texas, where Ola Mae was born on January 19, 1939, at a relative's house, before returning to El Dorado.

The way of the land was hard; the way of the people was harder.

CHAPTER TWO

I'M GONNA SING LIKE JIMMIE

"I'm gonna sing just like Jimmie Rodgers. I can yodel, too. Yod-da-ly-ee-ee, see there," my eleven-year-old brother, Sonny, told his younger brother, Billy. "If I had me a guitar I could really sing like him."

"I can sing like Jimmie Rodgers, too," Billy said.

"I'm gonna sing like Jimmie. You can sing like someone else, 'cause I'm gonna sing like Jimmie my whole life, but I've got to have me a guitar."

"Sonny, if you can sing like Jimmie, so can I."

"Okay," Sonny hollered at him, "let me hear you try. Come on, just try to yodel."

Billy let out a Yo-del-le-ee-ee you wouldn't believe. Sonny just stood there looking at him. "All right then, but we've got to have a guitar."

Sonny loved to listen to Jimmie Rodgers. After school he'd put on some of Jimmie's old records and get his head as close to the speakers of that old Victrola as he could. This way he could close out all the outside noise in order to hear the beautiful voice of the master, Jimmie Rodgers. Sonny knew, even at that young age, that somehow music was going to be his life. It was already in his blood.

One afternoon Sonny came running home from school excited. "Momma, guess what? I've been asked to sing at school."

Momma came out of the kitchen wiping her hands on a towel. "What is it you're gonna do?"

"My teacher found out I can sing a little bit, and asked me and some other kids to sing and stuff for the school assembly," Sonny said excitedly.

Momma grinned. "Okay, what are you gonna sing? Do you have something picked out?"

"Well, I was thinking 'bout maybe singing 'South of the Border,' you know, that Gene Autry song."

Momma said she thought that would be fine. "Do you remember all the words? Let me hear you sing a little of it."

Sonny stood up in the middle of the room and started singing, "South of the border. . . ."

All our brothers and sisters had come to hear so Sonny had an audience. The only thing wrong was little Billy singing right along with him.

"All right now," Momma instructed Sonny, "remember, don't just stand there like a statue, you gotta move around a little bit, throw that head around, you know, be alive."

"Momma, I'm gonna be all over the place. You'll be proud of me, I'll betcha."

Momma nodded her head and smiled. "I'm already proud of you, son, but let's try it again and show me something."

Sonny started singing again. He was moving his head around a little, and pretending to hold a microphone.

Momma noticed that even his feet were moving. "This might work a little better if you had some shoes on."

"Momma, you know I don't have any shoes to wear on stage when I sing."

Momma came over and put her arms around his neck. "Well, let's see, you're gonna wear those khaki pants and white shirt . . ."

Sonny interrupted, "And my blue and white scarf."

"Okay, try on my new shoes. I only bought them last week and I haven't even wore them anywhere."

Sonny looked at Momma and hesitated. "I can't wear girl's shoes. Everybody will laugh at me."

Momma just grinned. "No one will know, your pant legs will come down far enough to cover the shoes. Now don't be silly, here, try 'em on."

Sonny tried the shoes on and, wouldn't you know it, they fit. *Just my luck*, Sonny thought.

The show was held at the Parker Chapel Hill School just outside of El Dorado, Arkansas. When Sonny came on stage he could see the auditorium was full. His teacher started playing the intro on the piano, and Sonny began singing "South of the Border." His voice sure sounded fine that day. He looked out over the audience and saw Momma. She was moving her head around and kind of squirming in her seat. Sonny started moving his head around and his body began to sway just a little.

He glanced down at Momma's shoes and smiled. He thought, *Boy, isn't this something.* When the song was finished everyone in the audience clapped their hands and hollered to him. He smiled at everyone, took his bow, and realized that Momma was right. *Daddangit, I should of danced all over the place,* Sonny thought.

Sonny said, "Hey, Momma, let's go over to Uncle Lawrence's house. You know there's a black man that lives down the street from him, and he's got a guitar. He said he would show me some chords next time we came over."

Momma knew how much Sonny wanted a guitar. All he wanted to do was sing. He had just about worn out all those

Jimmie Rodgers' records. She wished there was some way to get him a guitar, but she didn't have the money to buy one.

"Sonny, when your Daddy gets home from work, maybe he'll take us to Uncle Lawrence's house."

Sonny jumped out of the car when they arrived at our uncle's house later that day. "Be back after awhile, Momma." He ran off down the street.

Uncle Lawrence asked Momma, "Where's Sonny going in such a hurry?"

She told him how much Sonny wanted to play guitar and about the black man who had one. "That's where Sonny goes every time we come over here."

Uncle Lawrence said, "Come on, Naamon, let's go find that boy. I wanna hear him play that thing."

Sonny was singing a Jimmie Rodgers' song and trying to play the guitar at the same time. "Let's see, this is the key of C and it goes to F and back to C, then to G and comes back to C again, is that right?" Sonny asked.

The black man watched young Sonny try to change chords while singing. "Boy, that's right and it's gonna take some practice, but you sho' do sound good. Now let's try it again."

Uncle Lawrence, Daddy, and Momma walked up while Sonny was singing. They stood and listened a few minutes.

Uncle Lawrence said, "Sonny, that guitar sure does sound good. Think you'll ever learn to play it? I mean, you know, real good?"

Sonny looked up from the guitar. "I'm gonna play just like Jimmie Rodgers, and you know that's good."

Uncle Lawrence walked over and said something to the black man. He reached into his pocket and gave the black man two dollars and fifty cents. He turned around. "Okay, Sonny, let's go home and bring that guitar with you."

It wasn't long before Sonny could sing and accompany himself on the guitar. He would play Jimmie Rodgers' songs for hours. He knew every one of them by heart. Sonny not only knew how to sing and yodel, but how to play the guitar just like his idol.

Radio Station KELD in El Dorado was planning a children's show, and they invited Sonny to appear. Momma called the radio station and asked the disc jockey if it was all right to bring Sonny's younger brother, Billy, for the show. The man said he thought that would be just fine. He would put Billy on the radio, too. Momma gathered my very excited brothers into the car and headed to the station. The boys sang all the way there.

Jimmy Page was the disc jockey for the children's program. When the threesome arrived, Jimmy said hello to Momma and asked Sonny which song he wanted to do on the show.

"I'm gonna sing 'God Bless America.' Do you think that'll be all right?"

Jimmy said that would be fine, and then asked Billy what he wanted to sing.

"Over the roof top, way up high," Billy confidently replied.

Jimmy smiled at Billy. "I don't think I've heard of that one, but that's okay. It will be fine. Okay, everyone, airtime is in two minutes."

"Hello, everyone, this is Jimmy Page, welcome to our children's show here at KELD Radio. We have some great talent here that we're all very excited about. We have Sonny Frizzell and his younger brother, Billy, with us today. Now, we know some of you out there in radio land have heard young Sonny sing, but I think this is Billy's first time to sing in public and especially over the radio. This is exciting! First, let me introduce the very talented young singer, Sonny Frizzell." Jimmy motioned for Sonny to step over to the microphone standing in the middle of the room. "Sonny, we're glad you could be here with us today, are you ready to sing for us?"

Sonny kind of cleared his throat. "Yes, I'm ready."

"Okay, what song will you sing?"

Sonny smiled. "Jimmy, I'm gonna sing 'God Bless America,' and it goes like this." Sonny sang that song with feeling, I tell you. Twelve-year-old Sonny sang like it was gonna be the last song he'd ever sing. His head moved around the microphone, his arms and shoulders shook a little bit, and his feet kept time to the music.

Jimmy couldn't believe what he was seeing and hearing. Afterward, he kept saying, "Sonny, that's great, that's just great. That's young Sonny Frizzell, and that's the kind of talent we're gonna have here every week on KELD Radio. Sonny, thank you very much and we want you back with us on a steady basis, okay?"

Sonny was grinning from ear to ear. "Thank you, and I'll be back."

Jimmy said, "Next, we have Sonny's younger brother, Billy. Hey, Billy, what song do you have planned for us today?"

Billy stepped up to the microphone. "Over the roof top, way up high."

"Billy, I don't remember that song, but we sure are ready to hear you sing it."

Billy started singing: "God bless America, land that I love. . . ." Billy sang that song word for word just like Sonny did only minutes before. When he finished, Jimmy just smiled and shook his head. "That was great, Billy, just fine and, you know what, I think I have heard that song."

"You know, I bet I can fly just like Superman, if I had something to use for a cape," Sonny said.

Daddy was working; Momma was cleaning house. Sonny, Billy, and Lesley were playing in the backyard. They'd been running all morning. At that moment they were sitting on top of a little tool shed about six feet tall. Sonny thought for a moment. He looked around and saw where Momma had hung the wash to dry.

"Lesley, go get a sheet and a couple of those towels over there on the line, and I'll show you and Billy how to fly just like Superman."

Lesley jumped down from the shed. He ran over and grabbed a sheet and two towels. Sonny reached down and helped Lesley climb up.

"Okay, I'll go first, just watch me." Sonny tied two ends of the sheet around his neck and shoulders. He stood on the edge of the tool shed and jumped. Much to his surprise, the sheet didn't do anything but cover him as he lay on the ground.

Billy asked, "What happened, Sonny? Did you fly any?"

Sonny stood up. "Naw, I just dropped, but I know what happened. I wasn't high enough. This shed is just too small. Come on, you guys, follow me." Sonny ran toward the house with the sheet flowing out from his neck. He realized that the faster he ran the more the sheet flowed out into the wind. Sonny ran around the house with Billy and Lesley trying to keep up. Billy had tied one of the towels around his neck and began to run. His little fat legs were jerking up and down rapidly as he tried to keep up, but they were no match for his brothers' long, skinny legs. Lesley stopped just long enough to tie a towel around his neck and then he was bringing up the rear.

Suddenly, Sonny stopped and grabbed a ladder. He leaned it up against the house and started to climb. Over his shoulder he yelled, "Follow me to the top." Up they went, three little Supermen, a sheet and two towels. Lesley started over to the edge with every intention of jumping.

Sonny grabbed his towel and pulled him back. "Lesley, sit down. Nobody is first before me. Always remember to follow me because I'm the leader." Sonny walked over to the edge and looked down. "All right, I'm gonna jump. You watch me fly. Then you can both jump." Sonny adjusted his sheet, made sure the ends were tight, and then he jumped. Once again the sheet did not open, and this time Sonny landed hard.

About that time Momma came out with another load of wash. She saw Sonny on the ground with her once clean sheet. She looked around and saw Billy and Lesley standing on the edge of the roof ready to fly. "Hold it right there," she said to them. "Don't you jump and I am not kidding. Sonny, you get up from there. Are you hurt?"

Sonny unwrapped the sheet and got up. "Momma I'm not hurt, I was trying to fly."

Momma took her son by the arm. "Not with my sheet you're not. Take that off and help your brothers down from there."

Sonny, Billy, and Lesley strolled into a drugstore on Main Street one afternoon and started looking at comic books. Lesley saw Sonny slip a comic book under his shirt so, thinking if one is good two must be better, he slipped two under his shirt. Billy saw his brothers slipping comic books under their shirts so he took one too.

Unfortunately, or perhaps fortunately, the store manager saw the boys hiding the comic books under their shirts.

He slipped up behind the three little thieves. "What're you boys doing with my comic books?"

Sonny saw him first and ran for the door. Lesley took off when he saw Sonny running. Billy saw his two brothers bolt for the door, so he did, too, or at least he tried. The manager grabbed for him and got a piece of his shirt, but that's all he got. All the comic books were lost in the mad dash for the safety of home. All three boys made it home just in time to meet the police.

Billy saw the cops first and escaped out the backdoor and made a beeline for their hideout in the woods. Sonny and Lesley stood their ground until Daddy's belt lifted them off the ground.

No one went to find Billy, but every so often one of the boys would open the back door and holler to him. "Billy, come on in and get your whuppin'. Momma's made a nice peach cobbler and, boy, it's good!" Billy stayed in that little hideout for three days. Everybody just waited.

Finally here he came. "Okay, Daddy, I'm ready for my whuppin', but can I have some peach cobbler first? I sure am hungry." When Billy got his whipping, Sonny noticed that Daddy didn't seem to be laying it on quite as hard as he had to him and Lesley.

Later Sonny said, "I know that Daddy kinda admired Billy's stubborn streak; he also knew that if it hadn't of been for Momma's peach cobbler, Billy would've still been out there."

The side of Momma's face was swelling up and it hurt like the dickens. She was lying on the floor. The pain and the taste of blood were nauseating. She hoped she wouldn't throw up.

Usually when Daddy got drunk as he was that night Momma kept away from him. He had caught her because she was six months pregnant and not fast enough on her feet. He held her arm and slapped her hard across the face. She dropped and just lay there not making a sound. Daddy staggered on out of the room.

Momma had already had two miscarriages between

Sonny and Billy. She didn't want to lose another baby. She opened her eyes when she heard Sonny's voice.

"Come on, Momma, here I'll help you."

Momma looked around the room. She saw all the kids watching her, and she could tell they were scared. They didn't make a sound; they just stared at her. "Okay, kids," she said softly. She didn't want Daddy to hear her. "Come on, we're getting out of here." Momma could hear Daddy cursing and rummaging through the kitchen.

"Hell, woman, I'll whip your ass all over this house," he said. "Get in here and put some food on this table. Don't make me come and get you." Momma grabbed Ola Mae and swung her around to sit on her hip. "Come on; let's go now," she whispered. She guided her children several yards away from the house. They hid in a ditch.

"Momma," Sonny was trying to calm the other kids. "Keep the kids here in the ditch. Daddy won't come out here. He'll eat whatever he can find then he'll just pass out. I'll go up and keep an eye on him. Then I'll come back for you, okay?"

Momma sat there with her arms around her precious kids. She hated for them to have to go through this. She knew it scared them and it would take days for them to get over this night. The baby was kicking pretty well, so at least she felt it was all right.

"I remember when I was about eight years old," Momma whispered. "We lived in Oklahoma. Momma was over at the neighbor's house delivering a baby. Me and my sisters were in the house. There was your Aunt OV, Eller, Ethel, and Sally. The boys were outside, your Uncle Doc, LB, and Johnnie. I don't know what they were doing, but it probably wasn't much. Johnnie saddled the old horse and said he was going after Momma, so he rode on off."

All the kids kind of moved in a little closer to Momma. They had forgotten about their drunken daddy in the house.

Momma kept right on talking as she sat there in that ditch. "Me and my sister, OV, went outside to watch your Uncle Doc milk the old cow. We were gonna help him, and maybe he'd let me milk her. Now the barn was about two hundred yards from the house, and we covered that distance laughing and pushing each other. Anyway, Doc said I could milk today. I hadn't gotten real good at it, but today I was actually getting some milk in the bucket. All of a sudden we heard this sound like a woman screaming, then again, and a third time. The old cow was jumping around and got away from your Uncle Doc, and ran on somewhere inside the barn. I was lying on the ground beside the milk bucket.

"About that time your Uncle Doc said, 'Run, run to the house as fast as you can.' He didn't have to tell us again. We were running fast and screaming, 'Someone open the door, open the door quick.' The door opened and we ran right on in the house. Ethel and your Uncle LB slammed the door shut. Then we ran to the window and saw Doc was running with the milk bucket just a-swingin', and behind him was a panther, and that big cat was catching up fast."

Momma stopped talking, stood up, and looked at the house for a long time. She couldn't see Daddy, but she could Sonny looking through the front porch window. He didn't move; he just stood there staring through that window.

Betty said, "What happened next, Momma?"

Momma sat back down and gathered her children close around her and continued her story. "Why, that big cat was about to catch your Uncle Doc, when all of a sudden Doc stopped and slung that milk bucket at the head of that cat. Milk went all over its head. The cat stopped running, but your Uncle Doc didn't. I'm telling you, Doc sure could run, but about the time he hit the porch so did that cat. Your Uncle LB had the door open. Doc ran through and LB shut the door right on that cat's neck. I was screaming, everyone was screaming, including that big cat. We were all tryin' to hold the door shut with that cat's head in it.

We were so afraid, then we heard Momma and Johnnie coming down the road, riding hard up to the house. Momma was shouting at the top of her lungs, 'Don't let go of that door.' We heard a gun shot, then we saw the light go out in that big cat's eye. Everyone just stood and stared, scared to death."

About that time Sonny came back. "Okay, he's asleep."

Our mother sure could tell a story with just enough humor in it guaranteed to get your mind off any situation. She was that way about life.

Momma knew it was only a matter of hours now before the baby would come; she'd already given birth to six other babies and she pretty much knew the routine.

"Naamon, why don't you go ahead and get the doctor. I'll be all right until you bring him back." Momma kind of smiled at her husband of fifteen years. He nodded back and went out the front door glad to actually be doing something. He wasn't too good at this baby thing, and he didn't like the waiting around. The kids were leaving for school. After our daddy drove off, Lesley was the first to reach our momma.

"Boy, Momma, I sure am excited. Now listen, when the baby gets here I'm the one who's gonna go tell everybody, okay? You know I can run real fast. The girls can't keep up, they'll only slow me down, so they can stay here. I'll go get Sonny and Billy, okay, Momma?"

Momma just grinned at Lesley and thought how small he was for his age. He was going on nine years old and wasn't no bigger'n a minute, but he was right, he sure could run. Momma nodded her head and hugged her boy. He took off like a shot through the house. Momma leaned back against her pillows and tried to relax. She knew that anytime now it was going to get a little rough.

Daddy's brother, Lawrence, and his wife, Ruth, came in the house. Ruth talked as she walked through the door. "All right, AD, come on, let's get that baby out here. There's more room on the outside than there is on the inside." She gave a little laugh and took Momma's hand. She could see Momma was about to do exactly that.

I was born at 8:30 A.M. on September 26, 1941. I was given the name of Louie David Frizzell. Ruth named me David from the Bible. No one ever said where the name of Louie came from. On the birth certificate it was spelled "Loui," so who knows. And, yes, Lesley sure could run. He ran all the way to the school to get Sonny and Billy. He was laughing and crying at the same time.

"We've got another brother, and his name is David."

CHAPTER THREE

LEFTY

The year was 1941, and a war was raging in Europe. Young men from all over the country were enlisting in the army. They couldn't wait to get into uniform and into the middle of the fighting.

Daddy and Momma had seven children. He didn't have to go, but they both knew he was going. He joined the army on my first birthday. All the young men were going, and besides, Daddy thought he looked right smart in that army uniform. Momma thought he only put it on so the girls would look at him.

Our mother, holding me in her arms and with the other kids gathered around, watched our father march off to war. It was wrenching even if marching off to war only meant going to Greenville, Texas, for his boot camp training. It was certainly quite a day.

Billy leaned over and whispered so only Sonny could hear. "Is Daddy really leaving for a long time?" Sonny told him that he thought Daddy was going away and might never come back, what with the war and all. Billy just took a deep breath let it out and said, "Wow, really!"

Momma had seven kids to feed and what little money she made taking in washing and cleaning up for others wasn't going very far. It just seems when things go wrong nothing will ever go right again. Day after day Momma would wait for the mail hoping there would be some money from Daddy. Nothing ever came. When he did write, he would say that any day the army would get his paperwork straightened out and the allotment would be on its way to her.

Sonny was about to turn fourteen, but he had to grow up in a hurry. Since Daddy was at boot camp and there was no money coming in, Sonny got a job at the local drugstore delivering prescriptions and Western Union messages. He was paid a few dollars a day. His salary, plus whatever tips the customers gave him, brought in at least enough to put some groceries on the table. He would run those prescriptions all over town, and I do mean run because he had no means of transportation. Sonny would come in from work at night tired and beat. He would take Momma by the hand and together they would go to the grocery store to spend what little money he had made that day. Laughing and singing, they would bring home food for the family.

Our father's sister, Carra Mae, always favored Sonny. She was proud of the way he took over the family, being so young and working the way he did. Carra Mae bought Sonny a bicycle, and when he saw that bicycle he just hollered out loud. Boy, now he could deliver more prescriptions and Western Union messages then anyone had ever done before in the whole history of the delivery business. He set out the very next day to prove just that.

Sonny would tie a string around his right pant leg to keep the bicycle chain from catching his pants. He peddled that bicycle everywhere. At night he and Momma would jump on that bike and ride down to the grocery store. They were more like pals than mother and son.

Sonny became really good at riding his bicycle. On Sunday afternoons he would say, "All right, chil'ens, everyone follow me for your weekly bicycle riding lessons." Sonny would rush out of the house with all the kids running after him. Every kid waited impatiently for their ride around the yard.

After each kid had their turn Sonny would say, "Okay, now I'm going to show you my trick riding. This is something that I don't want any of you kids to try because it is dangerous, dangerous. The first dangerous is because you could get hurt if you have a wreck and fall off. The second dangerous is because if I catch any of you kids trying to ride my bike I will kill you. Now for my trick of the day." Sonny, sitting on the handlebars backwards, rode up and down the street with all the kids hollering and running after him.

After Daddy finished boot camp he came home on a thirty day furlough, of which he spent a big part in the local domino and pool hall. One particular afternoon Daddy wasn't lucky. He had lost what little money he had. He stepped outside the hall. As he was looking around, he spotted Sonny riding his bike.

"Sonny," he hollered. "Come here." Sonny heard Daddy's voice before he saw him. He rode over to where Daddy was standing.

"How much money you got?" Daddy's voice was rough. Sonny reached inside his jeans and pulled out all the tips he'd made that day, a little over two dollars and fifty cents. He handed it over. Daddy took the money and walked back inside the domino hall. Sonny just sat there for a moment, watching our father, then silently rode away.

Momma was tired of living behind her mother-in-law. They didn't get along; they never had. Daddy had to report back to Greenville, Texas, for active duty. Momma wanted to move to her home town of Sulphur Springs, which was twenty-five miles east of Greenville, not only to be closer to Daddy, but also to her family. She missed her brothers and sisters.

Daddy didn't argue. He just said, "All right, get packed, we're leaving."

Daddy, Momma, and seven kids boarded the train in El Dorado, Arkansas, a few days before Christmas. We were bound for Sulphur Springs, Texas, with everything we owned, which wasn't much, because just about everything we owned we had on our backs.

Sulphur Springs is in the northeast corner of Texas, only a few miles southwest of Paris. At that time Sulphur Springs was a small, agricultural town with a population of about four to five thousand.

The Frizzells arrived at the Sulphur Springs train station early one morning. The town was alive and well; people were busy going places. The Frizzells were going places, too. Momma's brother, Johnnie, and his family lived not too far from the train station, and that is where Momma and Daddy were headed with their seven children.

Daddy was walking a little ahead, Momma was carrying me, and the rest of the kids were following. Seven-year-old Betty was bringing up the rear. She was pretty excited, this was her first time here and she had to see everything. It was lucky for her that she was seeing everything, especially the car that was making its way down the alley.

We crossed the alley ahead of Betty. She was walking along looking in all directions at once. When she saw the car, it was right on her. She had no time to run anywhere, so she just lay down where she was. The car went right over the top of her and just kept right on going. The driver didn't try to stop. It was probably a good thing that he didn't stop because, even though Betty wasn't hurt, Daddy's temper would have led him to try to kill the driver. No one doubted that.

Daddy may not have been the best husband or father, but he proved many times in his life that you didn't mess with one of his own. One time in particular comes to mind. He had found a little house in Sulphur Springs, moved his family in, and enrolled the kids in school. Daddy was getting everything ready to ship out to start his tour of duty for the army, when Billy came home one afternoon from playing with a boy up the street. They had started fighting and Billy had hit the kid in the face. The boy ran home crying. Billy came in and told Momma what happened.

"Momma, he said something to me I didn't like, so I punched him in the nose and he took off running."

Momma looked him over. "It don't look like you got hit or anything. Did you hurt him bad?"

Billy told her, "His nose was bleeding, but Momma, you know Sonny always told me if someone's gonna hit you, you should hit them first, so I did."

"All right, Billy. Go on and find your brothers and please stay out of trouble." Momma took his little dirty face in both hands, bent over, kissed his forehead, and added, "Okay?"

Billy ran out of the room hollering back over his shoulder, "Okay, Momma."

Billy stood on the front porch. He knew Sonny was in town and the other kids were playing around in back. He thought that maybe he would go to find Sonny and see what he was doing. He headed up the street. After two blocks Billy saw the boy he had fought with only minutes before. He walked up and said hello to the boy.

"I hope I didn't hurt you," Billy said. Before the boy could say anything his father came out of the house. He grabbed Billy by the arm and pulled him through the door of the house; he slapped him across the face knocking him down.

"I'm sorry for hitting your son." Billy cried. The man hit him again and again. The brute opened the screen door and threw Billy out onto the porch, and shouted, "I'd better never see you around here or anywhere near my son again. Do you hear me?"

Billy got up as quickly as he could and stumbled down

the sidewalk. He looked back and didn't see the boy's father, but the boy was standing there just looking at him. He didn't say anything.

Daddy and Sonny had just returned home when Billy came into the house. Blood was running from his nose and mouth. His arm had a big red welt where the man had grabbed him. Daddy asked, "What the hell happened to you, boy?" Billy said later it was funny that he didn't even start crying until he saw his daddy and his older brother. Billy told our father what had happened. Sonny was standing there kind of moving from one foot to the other ready for any kind of action.

Daddy took Billy by the hand and, with Sonny and Momma following right behind, headed back up the same street that Billy had so painfully just traveled. It was clear he didn't want to go back, but he was able to show our father which house belonged to the man who had just beaten him up so badly. Daddy stopped on the sidewalk leading up to the house.

"Everyone stay out of the way, don't move!" With that he stepped up on the porch and kicked in the door. The boy Billy punched was inside and ran into another room. The boy's father was standing in the kitchen. Daddy walked up to the brutal man and hit him in the mouth, knocking him down. He then kicked him in the ribs several times, grabbed him by the hair, and pulled him back through the living room over the busted door and out onto the porch. He put one knee in the man's chest and hit him in the mouth again. Teeth and blood went everywhere. "Now, you son-of-a-bitch, tell my boy how sorry you are."

Sonny was like Daddy in many ways. If he got riled he'd plunge head long, smack dab into the middle of whatever the problem was. One afternoon Sonny, Billy, and Lesley were walking home from school. Lesley was running a little ahead of the other two when he came upon three other boys. One of the boys said something nasty to him, so Lesley picked up a rock and chucked it at the boy. The fight was on or, more accurately, the chase was on. As I told you earlier, Lesley could run and he did too, right back to his older brothers. Sonny heard the whole story even before Lesley got there. You see Lesley could not only run, he could holler pretty loud, too. The other three boys were about Sonny's size. They knew some pretty good curse words, which they proceeded to use on Lesley. Sonny walked up to the one who was doing most of the talking, aimed for his eye, then struck with his left fist. The boy dropped to his knees. Lesley ran up and kicked him. Billy ran home, and Sonny started swinging at the other two.

The boy that Sonny had punched yelled to his friends, "Watch out he's a lefty, he's gonna hit you with his left hand, he's a lefty."

Our mother was sitting on the front porch rocking me when Billy ran up crying. He told her that three big boys were beating up Sonny. Momma came off the porch and grabbed Billy by the arm. Still carrying me, she made her way back to where Sonny was holding his own with those three boys. Lesley was kicking, running, and screaming.

Momma looked Billy right in his little scared face. She told him that he had better get in there and help his brothers or she was going to whip him herself. She let go of his arm. He turned around with tears in his eyes, but he ran into the middle the fracas with both fists flying. The fight was soon over.

After that fight, and possibly a few more, the boys around town started calling Sonny by a name that was to become known throughout the country music world . . . Lefty . . . Lefty Frizzell.

CHAPTER FOUR

PLEASE BE MINE, DEAR BLUE EYES

Our father received orders for Europe. He had been at the Greenville base a little over a year and was excited about leaving. He had never been anywhere except to Arkansas, Texas, and Oklahoma, and he was pretty eager to go. It didn't take him long to pack, and after giving last orders to our mother and the kids he boarded a bus to Houston. In no time at all he was standing on foreign soil.

Bob Green and his wife took a liking to Momma and us kids. Bob owned two large farms just outside of Greenville, Texas. They had no children of their own and they had a lot of room for kids to run and play, so they allowed the Frizzell family to move into one of the farm houses. After moving to Greenville, Sonny, who was now beginning to be called Lefty by a few friends, no longer attended school.

Every Saturday people came from all over the country to downtown Greenville to the Treadway Market, which was something of a farmers' market. Some came to talk and shop. Old men came to play checkers and dominos, or just to see who could tell the biggest lie. Women came to gossip and buy material for clothes for their families. Girls came to flirt with the boys; boys came to chase the girls. Momma and Sonny came to sing and play music.

Sonny tuned his guitar and threw the old homemade strap around his shoulder. Standing up, he hit a C chord and starting singing a Jimmie Rodgers song:

> "I had a friend named Campbell.
> He used to rob, steal and gamble."

Sonny was moving around, singing, and playing. People began looking up from whatever they were doing. They quit talking to each other. Everyone was paying attention to this curly-haired, guitar-playing young man.

Sonny then broke into Jimmie's famous yodel: "Yod-da-ly-ee-ee, Yod-da-ly-ee-ee, Yod-da-ly-ee-ee, Yod-da-ly-ee-ee, Yod-da-ly-ee-ee."

Sonny was really getting into the song and the audience was, too. Everyone was clapping their hands to the beat, some were stomping their feet. Momma jumped up from her chair and broke into the Charleston. Sonny kept right on singing and yodeling: "Yod-da-ly-ee-ee, Yod-da-ly-ee-ee, Yod-da-ly-ee-ee, Yod-da-ly-ee-ee, Yod-da-ly-ee-ee." When the song was over people gave him great applause, and everyone yelled for more. That's when our mother would pass the hat.

Around that time, Sonny met another Greenville, Texas, boy named Gene Wentworth. Gene played the guitar a little, so he and Sonny started playing weekend parties and dances, anywhere people gathered to forget some of their everyday problems. Momma would go along, too. She had a very special way with people. Everybody loved the pretty little lady with the great personality and her good looking, talented son. They were invited everywhere. After a time she didn't even have to pass the hat.

Musically, Sonny had been heavily influenced by Ernest Tubb, and especially by Jimmie Rodgers. Personally, he was influenced by movie cowboys, like Gene Autry and Tom Mix, to name a couple. He loved the way they dressed from their hats clear down to their cowboy boots. Sonny wore a handkerchief just like them; first, because that was the cowboy look, second, because it helped to hide the birthmark on his face and neck and, and third, because our mother could sew them for him.

Momma would also make Sonny shirts with different kinds of buttons. Sometimes she would cowboy them up with snaps instead of buttons, and she would add embroidery. She could make them anyway he liked, and that suited him just fine.

To say times were a little rough would be an understatement. Our mother had it really hard. She was trying to rear seven kids, the oldest almost fifteen and the youngest only two. Her husband was in the army stationed out of the country. The government allotment check was not coming in yet. Sonny brought in some money which, added to what little Momma took in from washing and ironing, at least put food on the table. Momma did have to get away once in awhile. She would go and visit with friends, and Sonny would do the babysitting.

Our sister, Mae, recalled, "Sonny would gather us kids in the living room, and we'd sit on the floor or wherever. He'd hang a white sheet up from the ceiling and hook up some lights, and then he'd get behind the sheet and put on a show. He would act out every part. Sometimes he'd be a monster or maybe a cartoon character, or other times he'd just get his guitar and sing for us. He'd entertain us 'til Momma came back. One time he told Momma, 'It's better having them sitting there watching me than chasing them all over the place.'"

Mae laughed. "Actually, he did chase us all over the place a few times. We each had a stick horse and his was, of course, the biggest, the fastest, and the loudest. Brother Bill's stick horse was the prettiest one, though. He'd use Momma's mop so his horse would have a mane, and he would use a belt for the reins.

"One time we were playing stick horse; we were running

all through the house and everywhere. Momma was mopping the kitchen. David slipped on the wet floor and broke his right leg in three places. Somewhere, somehow, Sonny found a little red wagon and brought it home. He would make each one of us kids take turns pulling David around. We'd argue about it, but we did it. Sonny even made that fun."

Sonny was singing mostly Ernest Tubb and Jimmie Rodgers songs, but he wanted to make up his own words, put his own music to them. One of his first songs was a love ballad titled "Please Be Mine, Dear Blue Eyes." There were probably several girls at that time who thought the song was written for them. We know that a lovely young lady by the name of Evelyn may have been one of them. Actually, the song was written for a very pretty blonde, blue-eyed girl by the name of Margaret.

Margaret was Sonny's first love, a love not meant to be. She came from a nice family living in Greenville. They didn't want their daughter going with a young man who had dropped out of school and didn't have any visible means of support, much less a boy who only wanted to sing and play guitar. In their eyes he even dressed funny and looked different from the other kids his age. They saw no future for their daughter with this boy. They wanted much more for her. He was told to stay away from her.

Margaret didn't agree with her parents, so every once in a while she and Sonny found a way to meet. Sonny poured out his young heart to her, but in the end Margaret did as her parents told her. She finished high school and wanted to go on to college. Her father found a school in Dallas, some eighty miles away, and arranged for her to live there with his brother's family.

Sonny was heartbroken. Our mother could see he was truly hurting. She tried to tell him to forget that girl. "Sonny, stop your moping around. You're only fifteen and you act as if the world is coming to an end."

Sonny let it come out. "Momma, you don't know, my world is ending. I don't want to do anything without her. I love her, Momma."

Momma hated seeing Sonny walking around wringing his hands. "Sonny, it don't matter how you feel really. They told you to stay away from her. Now they've sent her off somewhere. Besides there's girls all over the place; you can find another one."

Sonny looked Momma square in the face, and he gently put his arm around her shoulder. "I don't want any of those other girls and...hey." Sonny got really excited. His face brightened up; he even broke into a smile. "Momma, you know someone who can find her, your friend, you know, your friend Buttermilk Wallace. She knows everybody. Anyway, I think Margaret's down in Dallas, matter of fact, I know she is. She told me they have relatives there. That's where she is."

Momma could tell Sonny was just dying inside. "Sonny, we don't know where in Dallas she is. Dallas is a big place. We'll never find her down there." She was hopeful that he would give up on the crazy idea of trying to find Margaret.

"Momma, I'm going with or without you. You don't know how I miss her. I'm going crazy out of my mind. I don't know what else to do. I've got to try."

Momma hugged Sonny close. "You really are crazy if you think you can find her in Dallas."

"Buttermilk Wallace knows everyone and everyone knows her. Let's go over there right now. I'll bet you she can tell us exactly where Margaret is." Lefty cried out.

"All right," Momma agreed. "But if she doesn't know, that's as far as I go, do you understand?" Sonny nodded and headed for the door.

Buttermilk Wallace had lived in Greenville for a long time. Everyone knew and liked her. She made and sold dairy products like butter, buttermilk, milk, and clabbered milk. People would buy the clabbered milk to make bread and rolls. Sonny was right, Buttermilk knew everyone. She sold her dairy products, but the advice and gossip were free. If you needed to know anything about anyone, you could ask Buttermilk Wallace. She could give you the skinny on everyone in town.

Buttermilk and our mother got along just fine. They had spent many hours together sitting out on Buttermilk's front porch gossiping. They talked and laughed about things they did in the past, things they might do today or tomorrow, but especially what other people were doing.

"Hello, Buttermilk," Momma said. "I need a block of that butter and I hope you got a minute to spare."

"AD, come on in." Buttermilk was busy with the churn. "I'm making fresh butter right now. Besides I always got time, nothing more important than spending time with friends. I haven't seen you in a while. You been busy with that boy of yours? He sure sings good, don't he?" Buttermilk stopped churning. "AD, come on out to the porch, I need a break anyway. You want a smoke?" With that she opened a can of Prince Albert. She picked up a small book of cigarette papers and rolled a couple of cigarettes. "Here you go," Buttermilk handed Momma a cigarette. "Sit down here now and tell me what you've been doing."

Momma took the cigarette. She sat back in her chair and lit up. "You know my boy, Sonny," she took a big drag on her cigarette. "Well, he likes this girl, and this girl's family has taken her somewhere. He can't find her; it's driving him crazy."

Buttermilk puffed a cloud of smoke into the air. "Ain't that a shame. AD, you want a cold glass of milk? What's the girl's name anyhow?"

Momma took the glass of milk. "Margaret's her name. She's got blonde hair and blue eyes. She's very pretty, but I don't know anything else about her."

Buttermilk sat there thinking for a moment. "I know who

she is. I know her family. They're kind of uppity. They don't buy nothin' from me, so I don't know them real well. She is a pretty girl, though. Your boy's stuck on her, huh?"

Momma smiled. "He sure is. He just paces the floor, wringing his hands and making up love songs about her. I think he'll go crazy if we don't find her. Think you can help us?"

Buttermilk flashed a smile. "Don't you worry about nothin'. Before this day is out, we'll know everything there is to know about his sweet blonde, blue-eyed little Margaret. Now what else is going on, AD? How's your soldier boy doing?"

Sonny sat down one afternoon, picked up his guitar, and wrote his first song—a love song to Margaret.

PLEASE BE MINE, DEAR BLUE EYES

Got me a girl the other day.
She don't like me much they say,
That she talks more bout her other boy friend.
She's the girl of my dreams and
I love true it seems.
Darling, my poor heart just won't give in.
Met you, dear, I was surprised
When I saw your two blue eyes.
Darling, my poor heart was filled with joy.
I was glad till I heard the news,
But there's where I caught my blues.
For they said you thought more of the other boy.
You've been with me, you like me some,
But your love for me is none.
Please don't tell me, dear, I know that I would cry.
For it always makes me blue

To think I can't have you.
Please be mine, yes be mine
Dear blue eyes.
Dear, I'm happy when I'm with you.
I'm not sad, and I'm not blue.
It will hurt me to tell you goodbye.
Seems like my dreams they came true,
When you said, dear, I love you.
Please be mine, yes be mine,
Dear blue eyes.

The paper with Margaret's address in Dallas was neatly folded and placed in Sonny's shirt pocket. He had talked our mother into taking him to Dallas, and he was excited. He jumped up early that morning and got dressed in his favorite black slacks, boots, and a brand new white shirt that Momma had made for him. It had western stitching over the pockets, across the back, and around the sleeves. Sonny tied a scarf around his neck, and then he went about waking up everyone else in the house.

"Come on everyone get up, get dressed, and get in the car."

Sonny was happy for the first time since Margaret was sent away. With Sonny's help, Momma and the kids got ready pretty fast.

"Momma, you sure look good in that hat, are you ready?" Sonny was almost pulling her to the door.

"Yeah, I'm ready. Now don't get your hopes up too high. You still may not be able to see her." Momma was trying to prepare Sonny for what she believed was going to happen.

"Oh, Momma, I'll see her all right," Sonny laughed. "Us driving all that way will show them how serious I am. Oh, I can't wait! The kids are all in the car, so let's go. Oh, wait! I can't forget my guitar."

The drive from Greenville to Dallas was filled with talking, laughing, pushing, and shoving. In a car filled with six kids, a half-grown, love sick boy, and a mother who was no more than a kid herself, we covered the eighty miles in no time at all.

Momma pulled over to the curb in front of the house. "Okay, kids, do not open these doors. Everyone stays in the car." All of the kids were asleep except one. Eight-year-old Betty wasn't about to go to sleep. She didn't want to miss the performance on the porch.

Sonny was nervous as he and Momma walked up the steps to the front door. He knocked, and a lady in her mid-thirties answered the door.

"Hello, can I help you?"

Sonny tried to clear his dry throat. "Uh, hello, ma'am, my name is Sonny Frizzell, and I wonder if maybe Margaret is home. We've drove all the way from Greenville to see her. Oh, this is my mom."

The lady looked from one to the other. "You know Margaret from Greenville?" she asked.

"Yeah, we're great friends," he said. "Is she here?"

"Well, she was a little while ago. Let me see if I can find her." The lady turned and standing right behind her was Margaret. Margaret looked at Sonny and smiled. They both knew this was right. His coming all that way was right, at least for the last time.

The lady grabbed Margaret's arm. "I'll bet this is the young man your father warned us about, and I promised I'd look after you."

"Aunt Helen," Margaret said softly, "it's all right. I'm not going anywhere. We'll

stay right here." With that the young girl pushed by her aunt. She caught Sonny's arm and they walked to the far end of the porch.

Our sister, Betty, was watching closely. She saw how our mother was talking a mile a minute to the lady to keep her distracted from Sonny and Margaret at the other end of the porch.

Boy, this was better than the movies, Betty thought.

"Margaret, I've missed you something terrible," Sonny exclaimed. "When you were gone, and I couldn't find you, I just wanted to die."

Margaret looked him in the eyes. "You've got to forget about me. My father would kill us both. If he knew you were here, he'd be so mad. If he finds out you came here, I don't know what he may do. He is determined to keep me away from you."

Sonny took her hand. "Why doesn't he like me? I haven't done anything to him or to hurt you, and I never will. I just can't understand why."

"He doesn't think you'll ever be worth anything. He says you'll never amount to a hill of beans." Margaret lowered her eyes. "He just doesn't like your looks, he told me so." Tears filled her eyes.

Sonny put his hand under her chin and raised her pretty head. When their eyes met, he made her a promise. "One of these days I'll be back. I'm gonna drive up in the biggest car ever made. I'm gonna have more money than your old man has ever seen, and when I do he's gonna remember me. He'll know who I am. One of these days everyone will know who I am. I promise you."

Sonny heard of a store in Dallas that made and sold western suits. He felt that he had to have one, maybe something like Gene Autry might wear. "Momma, listen, you know if I'm going to be a singer, I've got to look like one. I can sing and play my guitar, but I need a cowboy suit. Now I know that a hundred dollars is a lot of money, but if you'll buy me that suit I know I can pay you back."

"Ah, Sonny," Momma sighed. "Right now I don't have that much. We'd have to pay something down and maybe pay it off later. I don't know."

Sonny thought about it for a moment. "Momma, listen, if you'll give me twenty dollars, I've got ten, I believe they'll take that much as a down payment. Then, by the time they get it made, we'll have plenty of time to get the rest of the money. Momma, please, I've just got to have it."

Momma stopped what she was doing and put her arms around Sonny, and hugged him tight. She thought about how hard he worked and what he'd been through. She thought about his riding a bike through the rain and mud just to make a few pennies, which he shared with the family. She just couldn't say no to him.

Everywhere one Frizzell went, everybody went, so she packed all the kids into the car and drove the eighty miles to Dallas, again, where Sonny bought his special cowboy suit.

Sonny was excited about his first show suit. "I'll wear it only when I'm on stage, Momma. You're gonna to be so proud of me someday. And, Momma, when I do make it, you'll never want for anything, I promise!"

Sonny picked out the material for his suit, a man took his measurements, and said the order would be ready in about two to three weeks. Momma loaded everyone into the car and headed back to Greenville.

When the store called and said that Sonny's suit was ready everyone was excited, down to the smallest kid. We all jumped into the car and laughed and sang all the way to Dallas. Sonny was beaming. He couldn't wait to see himself in his special suit.

When he tried it on and looked in the mirror, he knew that somehow, someday, he would wear that suit singing in front of huge crowds. He knew that people would come from miles around to hear him sing and see him wearing his special suit.

Back home in Greenville, with the kids all seated on the floor, Sonny stood in the middle of the bed wearing his new suit; he didn't want the pant legs to touch the floor. Sonny sure looked like a star.

Wait a minute. . . . he thought, *Sonny Frizzell, no, no not Sonny . . . Lefty Frizzell. Yeah!* He looked at himself in the mirror, kind of smiled and said, "Lefty Frizzell, you sure do look like a star . . . ah!"

CHAPTER FIVE

TRAVELIN' BLUES

Every Saturday night Lefty and our mother would play at some house party, the Treadway Market in Greenville, or anywhere they could. Well, I guess Lefty would play and Momma would dance. Between the two of them, they kept the house rocking. Finally, Lefty landed a Sunday afternoon show at KPLT Radio in Paris, Texas. This was a major step. Now he was a radio performer, and even though KPLT was only a 250 watt station he could tell that more people around the country knew him. This was really when Lefty realized how powerful radio was. He now knew that he could reach more people by radio than he could by singing somewhere on Saturday nights. Plus, he actually got paid for singing without having to pass the hat. Lefty was now a professional singer.

One afternoon after the radio show in Paris, Momma, Gene, and Lefty dropped by a soldiers' free hotel in Sulphur Springs. Lefty and Gene got their guitars and started playing. It wasn't long before Lefty noticed a beautiful, dark-haired girl staring at him. She probably hadn't seen too many boys who looked like Lefty with long, dark curly hair hanging down over his forehead, and wearing a beautiful handmade cowboy shirt and a matching scarf around his neck; a young boy who could sing and play with a smile that could light up Dallas. No, there weren't too many boys around like him. Lefty played a Jimmie Rodgers' song, "My Rough and Rowdy Ways," and then he put down his guitar and walked over to the dark-haired girl.

"Hello, my name's Lefty. What's yours?"

"Well, my name is Alice. Is your name really Lefty? I've never met anyone with a name like that."

"Yeah, it's Lefty all right, but my family still calls me Sonny. Do you like my singing?"

"Uh huh!" Alice smiled. "I think I've heard some of those songs, and you sing 'em pretty good." Alice went on to tell him that her aunt and uncle ran the hotel. "I come over once in awhile to visit, and I'm really glad I came by today."

Lefty smiled. "Maybe I'll see you again soon." With that he walked away, packed up his guitar, and left.

On the way home Lefty told Momma about meeting Alice. He told her that Alice's aunt and uncle ran the hotel where they had just been.

"I know them, that's Ruby and Lewis Satterfield," Momma said. "I've invited Ruby over to the Treadway Market next Saturday, and maybe if I ask her to she might bring Alice over there with her."

Lefty grinned. "All right."

Alice came to the Treadway Market the next Saturday with her Aunt Ruby. Lefty made quite a sight that day with his long, curly dark hair, white cowboy shirt, and a bright yellow scarf. Why, it was enough to take a girl's breath away.

Alice pointed out Lefty to her aunt. "That's him over there," Alice whispered. "I think he's getting ready to sing, listen."

"Hello, everyone, my name is Lefty Frizzell. I've got a song for you." With that Lefty sang:

"I'm a pistol packing poppa,
And when I walk down the street,
Yod-da-ly-ee-ee, Yod-da-ly-ee-ee."

Alice was impressed with what she was hearing and seeing, and she really couldn't believe it when Momma jumped up and started dancing all around the room.

"Aunt Ruby," Alice breathed, "have you ever seen anything like him before?"

Aunt Ruby thought for a moment. "I don't think I've ever seen anything like either one of them before. They are both something." She was laughing and clapping her hands along to the music, having the time of her life.

Lefty and Alice started a relationship that would span the next thirty-one years. The beginning years were really something to talk about, unbelievable ups and downs, arguing then making up, knock down drag out fights. Alice could hold her own, too, no doubt about it. They could argue about anything, fight at the drop of a hat, then just as quickly be making over each other totally in love. More important was that they were always there for each other.

Alice Lee Harper was born July 1, 1928, in Winnsboro, Texas. Her father's name was Luther Thomas Harper, and her mother's name was Mina Dickey Harper. She had one younger brother, Luther Thomas Harper Jr.—everyone just called him Junior. Alice's father moved his family around doing farm labor in and around Sulphur Springs. Her mother died of pneumonia about the time Alice reached school age.

After his wife's death, Luther Sr. took to the road leaving Alice and Junior at Ruby's house in Sulphur Springs or their grandmother's house in Winnsboro. Luther eventually returned, remarried, and settled down in Mt. Pleasant. He left again when he joined the Seabees.

Lefty and Alice's romance flourished throughout the spring of 1944. By summer they were seeing each other as much as possible. Lefty would play and sing at every event imaginable, and every Sunday he traveled to Paris for his weekly radio show. Alice never missed listening, even though the station barely reached her father's house in Mt. Pleasant.

When they couldn't be together, they would write letters. The letters would say how much they missed each other and what they planned on doing when they were together again. Lefty would sometimes tell Alice where he was playing, towns like Sherman and Dennison. He would tell her when he would be back. Their relationship kept growing through that year.

Lefty had been on the road for three and a half weeks playing every club and dive in northeast Texas. He was really glad to be home, and he had to tell Momma everything he had done. She wanted to know every detail of the tour. She couldn't get used to his being gone without her, and she missed going to the dances with him.

After awhile Lefty said, "Momma, I want to go pick up Alice tonight. We'll probably see a movie or something, but I've got to see her. I've missed her real bad. You know we've been writing to each other and, Momma, I think she loves me. At least, she says she does."

Momma put her arm around his shoulder. "Do you love her?"

"Momma, sometimes I do." He smiled. "Well, most of the time I do, I guess. All I know is I think of her all the time, and when I'm not with her all I can think of is being with her. Most of the time I can't get my mind off her. Even when I'm singing, it seems like I'm singing my songs right to her." Lefty paused, then asked, "Is that love, Momma?"

Lefty talked Momma out of the car keys, and within an hour Alice was sitting next to him. He was trying to drive and she was hugging and kissing him.

"Sonny, don't leave me like that again. I just miss you too much. I don't want to be here, there, or anywhere if you're not with me. You know I sure do like getting your letters. I've never got a lot of letters before. You know, I'll bet I've never written or received as many letters as we've sent to each other in my whole life." Alice was talking a mile a minute.

Lefty laughed. "You know I can always leave you long enough to write you a few more letters."

Alice punched him. "You got anything to say to me, you can just tell me in person from now on." They drove around most of the night laughing and talking. They finally parked somewhere between Greenville and Sulphur Springs. It was decided then that they would never be apart again.

"Momma, we want to get married." Lefty and Alice ran through the door waking up everyone in the house. It was just getting daylight. "Momma, listen, we've been out all night long. I can't take Alice home now; we've got to get married."

Momma slowly got out of bed. The other kids were waking up trying to figure out what was going on. "Sonny, being out all night isn't enough reason to get married. There's got to be more to it than that."

Lefty hugged Momma. "Yeah there is. We love each other, Momma, and we don't want to be away from each other anymore."

Alice added, "We want to be together for the rest of our lives, AD. We love each other so much." Alice ran over to Momma and they hugged each other. They both cried a little, too.

"Now, listen you two, there isn't any other reason is there?"

At first neither Alice nor Lefty knew what Momma meant. Finally, it dawned on them what she was asking.

"No, Momma, nothing like that. We just want to get married."

Momma put her arm around Lefty's shoulder. "Sonny, you're too young to get married. You haven't had very many girlfriends. You're just too young. You're both too young."

Lefty hugged her. "Momma, you and Daddy got married at about the same age as we are, and besides, I've had other girlfriends. I just don't want to marry them."

Lefty and Alice were both laughing and crying. They jumped up and started dancing around the house. All the kids saw Lefty and Alice dancing around, so we followed along doing the same thing.

Lefty was singing, "We're gonna get married, we're gonna get married."

Alice and all of us kids chimed in, "We're gonna get married, we're gonna get married." Ola Mae and I, the two youngest, didn't even know what we were singing about, but we knew that something exciting was about to happen. We knew it was time to dance.

Lefty was driving with Alice between him and Momma. I had the best seat in the car, on Momma's lap. The other five kids were in the back. We were headed to Hugo, Oklahoma, to Aunt OV's house. Momma hadn't seen her sister in a while. When she told her that Lefty and Alice wanted to get married, Aunt OV just took over.

"Okay, let's go downtown. I'll stand up for Alice and, AD, you stand up for Sonny. We'll get this done. Come on, let's go."

Momma already had seven kids. She thought, *What is one more?* She took Alice in and treated her like her own.

Lefty and Alice were young, in love, and married, but they were still kids. They loved to play games like hide and seek. All the kids would search for them, but sometimes they just couldn't be found. Alice would even play jacks with the smaller kids. Sonny and Alice would play card games, running games, all kinds of kid games; however, the one they liked the best was "Take the mattress into the woods." This was a game that only the two of them could play. The rest of us just had to sit that one out.

There was a pond down the road about a half mile from the house where all the kids would go swimming. One day Alice asked Lefty to take an old door down to the pond so she could float on it and sunbathe. Lefty told her how crazy an idea that

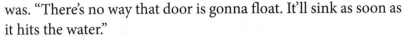

was. "There's no way that door is gonna float. It'll sink as soon as it hits the water."

Alice whined, "Now, Sonny, come on, it'll work; don't be so lazy."

Lefty picked up one end of the door and told Billy to grab the other end. "Alice, this door will never hold you. Even if it don't sink, it will as soon as you get on it, that's for sure."

Alice didn't even look at him. She just started walking toward the pond, then said back over her shoulder, "It'll work and I'm gonna float all day on it, so come on."

Lefty and Billy finally got the door down to the pond. They threw the door into the water, and everyone just stood there and watched as the door sank out of sight.

"Momma," Lefty walked out onto the front porch where Momma was sitting in a chair. "My life is over, over before I ever did anything." Lefty sat down beside our mother. He ran his fingers through his curly hair and kind of slumped back into his chair. Momma had been thinking about our father, about how much longer it would be before he got discharged from the army, and would be coming home. A lot of things had changed while he had been gone, and to tell the truth she was dreading the day he would return.

"What did you say, Sonny? I was thinking about your daddy; about when he's coming home, about how we're gonna tell him about you getting married and all." She was also trying to figure out how much farther down into that chair Sonny could scoot.

"Momma, I'm gonna have a baby," Lefty softly cried and he seemed to sink a little farther into the chair. Alice walked out onto the porch just as Lefty said, "Why, I'm just now old enough to be looking at girls. I'm too young to be married and too young to be having a baby."

If this hadn't been such a serious moment, Momma would have laughed out loud, but seeing Alice standing there getting madder by the minute, and her boy slumped down into that chair, she knew this was no laughing matter.

"Now wait a minute, Sonny, you know you can't have a baby."

Alice interrupted, "He's not having a baby, but I am, and I'm not gonna have my baby here, I'm leaving. And I'm going right now." Alice went back inside the house and threw a few clothes into a paper bag. She came back through the door nearly taking the screen with her. Off the porch she went heading down the road. Billy and Lesley were right behind her.

"He didn't mean those things," Billy said. "Come on back now, Alice, please!"

Lefty and Momma watched Alice go down the road with Billy and Lesley right beside her. Billy was trying to at least slow her down. Lesley was crying and begging her to stay.

"I guess I better go get her," Lefty said as he tried to get up from the chair.

Momma was watching Alice huffing and puffing down the road when her mind went back to our father. She thought of when he would come home, and how he would be shocked to find their oldest boy of sixteen not only married but going to be a father himself. *Oh my God, how much more time do I have, how am I gonna tell him? Oh my God.*

Eventually, Lefty caught Alice. "Alice, please don't go, you know I was just kidding.

Please stay, Alice." After begging and pleading with her for a while, Lefty finally convinced Alice to stay.

The Reverend Lewis E. Satterfield and his wife, Ruby, still ran the service men's free hotel in Sulphur Springs, Texas, the place where Lefty and Alice had first met. One day Ruby stopped by our house to visit and talk about a way to make some extra money.

"AD, listen, you know Lewis collects money around town to help support the service men's free hotel. All the collectors wear these uniforms. You just put these on, take a tambourine, and walk around town into the stores and different businesses collecting money. All you do is walk up to someone, shake the tambourine and ask, 'Would you like to give to the cause?' People will drop change into the tambourine. After a day's work you come to the hotel and we'll take our cut; you can have the rest, that's all there is to it," she paused. "What do you think?"

"You know, this is something I think I can do. I can shake that tambourine right along with the best of 'em."

Alice laughed and said, "So can I, just wait till they see me."

Lefty was shaking his head. "I just can't do something like that. I could never walk up to someone, shaking a tambourine, and ask for a handout. I just can't do it."

"Sonny, it's not a handout, it's for the cause." Alice looked right into Lefty's eyes. "Besides we need the money, you know, for the baby and things."

"All right, I'll go. I'll drive; we can cover a lot of ground using the car. We can go everywhere, but remember I have to be back for my radio show every Sunday. I'm not going to give up my music."

With Lefty driving, Alice and Momma collected money "for the cause" from Sulphur Springs and Greenville all the way to Dallas and Fort Worth. Things were going fine, just fine, until one day in early September.

A taxi cab drove into the yard and our father stepped out of the car.

Our father joined the Army Air Corps in Little Rock, Arkansas, on September 25, 1942, one day before my first birthday. The next day he was sent to Greenville, Texas, for basic training. After boot camp he moved our family to Sulphur Springs. He spent a little over one year at the Greenville training base before receiving orders to ship out, beginning his foreign service tour of duty. He was involved in the Normandy, Rhineland, and Northern France campaigns.

Daddy was awarded several decorations and citations; the campaign medal with three bronze stars and the good conduct medal, the bronze star medal, the Purple Heart, the American Campaign Medal, the European-African-Middle East Campaign Medal, and the WWII Victory Medal, all of which were authorized on a document issued May 1, 1969.

He was sent to Fort Sam Houston, Texas, where he was released from active duty on September 9, 1945. He caught a bus to Sulphur Springs some 327 miles north, arrived there the following day, and took a taxi home where his wife and seven children, plus one pregnant daughter-in-law, were living. He returned to a home and family he hadn't seen in one year, nine months, and twenty-one days. He walked into a home where no one was expecting him.

Our father stepped out of the cab, reached back in and retrieved his duffle bag, and paid the driver. Then he just stood there looking at the house. He didn't recognize the car parked in the drive. He could see his oldest daughter, Betty, staring at him over the fender of the car. She said nothing. The other kids, Lesley, Johnnie and Ola Mae, came around the corner of the house running and laughing. I was four at the time and brought up the rear. We seemed to all see him at the same time. Everyone stopped; there was not another sound. Daddy walked past the car, and us, and went right up to the house. He opened the screen door and stepped inside.

Sonny was sitting on the couch playing his guitar with

Alice beside him. Billy was on the floor with an oatmeal box between his legs hitting it like a drum. They were all singing "Chattanooga Shoeshine Boy" at the top of their lungs.

Our mother was in the kitchen making dinner and singing along. The house was full of music and fun, inside and out, until now.

Sonny saw Daddy first and yelled, "Hey, Momma, Daddy's home."

Momma came to the kitchen door. She saw her husband for the first time in almost two years. "My goodness, you surprised me, why didn't you let us know you'd be coming in today?"

Daddy threw his duffle bag in the corner. "I'm home all right, what the hell is going on here?" He looked around and saw Alice for the first time. "Who's this?" Billy was already scooting on his butt trying to get away into another room.

Sonny got up and laid his guitar down. "Daddy, this is Alice, we're married!"

"The hell you say!"

"We're gonna have a baby, too!" Lefty shot back.

Alice simply didn't know what to do. She didn't know whether to get up or just sit there. She probably felt like running. Billy was squeezed up against the wall and didn't move.

Momma came further into the room. She could see her kids were all confused and scared. "Naamon, Sonny wrote you a letter telling you he'd gotten married, and we figured you knew."

Daddy was still dressed in his army uniform. He was so mad that he took his hat and threw it against the wall. "You figured I knew! How can you figure anything, you stupid ass? I'm over there getting shot at, damn near killed, and you all over here living high on the hog with my money, not a one of you working, nobody doing nothing. Whose car is that in the drive?"

Momma cried out, "That's mine! I traded the old junk car you left and bought a good one. I didn't just use your money either. We worked; we all worked. We've been working and we saved our money."

Dad hit her across the mouth. She went flying back into the kitchen. Betty and Lesley were looking in from the screen door. They started screaming. Ola Mae, Johnnie, and I heard them so we started screaming, too. Sonny ran over to Daddy.

"Don't hit her again; she's done nothing. You come home after two years and the only thing you can think of to do is knock Momma around." Sonny stood there expecting Daddy to hit him, but he didn't. He stopped and looked at Sonny.

"Why are you so skinny, boy?" he asked. Then he nodded toward Alice. "How long's she got?"

Sonny looked over at Alice, he could see she was scared to death. Billy had melted into the wall at this point. The other kids quit screaming except for me.

Momma said, "Betty, go get David. Walk him around and stop him from crying."

She pulled herself up from the floor.

"She's got about five months to go, Daddy," Sonny said. He walked over to Alice and helped her up. "Honey, this is my daddy."

Alice walked over to Daddy with her head down. "Nice to meet you, Sonny has talked about you a lot." She finally raised her eyes to look him in the face. Daddy liked her right off.

"Okay, listen to me, all of you. I'm here to tell you the boom is over. We're gonna get down to business here; everyone will have something to do. We all work around here; the laying around at this house is done. I'm back now and the boom is over." With that Daddy walked into the kitchen.

Momma looked over at Alice and whispered, "What boom is he talking about?"

In the days following our father's return home, he became more and more upset over the changes Momma had made while he was gone. Changes like putting beds in the house instead of pallets on the floor and curtains on the windows. For the first time she had a sofa in the living room. She even had a better car than the one he had left behind. Daddy was ready to go somewhere else, to start over with him in charge.

Our mother had two older brothers who were living with their families in New Mexico. One of them, Johnnie, lived in Hagerman and the other, RA, known as Ray, lived in Roswell. Both made a living picking cotton. The thing that appealed to Daddy about picking cotton was the whole family could work, kids and all. Everyone pulled his or her own weight. I was four years old and the smallest of the Frizzell children, so I didn't have much weight to pull. Bill and Sonny were a different matter all together.

Daddy thought, *Yes, this a great idea. Everyone working together, seeing how hard it is to make a living. Might do em' all good, besides, I've spent the last three years serving my country, risking my neck. They can work right beside me, and I'll show em' all how it's done.*

It could have been moving to New Mexico, living in the desert, or maybe the picking cotton part that prompted Lefty and Alice to make another assault on Dallas. They had a few dollars saved, and with the help of Daddy they bought an old Model A car.

Lefty said to Alice one day, "You know, Daddy's gonna move everyone out of here. I've heard him talking about going to New Mexico. Boy, I just don't wanna go. There's nothing there but sagebrush, sand dunes, and rattlesnakes. Besides I don't think I can pick cotton, it'll tear up my hands. It'll make it hard to play my guitar. You know what? I think if we try Dallas one more time, I'll bet I can find a playing job. I'll never amount to anything picking cotton."

Alice smiled. "You're right, anything will beat going out there with them. I see no future at all in New Mexico. I believe Dallas will do just fine by us."

Lefty went to Daddy and told him of their plans. Momma helped Alice pack what little clothes they had into one small suitcase. Off they went to find their future in Dallas, two very determined people, both seventeen years old. What a pair they made; one five month pregnant girl and a very skinny, curly headed, guitar strumming country boy.

Mother's nephew, Robert Anderson, her sister Ethel's oldest boy, lived in Dallas. Lefty drove to his house because he knew Robert would put them up until they could find work. Alice found a job as a waitress at the Odd Penny Café. Robert drove Lefty from one honky-tonk to another. Sometimes a club owner would ask him to sing a few songs and others just told him no. Outside of town the boys found an old, run-down honky-tonk by the name of the Old Top Rail. This dirty little place was so rough, the owner would kick drunks out and later go out and kick 'em back in.

"My God," Lefty said to Robert, "I kinda hope this guy don't need a singer." As luck would have it, the owner did need a singer to work with his house band. He asked Lefty to sing a song for him. Lefty did and got hired on the spot; he was told he could start Friday night.

Lefty was so excited he could hardly wait to get back to town to tell Alice.

They found a little motel room they could rent by the week and moved in. Lefty started singing his heart out that Friday night. He knew a lot of Ernest Tubb and Jimmie Rodgers songs and every once in awhile he would sing one of his own. "Please Be Mine, Dear Blue Eyes" still worked for him. He had a way with an audience. He would have them dancing one minute and crying in their beer the next.

Things went really well the first weekend. The cotton

fields of New Mexico never crossed his mind as he sang one Jimmie Rodgers song after another. Alice's work was going all right, too. She thought she could do this job in her sleep. She probably did, too, in her dreams, sleeping in her little room and waiting for her man to come home from work smelling like smoke and whiskey. But that was all right; that was okay. At least they were happy. They were making their own way and they were not in New Mexico picking cotton. Things would only get better, or so she thought.

Lefty was going on his third weekend at the Old Top Rail club. When he went to work that Friday the club owner called him aside. "Lefty, you've done a good job for me. I personally like to hear you sing, but the band's complaining. They don't want to play those simple little songs you've been singing. They want to play some Bob Wills-type songs, you know, something with more than three chords in them. Now, understand I can't afford to lose my band. If they walk out I'll have to close this dump, and I can't do that."

Lefty didn't want to believe what he had just heard. "I'll learn some Bob Wills' songs or anybody else's songs. I just need to work. My wife is pregnant and I got to make some money."

The club owner just stood looking at Lefty, then he said, "Well, the boys in the band tell me you sing pretty good, but you're not a musician. They don't think you'll ever be; they don't want to work with you anymore. I'm sorry Lefty," he paused. "So here's what I owe you and a few dollars extra. Good luck to you." With that he turned and walked away.

Lefty stood staring at him. He didn't know what he could have done to deserve such bad luck. He stood there with his guitar in his hands, his head bowed and his heart broken, took a deep breath, and made for the door.

My God, he thought, *what'll I tell Alice?*

Five short years later the same guy, whom they said could sing pretty good but was not a musician and would probably never be, was the number one country music singer in the world. He went on to become a country music legend. Anyway, that was later, this was now.

Lefty and Alice made it back to Greenville just in time to pack the old station wagon, for which Daddy had traded Momma's fine car; eleven people with their belongings piled in and headed for New Mexico.

When the Frizzell family pulled into Roswell, New Mexico, the first thing Daddy did was rent a little house next door to Momma's brother, RA. The next thing we did was start picking cotton. Of all the things Lefty hated, picking cotton was at the top of the list. Daddy, Bill, and Lesley were the best pickers, then came Johnnie Lee and Betty Jo, Momma was next, followed by Ola Mae and me. We think Lefty was somewhere between Ola Mae and me, but he tried; he was there.

Most of the workers would pick just the cotton and leave the bolls and stalks. Lefty, on the other hand, put everything in his sack: cotton, bolls, stalks, and dirt clods. He would add a rock or two if he could find some. If one of the kids came up missing, the first place everyone would look was Lefty's cotton sack. The entire family would try to fill their cotton sacks at the same time so that we could go to the scales and trailer together. Everyone would line up at the scales and put their sacks on for weighing. That weight would be written under each picker's name. At the end of the day Daddy would check to see who was doing the most work.

There was a large wooden plank lying across the top of the trailer. This was so a person could climb up the side of the trailer, walk across the plank, and dump their cotton sack after it had been weighed. The kids would climb up on the trailer and do somersaults off into the cotton where we would jump around. Most of the time the cotton was really nice and soft, except where Sonny had emptied his sack. In that spot there would be cotton stalks, rocks, and all other matter of debris. Everyone knew that Sonny had been there.

There were times when Lefty and Alice would just lie down on the sack and dream about being somewhere else, anywhere else. He would talk about playing his guitar and singing to big crowds. Alice would talk about having their baby and how good a mother she was going to be. Then someone, or something, would bring them back to reality. Reality was being in New Mexico ,out in the middle of a field sitting on a cotton sack, but if two people could live on dreams alone those two would have been rich.

Momma's younger brother, Doc, had just been released from the Army. He came to Roswell to see his sister and his brothers, Johnnie and RA, but he was eager to go on to Oklahoma where he had been sending money throughout his enlistment to his older sister, Ethel. He would have to go right through Texas, and Lefty and Alice were not going to miss this opportunity. So when Doc left he had three extra passengers with him, Lefty, Alice, and the baby who was to be born in less than two months. This time, instead of Dallas, Lefty and Alice got off in Waco, Texas.

Lefty and his long time friend, Gene Wentworth, went to work for the Reverend Lewis E. Satterfield, National Commander of the American Rescue Workers Association in Waco. He was the same Satterfield who had run the service men's free hotel in Sulphur Springs where Lefty first met Alice.

The Reverend had relocated his organization to the Provident Building, 404 Franklin Avenue in Waco. Lefty and Alice had a room on the third floor of this beautiful hotel.

Everything was certainly looking better here than the cotton fields of New Mexico. Lefty's job was to drive a car with three or four other guys to an area around Waco, and then they would walk the streets with a tambourine soliciting money for the American Rescue Workers Association. Lefty and the boys were dressed in uniforms similar to suits worn by the Salvation Army. They would canvas one area, then move on to another. Lefty hated this kind of work, but not as much as picking cotton. He didn't like asking people for money, it was like begging to him. Besides, he had already helped Alice and Momma doing this same thing back before Daddy came home from the service. He had only driven the car, but he didn't like it then either. When the boys had taken all Waco had to give, the Reverend decided it was time to branch out to other places, other cities.

Alice's time was growing near. Lefty wanted to be there with her when the baby was born and so he was. Lois Aleta Frizzell was born February 16, 1946. They brought her home to the hotel and made her bed in a drawer from a cedar chest. Lefty was back on the road soliciting the next day.

The American Rescue Workers hit the road relying on the charity of strangers in San Antonio, Houston, and other south Texas cities. When these had been exhausted, they toured west Texas cities, such as Abilene, Odessa, Midland, and Sweetwater. Lefty would write letters to Alice telling her how lonely and blue he was. He promised to send money as he made it. One letter he wrote from Odessa stated he had earned fifty-three dollars and fifty-five cents. He told Alice that between him and his friend Gene Wentworth they lacked eighty-four cents of making a hundred dollars.

In one of the letters, Alice wrote to Lefty insisting that he call her. His letter dated May 8, 1946, made reference to the phone call. He wrote: "Well I want you to know how much the phone call was, it was $4.54, I hope you like that, I sure don't."

Lefty would write Alice letters from whatever town he was in and ask her to write to him at General Delivery in the next city where he would be working.

Lefty wrote another letter on May 16, 1946: "Well we've

been gone about three days now and I haven't made a darn thing yet, we sure haven't been doing so good." Lefty was writing songs on some of these lonely nights away from Alice. In the same letter Lefty stated, "I've started writing two songs, one is, 'I Hope You're Not Lonely While I'm Gone,' 'I Like to Hold You in My Arms, but I'm Too Far Away.'" Lefty also mentioned how big the city of Amarillo was and later sent her a postcard. He sometimes closed by saying, "Sweetheart, maybe I'll dream of you tonight. I wish I could for you're always on my mind. All day while I'm working and driving, I'm always thinking of you."

Reverend Satterfield later took his little crusade to some other states. Lefty wrote from Reno, Nevada: "Sweetheart, you said you prayed for me, well you must of forgot to pray Wednesday, for we got stopped in Reno. I got stopped before Lewis (The Reverend) did, I was put in jail for about three hours before Lewis was stopped, then Lewis was put in jail with me. Well, sweetheart, we had to stay around Reno for three days and then we got fined one hundred dollars each. Alice darling I wrote in a letter I had thirty four silver dollars just before we tried to work, sweetheart I had $43.00 when I got stopped, but honey it all went in on the fine.[…]Darling I wish I'd never came on this trip, I wish I'd stayed there with you now, because I just can't hardly stand it."

Lefty wrote Alice from Los Angeles, California, on June 25, 1946. One of the passages here shows just how bad the situation was: "Alice, darling, you cash this money order when you get it, and then make out another money order to the doctor in Waco. I'm sending you $11.00, you can take the one dollar and send the $10.00 to the doctor, you can have what's left."

Things were falling apart, the Reverend was going broke. When they got back to Waco, the Reverend sold his interest in the hotel and bought a house. Lefty knew it was time to figure out something else. The only thing he knew to do was head back to New Mexico.

Arrangements were made for Alice and the baby to go to her grandmother. Lefty hitchhiked his way to Wichita Falls looking for work, but he didn't find anything there. He then thumbed his way to Dexter, New Mexico, where we were living.

These heartrending letters were written by Lefty and Alice during those hard and lonely times. They tell of the cities where Lefty walked the streets asking for money from strangers for a cause about which he knew nothing. They tell a story of how two young people coped with being separated, having no money, and caring for a new baby.

By the time Lefty returned to New Mexico, Daddy, Momma, and the family had moved to Dexter, about fifteen miles south of Roswell. We moved into the Old Dexter Hotel. Momma's brother, Johnnie, and his family lived there, too.

Uncle Johnnie would take Lefty around the honky-tonks and night-clubs. Lefty carried his guitar and played. They passed the hat and Lefty made a little money.

The old hotel had a balcony over the second floor. Lefty would tell our brothers, Bill and Lesley, and our cousin, Junior Cox, to round up all the kids in the building and from around town. They would all gather down under the balcony.

Lefty told Junior, "Now, when I come out onto the balcony, you make sure they all clap their hands and scream and shout for me. Then I'll sing my songs and put you all on a show."

Lefty stepped out onto the balcony. "Hello, kids. Hey! Listen to this."

"For years and years I've rambled,
Drank my wine and gambled,"

Lefty sent for Alice and Lois in the fall of '46. They rented a small trailer in Roswell and did what had always worked for them in the past. They found Alice a job, and when that was done Lefty started making the rounds of local honky-tonks playing and singing to anyone who would listen. He knew how important it was to have his voice heard over the radio, so he approached KGFL's station manager, George "Jud" Roberts, at Roswell's oldest radio station. He made a deal for a fifteen minute show. Lefty had to get his own sponsors, but he had done that before. It wasn't long before his show had enough sponsors to go on the air. Showtime was 1:45 to 2:00 P.M. daily. Lefty's show was so popular it soon was extended to thirty minutes. Lefty's sponsors were The Arcade Billiard Coffee Shop, The Owen Brothers' Shoe Repair Shop, and a Planing Mill Company in Roswell. Most of the time Lefty did the show solo, but once in a while he would bring along another musician, a guitar player or maybe someone who could play the fiddle.

In every show Lefty would dedicate a song to our mother. She never missed one of his shows; she was so proud of her son.

Lefty would say, "I'd like to sing this next song to my mom. I know she's listening out there in radio land. It goes like this, Mom." Then Sonny broke into "Lonely and Blue."

Lefty used the show to promote his appearances through the next week. It wasn't long before he was drawing crowds wherever he was playing. Lefty went to a local dancehall called the Cactus Gardens where he met the New Mexico Playboys. The Playboys played at the Gardens on weekends. Lefty asked the band leader, Pat Espinoza, if he could sit in. Everyone liked Lefty so much that he was hired to front the band, not only at the Gardens, but also for any other road shows the band played around the valley. Lefty had no trouble persuading the owner of the Gardens to become a sponsor for his daily radio show.

Lefty was achieving regional and local stardom. He worked with the New Mexico Playboys during the week, played at the Cactus Gardens on weekends, and continued his daily radio show. He was in country music heaven, playing and singing full time and earning a living doing it.

Daddy's Uncle Troy came to Dexter and the two of them bought an old ice house. When they were off doing something else, Momma worked lifting and carrying ice out to the customers. Somewhere between working the ice house and looking after five kids she got pregnant again. Lefty was living and working in Roswell, Billy had hitchhiked to Ft. Worth and was staying with Alice's brother, Junior Harper, and the rest of us kids were living at home. One evening, Momma came in from working the ice house. She was four or five months pregnant, and she was having abdominal pains. Eleven-year-old Betty realized our mother was sick.

"Momma, here let me help you lie down. I'll get a wet rag and wash your face, it'll make you feel better."

Momma allowed her oldest daughter to help her to the bed. "Just let me rest. I am so exhausted and the pain is gettin' worse."

The house we lived in was small, only one room with two beds, a kitchen, and a bathroom. Momma was propped up on the bed. All of us kids gathered around. We stopped playing and sat there quietly. Even the youngest of us knew something was wrong.

Betty said, "Momma, tell me where you hurt, you know I can help."

Momma held out her hand to Betty. "You can help by fixin' something to eat. I know you kids are hungry. Betty, you go in the kitchen and fix some Cream of Wheat. Turn on the stove, get a big pot, and put some water in it."

Seven-year-old Ola Mae got up off the floor and came to

the foot of the bed. "Momma, you're just tired from lifting all that ice. If you get some rest, you'll be fine. You're just tired, Momma."

Momma sighed. "Yes, I'll be all right, and your sister's gonna fix you all something to eat. Johnnie, you go help your sister. You can make the toast."

Momma had the kids busy. We were all trying to help. Some of the fear disappeared. I crawled up beside Momma. This was my safe place.

The next morning, as he was getting ready to leave for work, Daddy called, "Betty, come here girl. Here's a bottle of medicine for your momma. You give her one spoonful after I leave and one about every three hours till I get back." He handed the medicine bottle to Betty and walked out. Betty walked over to our mother. Lesley was standing at the foot of the bed.

Momma was awake and she whispered to Betty. "Listen to me, however much he told you to give me, pour it out. I won't take any of it. Make sure you pour out only as much as he told you to give me. Do you understand?"

"Yes I do, Momma, but why?"

Mom looked at her and answered, "Because that stuff will kill me." Betty did as Momma told her.

"Go get another set of clean sheets and a couple of towels and bring them to me," Momma instructed. Betty was quick in doing what our mother asked her. "Now I don't want you to be scared, but there's a lot of blood in this bed. I need you to help me to the bathroom. I may be losing this baby, so while I'm in there you change the bed sheets, and then come back and get me. You can do this. You're big enough to help me. Now let's go."

Betty helped Momma from the bed. Momma leaned on her and they made it to the bathroom. While Betty quickly stripped the bloody sheets from the bed, she could hear our mother in the bathroom softly crying and moaning. Betty poured cold water in the tub and put the bloody sheets in it to soak. She spread the clean sheets onto the bed and left the towels there for our mother. She knocked on the door to the bathroom.

"Momma, I'm here, when you're ready, I'm right here."

"Betty," Momma said softly as she opened the door, "you will have to change these towels often. Even if I'm asleep, you check, and if you need to change them do it! Okay?"

Betty said she would. "You just try and sleep, Momma, and I'll take care of you." Betty changed the towels several times that day.

Early in the afternoon Ola Mae tried to wake our mother. "Momma, I'm hungry. Momma, wake up, I'm hungry."

Momma slowly opened her eyes. She could barely see Ola Mae standing there.

"Momma, I'm hungry, please get up." Ola Mae was still trying to wake her.

In a very weak voice Momma told her, "Go into the kitchen, get you a piece of bread and put some meat grease on it. You eat that for now, go on, baby." Ola Mae ran off into the kitchen.

Momma fell back to sleep. Betty was having a hard time getting her to wake up even to go to the bathroom. When she finally got her out of the bed, Momma left a trail of blood across the floor, and this scared Betty.

"Momma, you're bleeding more today than yesterday."

Momma kept on walking toward the bathroom. "It's all right, Betty, just get those towels off the bed. It's gonna be all right."

This time Betty was not so sure, but she stripped the bloody towels from the bed and laid out clean ones.

Mom made it back to the bed. "Bring me all the clean towels you got, girl, I'm gonna need a lot more."

That afternoon Lesley came in, and Mother was in and out of sleep. Betty checked in on Momma and looked under the covers. "Lesley, I need you to help me. Come here and look at this!"

Lesley walked over to the bed. He moved Betty to the

side and pulled back the covers. He just stood there for a moment, and then gathered everything into the bloody towels. He told Betty to get him a box or a paper bag. Betty brought a shoe box to him.

Lesley put the towels into the shoe box and said, "Betty, you clean Momma up as good as you can, and then call the kids. It's time for a funeral." Lesley and Betty were the only two that knew they were burying something other than a bird. Lesley was a little over twelve years old when he buried Momma's baby.

Daddy came in about six o'clock that night. He glanced over at Momma and then he went into the kitchen and found something to eat. Troy came in a few minutes later and walked over to the bed where our mother was still asleep. He tried to wake her, but she did not respond. Troy was not a doctor, but he was smart enough to know our mother needed to be in a hospital. He turned to Daddy, "Hey! AD needs a doctor and you damn well better get one fast."

Lesley said, "I'll go." He ran out the door. Cousin Junior Cox was standing outside and he ran with Lesley to find a doctor.

Lesley and Junior brought the doctor to the house. He took one look at Momma and called for an ambulance.

"We've got to get this woman to the hospital and right now. She's hemorrhaging." He paused and shook his head then softly said, "She's lost an amazing amount of blood."

Betty had not left the room. She was standing on the other side of the bed. She started to cry. "Momma, please wake up, if you go, I've got to go with you, Momma. Please, can I go? I can't stay here without you."

Lesley stood and watched the ambulance fade into the night. All was quiet except for the kids crying. Betty walked over and handed him something. She was crying hysterically as she went into the house. Lesley slowly opened his hand and saw the empty medicine bottle.

"Lesley, what's happened here?" Lefty had seen the ambulance leaving as he pulled up in front of the house. Lesley explained what had been going on the last couple of days, and handed Lefty the empty medicine bottle.

Lefty said, "I was just bringing Momma a new radio. She told me she wanted one; she didn't want to miss my shows. Lesley, you watch the kids, I'm going to the hospital." He yelled, "Hey, Betty, come here."

Betty came running out of the house with tears still streaming down her face. She put her arms out and Lefty hugged her close. "Betty, you probably saved Momma's life. You are a very brave and special girl. Tell me about the medicine bottle. How much of it did you give Momma?"

"Daddy told me to give Momma a spoonful about every three hours. After Daddy left Momma told me to pour out what she was supposed to take."

"How much did you pour out?"

"In three days I poured out about half the bottle."

Lefty thought for a minute. "You and Lesley have both done well, now let me go and see what I can do. I'll see you both soon." With that Lefty got in his car and drove off toward Roswell.

The ambulance arrived very quickly at the Roswell Memorial Hospital, and Momma was taken to an emergency operating room. The doctor told the nurse to get ready for a blood transfusion. "She's gonna need a lot of blood."

A nurse called Daddy in and started drawing blood. By this time other relatives of Momma's had arrived at the hospital. Uncle Doc had recently returned to Roswell. When the nurse asked for a blood donor, he volunteered. The doctor was in the process of prepping Momma for the blood transfusion.

Once the procedure was under way, the doctor knew it would take some time. He told Daddy, "Look, I'm gonna have to leave for just a minute. You pay close attention here and let me know if anything changes. If she starts shaking or anything out of the ordinary, call me immediately. Can you do that, Mr. Frizzell?"

Daddy nodded. "Sure I can, Doctor. I'll stay right here and call you if anything happens."

"I'll be right back." The doctor stepped out through the curtains.

The doctor hadn't been gone more than five minutes before Momma started shaking a little bit. Daddy touched her arm. "Okay, take it easy now, just be quiet. Stop moving around, you'll be all right." Her shaking became much worse very quickly. Daddy was trying to hold her down. "Stop that shaking. I'm gonna have to call the doctor if you don't stop moving."

At that moment the doctor came in and saw Momma shaking uncontrollably. He moved Daddy out of the way. "You know, maybe you had better leave. I don't think I'll need you in here anymore."

The next morning Momma was resting easy in her hospital room. Daddy was sitting in a chair looking out of a window. Momma had just drifted off to sleep when Lefty walked into the room. He had a little radio with him. Setting it down on the stand by our mother's bed, he reached down and plugged it in; Lefty didn't want her to miss the special song he had planned for her that Sunday. Lefty stood and looked at our mother for a long time without saying a word. Finally, he bent down and kissed her forehead. Momma woke up, but didn't open her eyes.

Lefty straightened up and looked over at our father for the first time since he had entered the room. Daddy was still sitting in his chair, but he turned to face his son. Lefty reached into the pocket of his jacket and pulled out the empty medicine bottle. He tossed it to Daddy.

"If she dies, you son-of-a-bitch, you'd better dig yourself a hole, 'cause I'm gonna put you in it." Lefty turned and walked out of the room. Evidently someone knew what was in the bottle, but the rest of us never found out because this episode was never talked about again.

CHAPTER SIX

I LOVE YOU A THOUSAND WAYS

L ife was going well for nineteen-year-old Lefty. His daily radio show had been extended from fifteen to thirty minutes. He and his band were working a lot, especially weekends at the Cactus Gardens. Alice worked and helped to pay the rent.

Lefty had not been with a lot of girls in his life. He had married Alice at the age of sixteen, but now he was a local singing star, and the girls found him. They saw him at the Cactus Gardens every Friday and Saturday night. There were many girls mooning over him, but one girl in particular had a huge crush on Lefty and she was willing to prove it. On a few occasions in the spring and summer of '47, she did just that. Two things were wrong with this situation: one, Lefty was married with a child, and, two, the girl was only fourteen.

This young girl and her friends followed Lefty and his band wherever they played. They particularly hung around the Cactus Gardens on the weekends. They would flirt around with the boys between sets. Everything was just fun. No real damage was done, until one evening in early July. After the dance, Lefty and three of the boys took the girl and her friend down to the Pecos River about twelve miles from town. Someone brought beer and the party was on. Lefty stayed with the girl who had a crush on him, while the other three boys had fun with the other girl. Things got out of hand and the girls ended up walking back to town. They had gone only a few miles when a policeman stopped. He asked the girls what was going on, and they told him they had just left a party down by the river.

"The party got a little rough so we decided to walk home," they explained.

The policeman asked their names and addresses, and then he wanted to know how old they were. The girls told him they were fourteen. He inquired if they were all right. He asked if they were hurt or anything. They assured him that they were okay; they just wanted to go home. The policeman drove them back to town. The girl that had the crush on Lefty planned to stay over-night at her friend's house, but when they walked into the house the friend's mother and father were waiting. They had seen the police car pull up and the girls get out.

The father said, "All right, I want you both to sit right there on the couch and tell me what's going on."

His daughter was scared and she said, "We went out to the dance. We were just having fun listening to the band and dancing with some friends."

The father got right in her face. "All right, then what happened? How come you came home this time of the night in a police car? And, little girl, don't you lie to me, I'm not in the mood for no lies."

His daughter was crying a little now. "We were invited to a party down by the river. We rode out with some of the boys, a couple of them were in the band, and she was with one of them." His daughter pointed to her friend who was looking very scared herself, staring at her hands in her lap.

"Before we go any further," the father said, "I'd better call your parents, what's the number?"

Under fire both girls confessed everything, even to the fact that this wasn't the first time they had been out with the band. They had been spending time with these boys and others for a little while now. The police were called and the girls gave the names of the boys involved.

Lefty and the other boys were arrested July 14, 1947, and accused of statutory rape upon a female minor under the age of sixteen years. Lefty entered a plea of guilty on July 16th, and was remanded to the custody of the sheriff. Bail was set at $1,500. He was released on bail July 23rd. After being found guilty, Lefty was sentenced to not less than two years and not more than three years in the state penitentiary. All but six months was suspended and time was to be served in the county jail. Lefty reported to the sheriff of Chaves County, George Wilcox, on August 21, 1947, to begin his sentence. The other boys pleaded guilty and received the same punishment.

The Frizzell family over the years felt they pretty much knew the facts of this episode. We knew that Lefty had pleaded guilty and, of course, we knew of the other boys' fate. All four boys spent six months in the Chaves County Jail. Their sentences ended on February 21, 1948.

The Frizzell family was recently surprised to learn there had been another boy involved. He was accused and convicted of raping the same fourteen-year-old girl for whom Lefty was paying six months of his life. That young man also pleaded guilty, but his sentence was deferred. He was arrested on July 15, 1947, and released on a $1,500 bail three days later. After the boy made bail there are no records of him. It is possible that this boy was a minor and his record was expunged. However, there's another possibility: sometimes the blindfold on Lady Justice slips and the scales tilt.

While Lefty was going through his legal battles and was out on bail, our family moved to Loco Hills, New Mexico, a little settlement halfway between Artesia and Lovington. Daddy had taken a job looking after an oil lease for a large company out of Artesia. The company furnished him with a truck and a house about thirteen miles off the main highway.

Daddy and Momma drove the seventy-nine miles from their house to Roswell in silence that early morning of August 21, 1947. They pulled up in front of the little trailer where Lefty, Alice, and Lois lived. It was early, around 6:00 A.M., and Lefty had to report to Sheriff George Wilcox at 8:00 A.M. at the Chaves County jail to begin his six month sentence behind bars. Lefty, Alice, and the baby were awake already. Daddy could tell that Alice had been crying, probably most of the night.

He put his hand on his son's arm. "Sonny, why don't Alice and the baby come on out and stay with us while you're gone? She doesn't need to be here alone. We'll be worrying about her and Lois. It might even ease your mind knowing she's with us and not here by herself."

Lefty sat slumped in his chair. "Aw, Daddy, Alice has a job and anyway she wants to stay close to me. The only thing I worry about with her staying here is that it's such a bad neighborhood."

Momma sat down close to Lefty and took the baby in her lap. "Sonny, if Alice wants to come out at any time, we'll come back and get her. I can help her with the baby if she does."

Lefty took Momma's hand. "Okay, Momma, maybe not right now, but probably she will later. Boy, I hate to go to jail, I wish there was something we could do."

Daddy said, "I've already asked that young fellow whose father owns the radio station. He said he would definitely talk to the district attorney. What was the D.A.'s name?"

"His name is G. T. Watts, and I'll bet I'll never forget his name. He did everything but bury me." Lefty sighed.

"I don't know if there's anything we can do right now, but maybe we'd better get going, it wouldn't do to be late today."

When Daddy pulled up in front of the courthouse, Alice began to cry again. Lefty was holding Lois and had his arm around his wife.

"Alice, please don't cry, this is something we have to do.

Crying just makes it harder. Look, you be sweet and take care of Lois." He squeezed her a little tighter. "Alice, you and Momma stay here in the car. I don't want you to come in and watch them take me away. Daddy will come with me. He can get all the information on visiting days and an address so you can write me, all that stuff. I'll say my goodbyes right here."

Alice was holding on to Lefty with her arms around his neck, crying. "Oh my God, this can't be happening. I can't let you go, Sonny. I'll be here waiting for you every visiting day. I'll only be right across town, that's how close I'll be."

Lefty noticed that Momma had started to cry. He got out of the car and went to where our mother was waiting. She put her arms around him and cried softly. "We'll look after her. You just don't worry about a thing."

Lefty held Momma. "Momma, I hate to leave you like this. We've been through a lot of things together, but nothing like this. When I get out I'll make everything right, I promise. I love you, Momma."

Daddy had walked around the car and stood waiting, ready to go inside the jail with Lefty. Tears were falling down his cheeks.

Lefty thought, *I think this is the first time I've ever seen him cry. I guess he ain't so tough after all.*

Lefty opened the door to the sheriff's office, stepped inside, stood there for a minute, and then said, "My name is Frizzell and I'm here to give myself up."

"Mr. Frizzell, right on time I see, that's good." The sheriff looked at our father. "Are you the boy's father?" Daddy nodded. "My secretary will give you all the information on visiting days and such. She'll explain the rules and regulations that we follow here." He looked over at Lefty. "Say goodbye to your father, son, and follow me."

The sheriff led Lefty out through another set of doors to the end of a long hall. There Lefty met the jailers, Burt and Red.

The sheriff gave Lefty's papers to Burt, and then he walked back out the doors.

Burt looked at the papers then over at Lefty. "I guess you're mine now."

Burt went inside a little storeroom and brought out some clothes and shoes. "Hey, Frizzell, empty your pockets, put the contents in this bag, and then take off your clothes and put these on." Lefty did as he was told, after which Burt gave him some bedding, two sheets, one blanket and a pillow. "Okay, son, I'll show you to your new home for the next six months. Follow me."

Lefty followed Burt through a steel door up three flights of stairs and through another steel door to the cellblock. The cell was about six feet by eight feet, had one cot, a sink, and a toilet at the back. Burt opened the cell door. "Okay, Frizzell, follow the rules, stay in line, and your time will go by fast. Is that a deal?" Lefty murmured something as he stepped into the cell. Burt locked the door, and Lefty was alone.

Lefty threw the bedding on the cot and looked around for a moment. He noticed a small barred window at the rear of the cell high above the toilet and sink.

Lefty thought, *If I stand on the toilet I bet I can see clear down to the ground.* He sat down on the cot. *Lord, I want to say how sorry I am. Never in the world did I think I would be in a place like this. I've never been this totally alone before, so excuse me if I cry a little. Lord, please look after Alice and Lois for me. I know I won't be there to help them when things go wrong, but if you're with them I know they'll be okay. I promise when I get out I'll make it up to them. They'll never want for anything. I'll do everything for them, and Lord, you know I can't stand to see my momma cry.*

The inmates could receive letters on Tuesdays and Fridays, and visiting day was on Thursdays. Momma would drive the seventy-nine miles to Roswell every Thursday to be with Lefty. In those six months she didn't miss very many days. Sometimes she would bring some of the kids, and whenever possible Daddy would come, too. Alice never missed a visiting day until she left for Texas in November of that year.

There were only three days a week to which Lefty looked forward: Tuesday and Friday, letter days, and Thursday, visiting day.

One letter Lefty wrote to Alice dated September 13, 1947, said how he hated for her to have to work so hard and so late. He was worried about her getting home safely, but the real reason he was writing was that he thought he had found a way to get out of jail, if she would help him.

"Alice, I'm writing trying to tell you how to get me out, if you knew what I had to go through here, you would sure try to help me….Alice, I want you to get a letter from the man you're working for, saying how much money you're making and that you really need me to help you. Also get a letter from the land-lord, Mrs. or Mr. Rogers, saying you have a baby that needs your care and that you have to pay someone to keep her for you.

"Alice, you can't make it without me, so help me get out and you'll never be sorry if you do….Please don't give up, go or call Mr. Whitmore (Mr. Whitmore owned KGFL radio.), tell him you're trying to work. Tell him what you're making. Carry the baby with you when you go. Alice, that's the way it's done. Alice, Whitmore could just say a word or two, or write a letter to the judge and I'd be free again. Go see the judge yourself, carry Lois with you, tell him your family's in East Texas, your mother died when you were four years old, show him the letters you get from everybody….I think I'm going to write G. T. Watts (the district attorney) tomorrow. He might come over to see you, if he doesn't come over to see you; you go over and see him Thursday. See the judge on Thursday, then come tell me what they said and I might get out soon you see. Alice, I'll be the happiest man in the world when I get out to you."

His letters were filled with remorse, about how he would never do her wrong again, how everything would be fine when he got out, how all the songs he wrote would be hers and Lois's. He closed this letter by saying, "Alice, darling, I really cry on Sundays, that's when we have church about three o' clock in the afternoon. I cry and think of you."

There is another letter dated September 19, 1947, following a visiting day: "Darling, you sure looked sweet to me yesterday and Lois did, too. I know you're taking good care of her for us. I didn't know I could miss you and her so much until now. Yes, darling, God has forgiven me. I know for I have prayed to him every night to forgive me and keep you and Lois for me.... Alice, hon, what I wouldn't give to hear some beautiful hillbilly music. You know you said you could hear Ernest Tubb singing. Boy, I sure would like to hear him. You don't never have anything up here like that. . . . Alice, darling, you remember what I told you to tell your family about me, don't tell them what really happened, please don't."

Lefty was so afraid Alice would leave him and go back to her family in Texas that he began making promises. He had already promised her all his songs, now he wrote, "You'll never have to work again when I get out. . . ." Further along in the letter he renewed his vows to her. "Now, Alice, honey, I swear to love, honor and obey in sickness and in sorrow until death do us part. I really do mean it too, honey, keep this letter and I'll prove it when I get out. . . . Kiss Lois for me, I have 149 more days. I'll sure be happy when they're over, won't you, darling? That's 19 more visiting days."

Lefty was extremely afraid that Alice was going to leave him or be unfaithful to him, or maybe both. In a letter written to her on October 7, 1947, Lefty said, "I see that you've got a girl-friend, Alma Lou, working out there with you. I hope you and her has lots of fun together, but I want you to remember this, whatever you do, you might as well tell me, because I won't be out thirty minutes till I know everything. I know one thing now, she's no good, but I hope you like her, I've known her a long time and you'll be sorry some day."

He went on to say that there were a lot of people out there that wanted to see them break up. "They want you to do something so they can have something to tell me, I hear everything that goes on out there now. . . . If you want to quit me and trifle on me while I'm down it's just up to you and then they will see just what they want to see. Please don't get me wrong, dear; I had rather die now than to give you and Lois up. I would lose my whole world. . . . I love you and Lois, but if want you to quit and part, now is the best time, just let me know. . . . Alice, sweetheart, I do know one thing. I do have two true lovers waiting for me that will be so true and there will never be no one else that can take my place in their hearts. They will always love me, just as I love them and someday I'm going to make them so happy. It's Lois Aleta and my mother."

Lefty explained to Alice in his letters that the guys in jail with him didn't believe there was a woman in the world that could be true, and that was what bothered him. "Hearing them talk about their wives doing them wrong, they say to me, 'how do you know what she's doing right now? Some other boy may be talking sweet talk to her'. . . . I once did think I could never love no one but Margaret ("Please Be Mine, Dear Blue Eyes") and I did put it in all my songs but, hon, I didn't write but three songs to her."

Lefty finally convinced Alice to look for another place to live. He told her the part of town they lived in was too mean and rough, and that he would feel better if she got a place in a better part of town. She moved into a one bedroom house in a nicer neighborhood, and found a new job at the Rainbow Drive-In.

It was a small, but nice house, and her job was a little better, too. Alice began to feel better. Being able to support herself helped a lot. Lefty asked our mother if Betty could help with Lois, so in early October Momma brought Betty with her to visit Lefty, and dropped Betty off with Alice. It took a few days for

Betty to get the routine down. Alice worked from 3:00 P.M. to 11:00 P.M., so she would leave around 2:30 P.M. and return home sometime before midnight.

Alice could walk from home around the block and catch the city bus. It would take her right to the front of the drive-in. The last bus ran at 11:15 P.M., and she couldn't afford to miss it. There were a few times she did, but on those occasions someone from work would give her a ride home.

Betty met a little Mexican girl that lived next door and became friends with her. They would play until Alice would leave for work, then Betty would have to watch Lois. Things were going well.

Lefty tried to get Alice to move from Roswell to Loco Hills where she could stay with our family. He tried coaxing her. "Alice, it won't cost you anything, and I won't be worried about you and Lois. Momma and Daddy will look after you and the baby, and you'll have the kids there to keep you company."

Alice didn't want to move out to Loco Hills. "Sonny," she reasoned, "it's too far away from you. Besides, it's so depressing and lonely way out there in the desert, and I don't get along too well with your family anyway. I just don't want to go there. I've been thinking about going back to Grandma's for awhile, at least until you get out."

Lefty tried hard to convince her to stay in New Mexico with Momma and Daddy. "I just don't like the people you're running around with, especially Alma Lou. Now I've told you she ain't no good; she's just playing up to you. I'd feel better if you would just go on out to Momma's and stay."

Alice didn't want to do that so she told him that she was going back to Texas to stay with her Grandma.

Lefty didn't like it at first, but finally he agreed. "Alice you may be right, I'd rather you be there than here in Roswell. I don't want you to ever move back here."

On the back of one of his letters dated November 25,

1947, Lefty wrote, "I hate that damn Alma Lou." He ended that letter with: "I love you, my sweet Alice, kiss Lois for me and please write." He signed it, "Your lonesome husband Sonny." Alma Lou, it turns out, was the girlfriend of one of the guys who went to jail with Lefty.

Lefty wrote to Alice almost every night. Most of his letters were just repeats of ones he had already written. They said things like, "I love you" and "I'll never be untrue to you again" and "I'll make things up to you when I'm free."

Lefty wrote several songs to Alice during this time, too, even though he didn't have a guitar with him. He wrote the melodies in his head and the words on paper. On September 26, 1947, Lefty wrote "I Know You're Lonesome While Waiting for Me." He later recorded it on one of his albums. It is a great love song, and if you listen to the music and read the words you know exactly how Lefty felt and what he was going through in jail.

Lefty wrote a lot of songs during this period of his life, and he later recorded many of them, such as the one above. Another song titled "I Had Two Angels at Home," was written on September 4, 1947. Possibly the best song written while Lefty was a guest of the county, or at least the most famous, is "I Love You a Thousand Ways." Again, Lefty wrote this song from the depths of his heart.

Lefty was sitting on his bunk after dinner one night. His heart was just sick over Alice, and he thought, *It's so hard to try and tell her how sorry I am, I know I've screwed up. Boy, what a dumb thing to do. If I could just tell her to her face, look into her eyes, maybe I could make her believe. God, I hope she doesn't leave me. I wouldn't blame her if she did, but I sure do hope she doesn't.*

Lefty looked around the little cell. He could hear the other inmates laughing and talking outside of his cell. Then Lefty heard Red's voice.

"Okay, boys, five minutes to lockup, everyone in your cell." Lefty didn't move, he just sat there knowing that things would calm down after lock up. The inmates would settle back to thinking of their own problems and things would get quieter.

Lefty's mind went back to Alice and Lois. "I know one day we'll forget all this, but right now it's almost too hard to bear. I don't know if I can stand this, being locked up with nothing better to do than to sit here and think. I believe this is just going to kill me. Momma sure has taken this hard. Anybody that would hurt his momma the way I have mine doesn't deserve to live anyway. I sure do love her; I've hurt her so bad. When I get out, I'll make it up to you, Momma." A tear rolled down his cheek. "I swear I will." Lefty was talking to nobody. Nothing but a lonely jail cell to hear him.

"Alice, please believe me, I love you. I'll prove it in days to come. I swear it's true, darling; you're the only one." Lefty stopped. "Wait a minute, if I had my guitar, let's see, 'I love you I'll prove it in days to come.' Okay, I'll write it down. The melody will go like this." Lefty sang very quietly, "'I love you and I'll prove it in days to come, I swear I'll be true, I'll prove it to you someday, I love you, in my heart you will always stay, I love you and I'll prove it a thousand ways.' Damn, what a song, I got to start all over."

Heart broken and filled with guilt, Lefty wrote one of the most important songs in country music history that night sitting on his bunk with tears in his eyes and no guitar in his hands. The only things he had in the whole world at that moment were his songs and his music. He carried the tune in his head, and; started singing. In his mind he no longer saw the gray walls of his cell. At that moment, he saw Alice and little Lois, and he was telling them, "I love you a thousand ways." If only for a little while, the music had set him free.

I LOVE YOU A THOUSAND WAYS

I love you; I'll prove it in days to come,
I swear it's true, darling, you're the only one.
I think of you of the past and all our fun.

I love you; I'll prove it in days to come.
You're my darling, you've been true.
I should have been good to you.
You're the one that's in my heart while were apart.
I'll be true, I'll prove it to you someday.
My love is for you, in my heart you'll always stay.
I've been so blue and lonesome all these days.
I love you, I'll prove it a thousand ways.
Bridge
I'll be nice and sweet to you,
And no more will you be blue,
I'll prove I'll love you everyday all kinds of ways.
Darling, please wait, please wait until I'm free.
There'll be a change a great change made in me.
I'll be true; there'll be no more blue days.
I love you, I'll prove it a thousand ways.
When I'm free.

(These were the original words, but Lefty changed them slightly when he recorded the song.)

We went to visit Lefty on Thanksgiving Day. Alice was on her way to Texas by this time. Lefty wrote Alice telling her how the guards let the prisoners out to be with their families for ten minutes. He recalled how surprised we all were when he walked out to be with us. Time was passing slowly, but it was passing. February finally raised its head and Lefty was closer to getting out. Alice was still in Texas, and planned to be back in Roswell by the time he was released. However, she didn't want to go back to Loco Hills.

In a letter Lefty sent dated September 25, 1947, he wrote, "Alice, sweet darling, remember it's up to you, if you want to come back or not, and remember who I told you not to talk to. Hon, you know just who you'll have to stay with and if you don't think you can stay with them you had better stay in Texas." Lefty was referring to our family. He knew Alice didn't want to stay with us.

He went on to write, "I do not want you here in Roswell and I don't want you talking to that damn lying Alma Lou, I've got a few things to ask you now when I get out, but just forget about it now darling, wait till I'm free."

Alice arrived in Loco Hills around February 2nd, and went with Momma to see Lefty during the next visiting day.

After the visit Lefty wrote, "Darling, when I get free, I'll try to put into words really how happy I was to see you and sweet little Lois Aleta."

Lefty ended that letter with, "Oh, yes, honey, you remember what I told you about A. L. I told you she wouldn't be true and wait for Barney; she's getting married tomorrow to some Dago."

The last letter Lefty wrote from jail was dated February 16, 1948. "Today is Lois Aleta's birthday, honey, I would give anything if I could have been with you and sweet Lois Aleta today on her birthday. Well it's too late for that, but I bet I'm with you and her on her next birthday when she's three years old, at least I pray to God I am. Honey, please don't be late getting here this coming Saturday morning, try to be here before six please. Red said he would let me out as soon as you get here and don't forget to bring my coat, and I'm gonna want something good to eat that morning for breakfast. Oh, Momma said Daddy was going to get my guitar out of hock for me. I'm so happy just three more days and I'll be free. Honey, don't forget, please don't you all be late coming to get me. I'll be so happy; it's been such a long, long time."

"Hey! Red, Red, are you there?"

It was Saturday, February 21, 1948, at 5:00 A.M. Lefty hadn't been able to sleep very much the night before because he was so excited about getting out.

Red walked up to Lefty's cell. "Boy, you're up early. What time are your folks coming to pick you up?"

"They're going to be here around six. Boy, I sure do hope they're not late. Now, Red, you told me I could get out at six if they were here to pick me up, so don't go back on your word. You know I've got to get out of here."

Red assured him. "I didn't lie to you; a promise is a promise. Besides, the sheriff already gave me permission to let you out. Okay, what do you want now? Let's see, it's only five in the morning. Do you want something to eat?"

"Naw, Red, I don't want to eat anything, but I'd sure like to take a shower. I'd like to be real clean when I walk out of here. I don't want to take anything from this place with me, especially not the smell."

"Okay, I don't blame you." Red opened the cell door. "Come on."

One hour later, Lefty was back in his cell and calling to Red. "Red, hey, Red. Red, what time is it? Is it six yet?"

Red shouted back, "Not quite, listen, if your momma told you she'd be here at six, she'll be here at six. I'll bet she's downstairs right now, so just hold your horses, relax."

Lefty had started pacing. "I can't be still, Red, please call down and see what's going on. Please, Red, just call." A minute passed and Red came into the cellblock. "Okay, Lefty, they're here. Have you got all your belongings?"

Lefty said he did and Red opened his cell. Lefty followed Red out of the cellblock and went down three flights of stairs where Burt was waiting. Burt handed Lefty the little bag of his personal belongings and the clothes Lefty had worn six months before.

"Lefty," Burt said, "check to make sure everything's there. Your mother brought some new clothes for you. I believe she brought you a pair of shoes last time she was here." Burt pointed to a little room behind his desk. "You can change back there."

Lefty came out looking and feeling like a new man.

"Look, son," said Red, "I'm not even going to walk you over to the sheriff's office. You know how to get there, just go out that door and down the hall. Everyone is waiting for you there. Oh, and Lefty, don't ever let me see you back here."

"Okay!"

Burt agreed. "Ol' Red is right, son, you got your whole life ahead of you; so don't spend another minute in here. Go!"

Lefty ran out, and didn't look back once. He went down the hall and opened the door. First he saw Alice and Lois. Alice came toward him crying. Lefty felt his pulse quicken. His heart was in his throat; he could hardly speak. He put his arms around his wife and baby. Tears were falling all over that sheriff's office. Lefty looked around and saw Momma standing, holding my hand. She had tears in her eyes, too.

When Lefty walked out of the sheriff's office on that chilly February morning, he refused to look back. As Momma drove away from the curb, Lefty *still* would not look back at the building where he had spent six months of his life. All he wanted to see and remember was the love in the smiling faces of his family.

Loco Hills was located twenty-five miles east of Artesia on Highway 82. The little settlement had a café, post office, a general mercantile store, a gas station, and the Greyhound bus stopped there. You could buy a ticket to anywhere in the real world right from that grocery store.

Lefty was mighty glad to see Loco Hills that morning as Momma drove him through on the way to the turnoff. It was another thirteen miles to the little settlement where we lived. Thirteen miles of dirt road called the Rub Board Drive because its ridges were similar to a washer woman's scrub board. No one in the car was surprised to see a dead rattlesnake every once in a while, draped across the barbwire fence that followed alongside the dirt road. You might also see a few dead coyotes with their ears missing because there was a fifty dollar bounty on them in that region. Of course, Lefty was glad to see and be about anywhere that morning after spending six months in the Roswell City Jail. He couldn't seem to hug and kiss Alice and Lois enough on the ride home. The other kids were waiting outside when the car drove into the yard. You didn't hear the name Lefty that day; everyone called him Sonny. This was all family and no one in the family ever called him anything but Sonny.

"I'm gonna fix you the best chicken dinner you ever had," Momma said. "Come on outside and we'll pick out the chicken. Now, let's be sure and pick the fattest one."

Everyone went out back to the chicken coop. Lesley opened the pen and went inside. The chickens went crazy, trying to fly, running around, squawking. Lesley cornered one, grabbed it, and brought it over to Sonny.

"What about this one?" Lesley held the chicken up so Sonny could get a good look at it.

Sonny looked the chicken over. He motioned for Lesley to turn it around. Lefty looked at it some more and then he said, "Look at her. She's looking at me and she's begging, 'please don't eat me, don't ring my neck.'" He solemnly asked Lesley, "Why don't we give her another chance; she just looks so innocent. Let's give her a pardon."

Lesley turned the chicken loose. He was enjoying the game, and all the kids were too. Momma, Alice, Lois, and Sonny were all around the outside of the pen hollering at Lesley.

"There's one, get that one," Sonny shouted.

"Over here, Lesley, this one's the fattest," Alice hollered.

Lesley caught another one. He held it up over his head and brought it to Sonny who looked at the chicken and motioned for Lesley to turn it around. Sonny kept looking at the chicken. He asked Lesley to turn it back around again.

"Lesley, I don't know how you did it but I believe you caught the same chicken," Sonny announced. Everyone started laughing. Lesley was laughing so hard he almost dropped the chicken. Instead he grabbed it by the neck and said, "Hell, that must mean she's coming to dinner." And he wrung its neck.

Life was better for Sonny, except for not being able to play music for a living. There were no clubs in the small settlement, and he had no bookings. So Lefty played for himself. There were five houses in that oil workers' camp, and one of them was empty. Sonny would take a chair, sit in the middle of it, and play his guitar. He would sing all the songs he had written while in jail. The empty house had a natural echo-sound, which Sonny liked, and sometimes he would sit there all day and play that guitar and sing those songs.

Sonny tried working with Daddy a little. It was hard, nasty work, but it was all there was. There was no other way to make any money, or "get away money," as Alice called it.

Every payday, Alice would count the money they had earned. "We've just got to save enough money to get away from here," she'd say.

There was nothing to do way out there in the desert, especially when Sonny was working. Alice would lie around and read romance magazines, and when Sonny came home they would do nothing together. There was no such thing as television and there was hardly any radio that reached them. The only entertainment was playing games with the other kids.

We lived in a shotgun house, long and narrow. There was no electricity or indoor plumbing. There was a front door leading into the living room, off to the left was the kids' bedroom, going on back toward the middle of the house was Daddy and Momma's room, after which was the kitchen. There was a side door leading out from the kitchen onto a long, narrow porch, to the right of which was Sonny, Alice, and Lois' room. Since it was just off of the main house, they didn't hear the commotion around midnight one night when Daddy and Momma got into a hell of a fight.

It seemed Daddy wanted to have sex and Momma didn't. Our father was calling our mother every name he could think of, then he started pushing her around. This woke up the kids in the bedroom that we shared at the front of the house.

Daddy was mad, really mad. "I'll bet you give that son-of-a-bitch to everybody else, but when I want it, hell, naw."

Momma didn't say anything, but she got out of bed and stood on the far side, keeping the bed between them.

Since there was no electricity, we used coal oil lamps, and though they were all turned off it was bright inside of the house. The windows were not covered and there were no doors to any rooms. Betty went to see what was going on; the other kids were hiding. Lesley silently went out the front door and around the house to wake up Sonny.

"Sonny, wake up." Lesley said as he knocked lightly on the door to the little room.

"What's going on?" Sonny asked on the other side.

Lesley said softly, "Daddy's beating up Momma again."

Sonny told him to wait, that he'd be right there. He got dressed quickly, and told Alice to stay in bed. He opened the door, stepped outside, and found Lesley standing there waiting.

"What's happened? How did this get started?" Sonny quizzed his younger brother.

"I don't know but, boy, is Daddy mad. He's hitting her pretty hard."

Sonny bent down and picked up a rock, the rock fit perfectly in the palm of his left hand. Sonny slipped through the door into the kitchen. It was dim, but he could see our father about fifteen feet away

"We all know you can whip Momma. Hell, we all know

that, you've been doing that for years. Why don't you come over here and try to hit me, you son-of-a-bitch," Sonny challenged.

Daddy looked around at Sonny, "You'd better get back outside that door, you little bastard. I'll mop the damn floor up with you."

Daddy turned and came into the kitchen so they were standing face to face. Sonny let go with his left fist and caught Daddy on the side of his face. Daddy fell into the kitchen table and then fell to the floor. He couldn't believe he had been hit so hard. Sonny had always been skinny. He probably weighed 125 pounds before going to jail, but he had put on about thirty pounds since. He had also been working with Daddy doing hard labor every day. Now Sonny was a solid 155 pounds, about the same size as Daddy.

Sonny stood over him. "Not quite like fighting a woman, is it? Get up, you sorry son-of-a-bitch, I'm gonna put you back down every time you get up."

Daddy got up fast. He rushed Sonny, and down the hall toward the living room they went. Sonny was trying not to let our father get a hold on him. He knew that if he did, Daddy would squeeze the life out of him. Cursing, punching and pushing, they went past Momma who was now standing on top of the bed. Sonny punched Daddy and Daddy tried to get his arms around Sonny. In the living room Sonny got a clear shot and knocked Daddy into a lamp stand. One of the corners left a permanent scar on Daddy's shoulder. As if our father couldn't have become any madder, he did right then.

Daddy screamed as he came up off the floor, and he pushed Sonny back into the wall with enough force to knock the air out of him. Sonny was swinging both fists now. He didn't care where he hit Daddy; he just wanted to hit him. Daddy had pinned Sonny against the wall and was trying to get his forearm across his neck. Sonny came up with his knee into Daddy's groin. His hold on Sonny loosened for a moment, and Sonny took this opportunity to get away. Back down the hall they went, all the way into the kitchen. Daddy let go with a roundhouse right. If he had hit Sonny with that, it would have taken more than the wall to stop him from flying. Fortunately, the right hand missed and Sonny clipped him, again, right on the chin. Sonny was getting the best of the fight now. Our father couldn't get his hands on him. Sonny would hit and move, hit and move again.

Sonny hit Daddy with a hard left knocking him into the kitchen cabinets. This time he was stunned. He had to lay his head on the counter. He was breathing hard, and blood was running from the corner of his mouth. Sonny stood there, waiting for Daddy to move. Daddy's hand went into one of the cabinet drawers and pulled out a knife. He brought the knife around and pointed it at his son.

Sonny stood his ground. "You've got a knife. You've pulled a knife on me, you bastard. Now you know what, you son-of-a-bitch, I'm gonna have to kill you."

When Momma heard what Sonny said, she screamed and fainted. The fight stopped. Daddy and Sonny both rushed in to find Momma out cold. For many years after that fight, Lesley kept that rock.

The next morning Sonny said to Alice, "You know, why don't you start packing? I think it's time we tried our luck somewhere else."

Alice agreed. The next day they walked the thirteen miles on Rub Board Drive to Loco Hills and bought bus tickets out of New Mexico. Lefty was one week away from his twentieth birthday.

Sonny turned to Alice and said, "Anyway, I'm tired of being Sonny. I'd like to be Lefty again, I think."

CHAPTER SEVEN

TIME CHANGES THINGS

Lefty, Alice, and Lois walked out of the Greyhound bus station in Lubbock, Texas, in the spring of 1948, less than twenty-four hours after they boarded it in Loco Hills.

Alice said to Lefty, "Are you sure it'll be all right if we go to your cousin's house. How well do you know him anyway?" Lefty was carrying his guitar and suitcase, and Alice held Lois.

"Look, hon, me and Cousin Andy are close. I'll tell you one thing, it would hurt his feelings if we didn't stay with him. You'll love him and his family, I promise you. They'll all love you and Lois; don't worry anymore about it. Come on, it's a long ways over there."

Our cousin, Andy Cummings, had moved to Lubbock from Dallas about a month earlier, and started a new garage door business; however, like any new business, it was a little slow getting started. Andy and his family were still trying to move into their house; things were scattered here and there.

The family was just sitting down to dinner when Lefty knocked. Mary, Andy's wife, opened the door. When she saw Lefty standing on the porch, she hollered. "Andy, you won't believe who's here."

Lefty and his little family stayed with Cousin Andy, Mary,

and their three kids. Lefty did a few odd jobs, and even worked with Andy a little. Lefty did anything to make a living, and a poor one it was, too. When all you want to do is sing and play guitar, believe me, nothing else will do.

One job Lefty got while they were in Lubbock, was at the Lubbock Hotel as a bellman. Sometimes, the guests would ask for a little more service than the hotel provided, such as, "Was there any whiskey to be had in this dry county?" Lefty was the right man for the job. He had made friends with a bootlegger not more then a block from the hotel, so it was a simple job of supply and demand. Lefty became very good at his work. The hardest part of the job was not to let the manager catch you bringing whiskey into the hotel.

One evening, a man came into the hotel with his wife and registered. Lefty put their luggage on his cart and said, "If you will follow me I'll take you to your room, sir." Lefty led the couple to the elevator.

Once inside the man said to Lefty, "I know you can help me, young man. Listen, I want to take my wife out on the town tonight, and I don't know where to go, but I'll bet you do, don't you?"

"Well, I might point you in the right direction," Lefty said. "Depending on what you're looking for."

The man looked Lefty over. "Well, you know, a little dinner, maybe a place that has a band where we can dance a song or two. Somewhere we can get a drink; you know, that kind of thing."

"Around here there are a few places to eat. Here in the hotel they've got a great restaurant, and there are several others. As far as a band goes, some places have live music, but that's mostly on weekends. Because tonight is only Thursday I don't know if I can help you with that one. Now, something to drink is another thing altogether." It was agreed that Lefty would bring a bottle up to their room around 10:00 P.M.

Lefty got them settled and told them where the dining room was. After receiving his tip he said that he would see them at ten o'clock. Everything was going along just fine. Lefty purchased the whiskey from his friend, put it under his coat, and walked into the elevator. Before the elevator door closed, the manager stepped inside.

"Hey, Lefty, you've been busy tonight. Every time I see you you're going in and out of the elevator. Boy, you must be raking in the money. Where are you going now?"

Lefty told him, "The man in 534 called. I don't know what he wants, but I guess I'll find out soon enough."

The manager smiled. "Yeah, I suppose you will. Oh, Lefty, I guess I'm gonna need to know where you're taking that whiskey you've got under your jacket." The manager stood there with a grin on his face waiting. Lefty thought, *How in the hell did he know?*

"All right, you've got me. Look I was just trying to make a few dollars. Man, it's so hard to make ends meet, and you know there's not a lot of money in bell hopping."

The manager shook his head. "I know, son, but you can't make it here like that. It's against the law. I should call the police. Did you know you could be locked up for a year because of this?"

Lefty shook his head. "Man, please don't call them. I'm sorry, this will never happen again, I promise."

The manager looked at the floor then back at Lefty. "You know, you've been a good worker, and I wouldn't want to see you go to jail when I know how tough it is to get by. So, give me the bottle and you go on home. You can pick up your wages tomorrow, okay?"

"Yeah, I will and thanks for not turning me in." Lefty handed the bottle of whiskey to the manager. "But, tell me, how did you catch me?"

The manager never quit smiling. "How long have you been working here, son?" Lefty told him going on two weeks.

The manager said, "Well, I'm surprised some of the other help didn't tell you. Every so often I stop the boys here in the elevator and ask them, 'Where are you taking that whiskey?' Sometimes they've got booze, sometimes they don't. I just figure that if you don't ask, how you gonna know?"

Lefty decided he was tired of Lubbock. It was time to move on. He and Alice said their goodbyes to Cousin Andy and his family, and they caught a bus to Winnsboro where Alice's grandmother lived.

Lefty didn't stay there long either. For a couple of months he had been listening to a new radio show live from Shreveport, Louisiana. The station was KWKH, and they broadcasted every Saturday night from Shreveport's Municipal Auditorium. The show was called the Louisiana Hayride. It aired for the first time on April 3, 1948. Over the next ten years the Hayride became one of the most popular live radio shows, second only to the Grand Ole Opry in Nashville.

Lefty told Alice that he wanted to audition for the Hayride, and that she and Lois could stay in Texas with her grandmother. So one day Lefty and Alice's brother, Junior, climbed aboard a Greyhound bus and headed south to Louisiana.

On a Friday morning Lefty and Junior pulled into Shreveport. They found radio station KWKH and learned that auditions were to be held the following Wednesday.

Lefty looked at Junior and grumbled, "I wish we'd known that. Now what are we gonna do for the next five days?"

The auditions were already under way on Wednesday morning when Lefty walked in with his guitar, Junior trailing behind him. There were a few musicians milling around, and Lefty asked one of them who was in charge.

The man pointed to a hallway. He said, "Go down there and it's the last door on your right. Do you need someone to back you? Everyone here plays an instrument of some kind."

"I don't know, I brought my guitar, but thanks, man. I'll

sure call you when I find out what's going on." Lefty walked down the hall, and when he got to the last door it was open. A very thin young man was coming out with his guitar in his hand. He was talking back over his shoulder.

"Okay, thanks, guys, and I'll see you on Saturday and, once again, you don't know how much I appreciate your believing in me."

Lefty heard a voice from inside say, "Hank, glad to have you on board, see you Saturday."

The man turned around and ran right into Lefty. He said, "Excuse me, I'm sorry, I didn't mean to run you over."

Lefty grinned. "It's my fault standing right in the door like that. Hey, how'd it go in there? Did you get a job?"

"Yeah, those guys are okay. Go on in make 'em cry and they'll love you for it."

Lefty shook his head. "Boy, I hope so, I could sure use a job, but anyway good luck to you, and my name is Lefty Frizzell."

The thin young man reached out and shook Lefty's hand. "I've got a feeling you're gonna be all right. Just keep playing that guitar and singing them ol' sad songs. The world is yours. I'm Hank Williams."

Lefty walked into the room and noticed how dark it was. He nodded to a man sitting behind a big desk. "Hello, my name is Lefty Frizzell. Thanks for taking time to listen to me."

The man said, "No problem, Lefty is it?" Lefty nodded. "Go ahead and sing me something."

Lefty sat down in a straight back chair and sang:

"I'm going to California where they sleep out every night,
I'm leaving you momma, 'cause you know you don't treat me right."

"Well, Alice I guess it didn't go so good," Lefty wrote. "They hired one guy for the show. I believe his name was Hank and I think it was because he had a band. Me and Junior are going to catch the bus in the morning and I'll see you in a few days."

Lefty was sure logging a lot of Greyhound miles from Loco Hills, New Mexico, to Lubbock, Texas, then up to Winnsboro, Texas, down to Shreveport, Louisiana, and now back up to Winnsboro. As if that wasn't enough, Lefty, Alice, and Lois boarded another Greyhound to El Dorado, Arkansas, shortly after the audition.

Once again, Lefty started to make the rounds of night-clubs. He worked a place called the Ace of Clubs, a nasty little honky-tonk where your fighting skills were worth more than your musicianship. I'm sure the thought of quitting altogether was in the forefront of Lefty's mind. If this was all he had to look forward to—people drinking, fighting, and busting heads—maybe he'd better find something else to do. So back to the bus station they went. Alice and Lois got off in Winnsboro, but Lefty stayed on the road. His feet never touched the ground until he stepped off of that Greyhound bus in Loco Hills. He looked around and saw our mother waiting for him.

"Momma, I should have just bought a round trip ticket."

As unbelievable as it may seem, Lefty ran into another musician, Ray Thurman, working on the same oil lease as our father. Ray lived only a few miles away. He played bass guitar and some fiddle, and he fronted a band called the Pecos Valley Ramblers based out of Artesia. When Ray heard Lefty sing, he introduced Lefty to the other players, and Lefty got the job as front man for the band. They played around the Artesia area, sometimes over in Roswell, even Lovington and Carlsbad. Lefty was doing all right again; he was making a little money. The clubs were not as rough as they were in Arkansas, so he sent for Alice and Lois. They rented a little room in Artesia and moved in, and

Alice got a job doing counter work at a corner drugstore. This was not unlike every other place they had tried. Lefty played his music while Alice did all she could to help out. I suppose this could have gone on forever, except that Lefty was destined for greater things.

A friend came by one afternoon and told Lefty that he had been offered a job in Big Springs, Texas, at a honky-tonk called the Ace of Clubs. Lefty's friend wasn't able to take the gig because of a family matter. He asked Lefty if he wanted to try and get the job. Lefty told him sure, if they would make it worth his while. So his friend called the club and told the owner about Lefty, and explained how great he could sing. The owner agreed to pay Lefty $42.50 a week, but they needed him by the next night. Everything was agreed upon. The only problem now was how to get to Big Springs by the next evening.

Lefty called our father about his job, and Daddy told him what he had to do to make it happen. Daddy came into town, picked up Lefty, and they went to find some kind of transportation. They found an old Studebaker that seemed to run pretty well. Daddy bought it and handed the keys to Lefty. "Hope this car will get you where you've got to go. Be sure to always check the oil, that's very important. Treat the car right and it will do well by you. If you run into any trouble let me know."

"Daddy, thank you, I'll pay you back, that's a promise."

Lefty and Alice packed the car and drove out of Artesia later that evening. They had no time to lose.

The next afternoon Lefty was cruising on down the road. They had just enough time to get there if they didn't run into any trouble. Of course, that's when trouble will come, right when you can't afford it. A tire on the passenger side blew out. He pulled over on the side of the road, barely getting the car to stop, and only then did he realize that he had never changed a tire in his life.

"Alice, have you ever changed a tire?" Lefty asked.

"Well, no, Sonny, I never have, but I believe we've got to

see if we have a spare and a jack."

Lefty was looking everywhere. "Where do you think I'll find one, Alice? Why don't you get out here and help me look."

Alice opened the car door. "Sonny, why don't you look under the car, you know, or maybe in the trunk. Here… I'll find it for you, just calm down."

After finding the tire in the trunk, under the floor mat, Lefty spent the next thirty minutes trying to figure out how to use the jack.

"Alice, I'll jack the car up and you take this tire iron, or whatever it is, and start unscrewing those big bolts. Quit talking to me, I don't want to hear your little voice right now."

"Aw, Sonny, you don't know how to do nothing, and you jump on me when I'm only trying to help."

"Okay, okay," Lefty said irritably, "take that tire off and put this one on. We've got to hurry, I'm gonna be late on my first day."

Alice took the tire off and was putting the other one on when she stopped and looked up at him standing there. "Don't worry, Sonny, you're going to get there. I'm gonna make sure of that, you can bet on it."

Lefty hollered back, "Oh yeah, I'm gonna get there all right, late, late, late, that's what I'll be and I won't have a job when I do, but I'm gonna get there all right."

Lefty was late when they drove up to the Ace of Clubs. He ran in and told the bartender who he was and asked to see the owner. The bartender pointed out Stella Simpson who was standing at the end of the bar.

Lefty walked over and said, "Hi, my name is Lefty Frizzell. I'm the fellow you hired to sing and I'm sorry I'm so late, you see . . ."

Stella interrupted. "Don't say another word, you can tell me later. Get your guitar and get up on that stage. Everyone in here wants to hear you sing, as a matter of fact, they're ready to

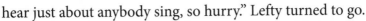

hear just about anybody sing, so hurry." Lefty turned to go.

"Oh, Lefty," Stella hollered after him, "welcome to the Ace of Clubs."

Lefty jumped on stage. He smiled and waved at the band, and then he walked up to the microphone and started singing:

"Good morning captain,
Good morning shine."

It looked like Lefty had really found a home this time. He was working for great people, the band seemed to enjoy playing and backing him, and he was making decent money. Lefty's repertoire included a lot of cover songs, but more and more often he was singing his own. He worked the Ace of Clubs for over a year, playing seven nights a week and an extra set on Sundays. The band played very few instrumentals and Lefty was the only singer. After awhile all the smoke and all the nonstop singing would get to him, but Lefty hung in there and never missed a night except for when our precious baby brother was born.

About the time Lefty had started playing the Ace of Clubs, Momma became pregnant again. Lefty, Alice, and Lois went back to Artesia for the birth.

A baby boy was born at six o'clock, Thursday morning, November 24, 1949. There were complications. It was believed that something was wrong with the baby's blood because the baby's coloring was an orangey-yellow. Dr. Hamilton, Momma's doctor, wasn't medically aware of the baby's problem and didn't know how to treat it.

Lefty and Billy were standing beside our mother's hospital bed. They were all trying to come up with a name.

Billy said, "Sonny, you always get to name the babies, but now it's my turn."

Lefty laughed. "Do you know why I name the babies and you don't? It's because I have an imagination," he teased. "You could never come up with anything original. Look at your own name, Billy Edgar, who would have ever thought to name a poor little baby something like that. You know what? I believe you must've named yourself. That sounds like something you'd come up with." Everyone laughed.

Billy grabbed Lefty around the neck. "Hey, how about your name, Orville? Man, that's the worst name I've ever heard."

Lefty grinned and hugged Billy. "You're right about that, ol' pal. That is without a doubt the worse name I've ever heard. Momma, tell me why you let anyone call me something like that."

Momma laughed. "You boys think you've got it bad. What about my name? How'd you like it if someone didn't even take the time to call you a real name, just gave you initials, how mad would you be about that?" They were all laughing and having a good time.

A nurse opened the door and brought the baby in, and gave him to Momma.

"What a good looking boy!" she said.

Momma looked at her baby. "How much did you say he weighed?"

"I believe he's six pounds and five ounces. Isn't he handsome? Look how long his hair is."

Momma took the baby and asked the nurse, "Is my baby all right? You know his coloring is a little....Is he okay?"

"Well, I believe he is, but I'll ask the doctor for you."

Billy said, "Why don't we call him Billy Ray? Sonny, what do you think of that?"

Lefty was feeling the baby's hair. "Momma, his hair is as long as a girl's, and look how black it is. Billy, I do like that name. What do you think, Momma?"

"I like it too," she said. "Billy Ray Frizzell it is then."

Dr. Hamilton came to see Momma. He told her how

beautiful her baby was, and then he explained what he thought was wrong with Billy Ray. "I believe your baby is having trouble with his blood. I'm running some tests now and maybe they'll tell me something. Right this minute, I don't know what to tell you, but I'll see you in a little while."

Billy Ray's condition only got worse. The doctor would take blood from our mother and give the blood directly to Billy Ray, but nothing worked. Billy Ray died four days after he was born.

When our mother's last child, Allen, was born in 1951, she finally learned about RH negative blood and what it means to a newborn baby.

I was eight years old when we buried our baby brother, Billy Ray. I stood between my brother, Sonny, and my sister, Betty. They were both holding my hands. I missed my mother so badly right then, but she was very sick and was still in the hospital.

I looked all around. My other brothers and sisters were there. Some of our aunts and uncles and their kids were standing around. I remember the preacher saying some words like, "...*the Lord giveth and he taketh away.*" I didn't know what was meant by that.

I looked up at Sister Betty and saw she was crying. I looked at everyone standing around me and they all were crying, too. The only one who wasn't crying was me. I didn't know what to do. About that time Sonny squeezed my hand. He must have known how confused I was feeling. I looked up and saw tears in his eyes.

Sonny bent down and put his arm around my shoulders. He spoke gently. "Remember me telling you about the angels, how once in awhile God will send one down to earth? It's not very often that someone like me and you would ever see one, but you know what?"

I whispered, "I don't know, what?"

"That's what Billy Ray is, he's an angel. David, do you believe that?"

I stuttered. "I . . . I . . . I guess so."

"David, listen to me, I promise, in my whole life, I will never lie to you and I'm not lying now. Billy Ray is an angel. He was with us for four days and God called him back. God needed him and he had to go back, but I'll bet we'll never forget him, will we?"

"No, I'll never forget him," I promised as the tears welled up in my eyes. "I'll never forget my brother is an angel and he's in heaven."

Sonny hugged me really close. "One of these days you and I will go see him. We'll walk around heaven with him, won't that be all right?"

"Oh ye . . . ye . . . yes," I cried, "tha . . . tha . . . that will be fi . . . fine."

Sonny stood up. I thought about it for a moment, and then I pulled on Sonny's arm. When he looked down I whispered, "So . . . So . . . Sonny, do you think it will be al-all right with Go . . . God if Momma co . . . co . . . comes with us?"

Sonny just stood there with tears in his eyes. He nodded his head and whispered, "Yes."

Daddy never really got into Christmas, birthdays, or any other special days, but Momma and the rest of us did.

We never had a Christmas tree except once. A few days after Christmas one year, some folks had thrown one away, and Sister Mae and I saw it at the same time. We both grabbed at it, and by the time we fought over it awhile and hit each other with it a few times there wasn't much left of that Christmas tree.

Momma did her best to make Christmas good for us. She

would send me out to find fresh, clean snow and she would make homemade ice cream. Brother Lesley would bring in rabbits and quail and Momma would cook up quite a dinner. Sonny and Alice were gone most of the time in those days, but they would always send us a box full of presents. We never thought of how they found the money to buy the presents, but Christmas to us was opening that box.

One year, I got a blue satin cowboy shirt. I wore it for every occasion. I wore it so much that Momma finally couldn't even keep it sewn together. I was seven or eight years old, and I'll never forget that Christmas and that blue cowboy shirt. Sonny was our Santa Claus.

I'm sitting here some fifty years later trying to write my memories down. I've thought of Billy Ray many times throughout the years. I can still see him lying in his crib. I can see his long black hair and I can see his wings. I never see Billy Ray in my mind or in my dreams without seeing his wings and my blue cowboy shirt.

I wrote this song for Billy Ray some years back.

WHERE IS BILLY RAY, MOMMA?

First came Brother Sonny, look at him run.
Next is Brother Billy
Just about to catch up.
Lesley, Betty and Johnnie Lee
I know they're somewhere near.
Mae, me and little Allen
Are bringing up the rear.
But where is Billy Ray, Momma?
Where is Billy Ray?
My brother lived for just four days.
Where is Billy Ray, Momma?
Where is Billy Ray?
Lefty became a singing star.

Billy played in the band.
Lesley fought in the Korean War
And made it home again.
Betty, Johnnie and Mae got married
To get away from home.
Me and little Allen were just two boys
With nowhere to go,
But where is Billy Ray, Momma?
Where is Billy Ray?
My brother lived for just four days.
Where is Billy Ray, Momma?
Where is Billy Ray?

Chorus
I know where Billy Ray is, Momma.
I know where he is.
He's in heaven with you and Daddy
Playing with the other kids.
Sonny, Lesley, and Johnnie Lee
They've all come home to you.
It won't be long 'til the rest of us
Will be coming home too.
I know where Billy Ray is, Mom
I know where he is.

CHAPTER EIGHT

IF YOU'VE GOT THE MONEY, I'VE GOT THE TIME

efty was glad to get back to Big Springs and to his job at the Ace of Clubs. He had written quite a few songs of his own, but he still learned all the current hit songs by Ernest Tubb or Hank Snow, and Little Jimmy Dickens was blazing up the charts. Lefty sang all of these songs, but in between he would sing one of his own.

Lefty was still getting a lot of mileage out of "Please Be Mine, Dear Blue Eyes" and "I Love You a Thousand Ways." One afternoon, Lefty and a couple of the musicians were practicing some new material at the club. Some players from another band came in and they all started picking and singing. Lefty sang "I Love You a Thousand Ways."

One of the boys said, "Lefty, I like your song as well as any song I've ever heard. Why don't you go to Dallas and record it?"

Lefty said, "I sure would like to, but not only do I not have the money, I wouldn't know where to go if I did."

"Our band is going to make a record as soon as we find the right song," the boy told Lefty. "And we're going to a guy's studio there, I think his name is Jim Beck. If you want me to, I'll find out what he charges."

"Boy, that would be good. How many songs do you record at a time?"

"I think you could put down three or four. You'd better take your own band with you. I'm sure the studio will have a band there, but it will cost you a bunch."

Lefty told him that he wouldn't even go if the band didn't want to go. Lefty found out a little later that for one hundred dollars he and his band could record up to four songs. Lefty called the studio and talked to Jim Beck. A deal was made and a time was set up to record in two weeks.

The day of the session, Lefty and the band drove up to Dallas. On the way the boys talked about what songs they would record. Lefty wanted to do one of Ernest Tubb's and, of course, one of Jimmie Rodgers'. No one thought much about what they would do with them after they were recorded. They just wanted to hear themselves on records.

After they arrived at Jim Beck's studio, and met Jim, they gave him the hundred dollars and Jim turned on the recording equipment.

The session was underway. Lefty sang a few cover songs, some Tubb and some Rodgers, but nothing that knocked Jim out.

He asked Lefty, "Hey, don't you have any songs of your own?"

Lefty grinned. "Well, yes I do, I've got a couple of ballads I like a lot." He sang "I Love You a Thousand Ways."

After the song ended Jim asked, "Don't you have any up tempo songs, you know, something with a beat?"

Lefty was quiet for a minute and then said, "Jim, I don't write fast songs very much, but I've got a few lines of one. It goes like this. Hey, guys, grab a D chord."

"If you've got the money, honey, I've got the time,
We'll go honky-tonkin' and we'll have a time."

Lefty stopped singing. The band quit playing. "That's all I got."

Jim Beck was so excited that he started screaming, "That's it, that's it, that's what I've been looking for. That's what I'm talking about. How long do ya' think it'll take to finish it?"

Lefty grinned again. "I don't know, let me think about it."

The guys in the band started throwing out lines. Jim may have said a word or two. Lefty didn't pay any attention to them. He just went off by himself, and eventually the song was written. Lefty and the boys stayed at the studio all night. By the next day all the songs were ready to record. Lefty recorded four of his original songs that day: "I Love You a Thousand Ways," "Please Be Mine, Dear Blue Eyes," "If You've Got the Money, I've Got the Time" and "Lost Love Blues."

Jim Beck knew he had a winner with "If You've Got The Money," but he wasn't thinking of Lefty singing it. He was thinking of Little Jimmy Dickens. Dickens was red hot on the *Billboard* charts at the time with hits such as, "Take an Old Cold Tater and Wait" and "Sleeping at the Foot of the Bed." Both were great up-tempo gimmick songs. Columbia Records had a huge star in Little Jimmy Dickens. Even today Jimmy's friends and people in the industry call him Tater.

Beck told Lefty that he wanted to see what he could do for him, but whatever he did it would cost him half of his songs. Lefty thought that half of something was worth all of nothing so they shook hands. Lefty went back to Big Springs and Jim Beck went to Nashville for a meeting.

The meeting at the Andrew Jackson Hotel in Nashville was for the purpose of finding songs for the next Jimmy Dickens' session. Present at the meeting were Little Jimmy, Don Law, the A&R man of Columbia Records, Jimmy's producer, and Troy Martin, a music publisher and a personal friend of Don Law. A couple of other guys were there also, possibly songwriters pitching songs or other publishers. Don Law had known Jim Beck briefly in Dallas, and he was expecting him to come by. Jim had sounded pretty excited when he had talked to Don a few days ago.

Jimmy was questioning his repertoire. "Don, we've been real lucky with these fast funny songs, and that's fine, but I'd like to find a good ballad. You know, something I can get into, something with heart. Don't you think I could sell a real strong, slow song?" Don had just played a demo of another up-tempo, funny song, which Dickens did so well.

"Yes, Jimmy, there's absolutely nothing that you can't sing, fast or slow, but of course, I wonder if your fans will accept the change."

"Well, Don, if we find a good one, we can discuss it then, all right?"

"Sure we can," Don said as he threaded another tape on the recorder.

When Beck got there a little while later, Don asked hopefully, "You've hand carried a tape of songs all the way from Dallas for us to hear. I sure hope you've brought us a hit."

"Mr. Law, I sure have. I may have more then one. Just put on the tape and listen for yourself." Beck looked over at Dickens. "This first song is a sure hit for you, listen."

Lefty's voice sang out:

"If you've got the money, honey, I've got the ti-i-ime,
We'll go honky-tonkin and we'll have a time."

After the song played through, Don asked Beck to play it again. Beck wound the tape back and once again Lefty's voice came out: "If you've got the money, honey, I've got the ti-i-me."

This time when the song ended Don asked Beck, "Who is the guy singing?"

"His name is Lefty Frizzell. He's working down around Big Springs, Texas. He came to my studio about a week ago and he and I put these songs together. I wanted you to hear this song; I wanted Little Jimmy to hear it."

Don looked over at Dickens, "Well, what do you think?"

"I'd like to take a copy and listen to it some more," Jimmy replied. "What else is on the tape?"

While Beck played the rest of the tape, Don was talking to Troy Martin. "I've never heard anyone sing like this Lefty. The way he rolls the words around in his throat before they come out of his mouth is unique. Hey, Beck, listen," Don walked over to Jim. "I'd like to keep this tape. I'll be in touch with you in a few days."

Word gets around the streets of Nashville pretty fast. Probably one of the men at the meeting told someone who told someone else, and before long Music Row knew about Don Law liking some new kid from Texas, who had a great song, something about "If You've Got the Money."

Before Jim Beck left Nashville he visited some of his friends. One of them was Jim Bulleit who used to be an announcer at WSM radio. Now he had his own record label called Bullet Records. He and Beck had been friends for a while, and over the course of a meal Beck told him about Lefty.

Back at The Ace of Clubs the bartender handed Lefty a note. It read: "Lefty my name is Jim Bulleit. I own Bullet Records here in Nashville. I talked to Jim Beck and he told me he was working with you. I'd like to talk to you and possibly meet with you. I will call you tomorrow at one o'clock at the club. Talk to you then."

At one o'clock the next day, Lefty was at the phone. "Hello, Mr. Bulleit, this is Lefty . . . .I'm doing fine . . . I've been working here at this club about a year now . . . Well, I'm glad you like my songs . . . .No, I haven't signed any publishing agreements of any kind . . . .You're coming through here this week? . . . Sure, I'll be here . . . .Okay, I won't say anything to anyone . . . .I'll see you the day after tomorrow . . . .So long."

Two days later Jim Bulleit and Lefty met and a deal was made. It gave Jim publishing rights on "If You've Got the Money,

I've Got the Time."

"Lefty, now that you've signed your publishing over to my company," Bulleit explained, "I'll be able to use my influence on Don Law of Columbia Records. Now that I've got a stake in the outcome, I'll help pull this on in. I know that Beck has been talking to Don, but now between all of us I think we'll get you signed."

Lefty and Jim Bulleit shook hands. "I'll see you in Nashville." Bulleit said.

Jim Beck had not covered all his bases. He did manage to get his name on Lefty's songs as half-writer without writing a single word. That was pretty good, but it would have been just as easy to get all the publishing as well. That wasn't all. Beck signed Lefty to a management contract and ended up booking him, too, but that was on down the road a ways. So when Beck found out that Lefty had signed away his publishing rights to his so-called friend, Jim Bulleit, he was furious.

Don Law called Beck wanting Jim to set up a meeting in Dallas between Lefty, himself, and another big shot at Columbia, "Uncle" Art Satherley. Uncle Art, as Lefty later said, was Mr. Columbia Records. He ruled the company from Dallas to Hollywood, while Don's territory was Dallas to the East Coast. These were two of the greatest record men ever to be in the business and they wanted to meet Lefty.

"This handshake is the same as a contract," Don Law told Lefty as he shook his hand after the meeting. "Welcome aboard, son." Lefty went to Dallas on June 15, 1950, where the two-year contract was finalized and signed. The contract called for four sides per year at a royalty rate of two percent of ninety percent.

Lefty's first session for Columbia Records was booked at Jim Beck's studio on July 25, 1950. Four songs were to be recorded. Lefty had been working on his own songs, and Jim Beck had a few other ones for him to hear. Finally, the songs were picked and sent to Don Law in Nashville for final approval. The songs were: "If You've Got the Money, I've Got the Time," I Love You a Thousand Ways," and "Shine, Shave and Shower (It's Saturday)." All three of these songs were written by Lefty, with Jim Beck's name added as co-writer even though Beck hadn't helped write them. The fourth song, "Cold Feet," was written by a friend of Jim Beck's named Aubrey Freeman.

The songs were ready, and Lefty was definitely ready, so on that Tuesday morning in July the stage was set. The session started at ten o'clock, so Lefty arrived around 9:30 A.M. While the musicians were setting up their instruments, Lefty went around shaking hands with everyone. Some of the musicians he knew, others he was meeting for the first time. On lead guitar was Norman Stevens, on bass was Bobby Williamson, fiddle was R.L. "Pee Wee" Stewart, and on piano, from Wichita Falls, was Madge Sutee. Madge was the one who really helped to give Lefty the honky-tonk sound that was to become his trademark. The band ran through "I Love You a Thousand Ways" a few times.

"All right, let's put one down," Don instructed from the control room. "'I Love You a Thousand Ways,' take one."

Lefty knew this was what he had waited for all his life, to make records, especially of songs he'd written, songs that now he could make come to life. He was born for this, for this day. He poured all the emotion from his heart and soul right into that microphone. This was the song he had written for Alice only a few years earlier while sitting in a jail cell in Roswell, New Mexico. It was immortalized on a record that day. Later it would be counted as one of the greatest country music songs of all time.

"If You've Got the Money, I've Got the Time" was put down next.

Don Law said, after they recorded it, "You can change anything you want to, but don't mess with the piano, that's great."

After the session Lefty went back to Big Springs where Alice and Lois were waiting. He was so excited that things were finally happening. It wouldn't be long now before his records came out, and he'd be able to play his music all over the country, maybe all over the world. It was finally his turn.

While Lefty was recording and spending time in Dallas, the Simpsons had leased the Ace of Clubs. The band Lefty had been working with scattered looking for work elsewhere. Some ended up in Albuquerque. Lefty and Alice packed and moved to Dallas where they began the long wait for the release of Lefty's first record.

Meanwhile, Jim Beck was trying to figure out how to better his deal with Lefty. Lefty had no manager, no booking agent, and no business sense at all. He just trusted everyone to do the right thing. Lefty was about to learn a hard, cruel, and expensive lesson.

Beck had already put his name on Lefty's songs as half-writer. He then signed Lefty on for management and bookings for a fee of twenty-five percent. Beck realized there was more money to be made from this young, talented, gullible boy if he could just think of it. First, he had to do something about Jim Bulleit. He talked Lefty into signing a letter stating that Jim Beck already had rights to "If You've Got the Money, I've Got the Time," and several other songs as well. This letter was pre-dated before Jim Bulleit had come into the picture, but not before Jim Bulleit licensed someone else to record "If You've Got the Money, I've Got the Time." A singer by the name of John Talley cut it, so when Lefty heard his song for the first time on the radio, it wasn't even him singing it.

While Jim Beck and Jim Bulleit were dividing up the money Lefty hadn't made yet, Lefty was starving. He had no job; he only had whatever he could pick up by singing here and there.

Beck didn't want to book Lefty anywhere before the record came out, because booking him at that time for some small amount would only hurt him later on when he asked for more money. Beck was right, but what was Lefty suppose to do? He was broke. They had nothing to eat and nowhere to stay until a man by the name of Morris Stevens saw Lefty and Alice at a club he owned, the Roundup Club, and offered Lefty a job at ten dollars a night. Lefty told Stevens that Jim Beck wouldn't let him work until after his record came out.

Morris Stevens expressed his concern. "Well, I understand why, but I don't understand how you're going to get by till then."

"Man, I don't know either. We are completely broke, and we don't even have a place to stay. We sure don't want to go all the way to Daddy and Momma's place. I'd like to stay here, but it may be impossible. I wish I knew when my record was coming out, at least if I knew, it would help, I think." Lefty worried.

Morris said, "Lefty I might be able to help after all. I have a club on the other side of town which I had to shut down awhile back. There's a little bedroom upstairs. Actually, Lefty, it's just a loft with a mattress thrown on the floor but to tell you the truth, I could use someone there to watch after the place."

Lefty smiled. "Morris, I'm a regular watchdog, just point me in the right direction and I'll be there a while ago."

"I've still got a lot of stuff over there," Morris added. "A bunch of tables and chairs, there's an old jukebox and several booths. I don't know what all, but I do know I don't want to lose any of it. I'd feel better having you there as long as you need a place to stay."

"Morris you're a life saver. You don't need to worry about a thing. Do you still have any records on the jukebox?"

"There ain't nothing but the blues on that jukebox," Morris laughed. "A bunch of race records and, boy, are they good. Lefty, have you ever listened to any of the deep blues records?

"Well, I haven't heard a lot but, if it's music, you can bet

I'm gonna like it." Lefty did like some of those records. When he wasn't at Jim Beck's trying to earn a few bucks, he was listening to the blues and waiting for his own record to come out.

When Columbia finally released "If You've Got the Money, I've Got the Time" on September 2, 1950, the record came out like an Oklahoma Blue Northern blowing across the airwaves. Every disc jockey in America was playing it. Even Hank Williams, who had a two sided hit going at the time— "Long Gone Lonesome Blues" and "Why Don't You Haul Off and Love Me One More Time"—would just have to move over. Every jukebox in every corner of America blurted out the fact that there was a new boy in town, and he was going to dominate country music for the next few years.

Everything Lefty did he did with great heart and soul, especially singing and songwriting. Lefty's voice was being heard everywhere. People could not get enough of the sound of his voice, and the way he slurred the words in his songs. He would hold one note then let it go and grab another one. He would worry with one word until all the emotion was wrung out, then he would go to the next. The way he sang was just as important as what he sang.

In the first few weeks of the record's release, disc jockeys tried to pronounce the name Frizzell. They called him Frassel, Frissell, even Frissell tail, but still, they played his record while they had fun with his name.

Lefty had a two sided hit. "I Love You a Thousand Ways" was right behind the hottest song in the nation, "If You've Got the Money, I've Got the Time."

Lefty's records were selling as fast as Columbia could press them; however, Lefty was still broke. He had to do something. Once again he sent Alice and Lois over to her family in Winnsboro, and he headed to Snyder, Texas, where we were living. Daddy had taken a drilling job just outside of town and moved the family only a short time before Lefty arrived.

Lefty and Robert Lee, our cousin, arrived in Snyder one evening before supper. After eating, Lefty lay down complaining of a stomach ache. By morning he was much worse, so Momma, Robert, and Brother Bill took Lefty to see a doctor. The doctor did a few tests and told Lefty he wasn't eating right. He had the beginnings of an ulcer. The doctor gave him some medicine and sent him home.

In a letter to Alice dated October 17, 1950, Lefty made mention of this problem. He asked her not to worry. He also told her that Momma, Daddy, and he went to Big Springs and talked a club owner into paying him one hundred and twenty-five dollars a night for two nights.

"Alice, everything worked out better then we planned. I'm just going to work at Big Springs Friday and Saturday night, $125 a night. I didn't know my records did so good there. I slipped into Big Springs. Momma, Daddy and I made the deal with the Casino Club. Oh yes, honey, do you have the ticket on Bill's watch that's in the pawn shop, I don't have it."

Three weeks after the release of Lefty's record Don Law called for another session. On September 21, 1950, everyone met at Jim Beck's studio. All the musicians had been changed except for one, Madge Sutee on piano. Jimmy Rollins played lead guitar, Buddy Griffin was on rhythm guitar, and Jimmy Kelly played steel guitar. Eddie Duncan was on bass and Eddie Caldwell played the fiddle. The Frizzell sound was well represented. Songs cut on this session were: "Don't Think It Ain't Been Fun Dear,"

"When Payday Comes Around," "My Baby's Just Like Money," and "Look What Thoughts Will Do." With Don Law producing, Jim Beck engineering, and Lefty singing, country music history was being made.

Lefty's contract with Columbia was redone. The original contract, signed only a few months earlier, was for two years with two separate one year options. The new terms were one year with four, one year options, and a royalty rate of three percent for the first three years and four percent for the last two.

It seems that Uncle Art Satherley, Vice President of Columbia Records' Western Division, may have helped put the new contract together, along with Don Law. The two men got together in Dallas just a few weeks after Lefty's records were selling out in stores and put this new deal together. The new contract was signed, giving each side a little better deal. This shows how well Lefty's record was selling. It is no wonder Don Law was quoted saying, "Lefty Frizzell, Columbia's find of the year."

Jim Beck was afraid someone would come along and steal his find of the year. After all, he was the one who really found Lefty, wasn't he? While Uncle Art was in town, Jim decided to talk to him. The two of them hammered out a deal to share in Lefty's career. The deal went something like this: a contract was drawn up giving them equal control of Lefty's career. Lefty's earnings from his songs and records would be split three ways: Uncle Art got one third, Jim Beck got one third, and one third went to Lefty.

It is important to remember that Jim Beck already had his name on Lefty's songs, giving him half of the monies the songs themselves made from airplay and sales. He collected all this without writing a word or a note of music. With half the rights to the songs gone to Jim Beck, this new contract included Lefty's half, plus his Columbia royalties of three percent, which would escalate to four percent in the last two years of his contract. So all these earnings would be split three ways, and this contract was for three years. Now all Jim and Uncle Art needed was Lefty's signature.

"Oh yes, I should mention what Jim and Uncle Art are supposed to do for their obligation to the contract." Lefty explained to me one night in 1956 during a tour of Texas. "Jim and Uncle Art told me that their main job would be to stop any problem from becoming a problem before that problem got to me," Lefty said. Then he laughed. "I should have realized the two biggest problems were standing right there in front of me. David, actually my biggest problem was trusting everyone. I thought they were my friends and would look after me, and boy, did they ever. Another thing they were supposed to do was to make sure I had good songs to record. That part should've been easy, since I was writing everything." Lefty ended with, "They took me for everything, my best songs, my best years, almost my want to carry on, but in the end I refused to give them that."

Everything Lefty did, he did with great heart and soul. It's too bad he met so many who had neither.

While "If You've Got the Money, I've Got the Time" and "I Love You a Thousand Ways," two of the hottest songs in America, were climbing the *Billboard* charts, Jim Beck decided it was time to start booking Lefty. He took out an ad in *Billboard Magazine* giving his name, address, and phone number for booking information. Lefty had been booking himself up till now in places he knew well, like Roswell and Carlsbad, and he was ready for someone else to do the booking. One of the first bookings Jim Beck made started in December of 1950. It was a tour of one-night stands through north and west Texas. Lefty traveled in a 1948 Buick with one or two members of the band. The rest of the band followed in another car. The musicians were mostly made up of Big D Jamboree musicians who had to be back in Dallas on Saturdays to play the Jamboree; therefore, the tour couldn't range too far from Dallas. At least Lefty was working while his songs were becoming consistently more popular. A problem during this early stage of booking was that, while almost everyone had heard his songs, no one knew who Lefty was. Name recognition hadn't caught up with the popularity of the songs yet, but that was soon to change.

The day after Lefty and the boys had played a show and dance in Amarillo, they were having lunch at a little restaurant before going on to the next date.

"Last night you boys played so good I'm buying the eats today." Lefty grabbed the bill and headed for the cash register.

Bill Callahan, one of the acts on the show, hollered after him, "Thanks, my man, you've done a great deed here today, and I for one am going to give you many more opportunities to re-peat your generosity."

Lefty and Bill left the restaurant ahead of the others. Lefty walked over and put his key into the lock to open his car door and found it was already unlocked. As a matter of fact, the door wasn't all the way closed. Lefty then noticed that his stage suit, which always hung in the back seat, was gone. He searched the car and the trunk. Nothing else was missing. Lefty was so mad he was shaking.

"Why would anyone want my show suit? They could've taken my guitar, why didn't they take that, too? Hell, it's laying right there."

Bill Callahan was looking in the other side of the car. "Lefty, didn't you lock the car, I thought I saw you lock the car door." He paused. "Someone passing saw your suit hanging there and either the door was unlocked or they jimmied it opened."

Lefty was beside himself by now. "Shit, I believe I locked the door, but hell, now I don't know. Damn, damn it. Why would they take my suit and not take an extra second and steal my guitar? You know what Bill? If I could find the guy right now, I'd either whip his ass or give him the guitar, too." Lefty never got over his suit being stolen. He talked about it for years.

"If You've Got the Money, I've Got the Time" was released by Columbia Records on September 4, 1950. By the end of October the song had skyrocketed to number one on *Billboard's Most Played Juke Box Folk (Country and Western) Records* chart and was listed as number two on both the *Best Selling* and *Most Played Billboard* charts. The flip side of the record, "I Love You a Thousand Ways," went to number one on the *Billboard* charts on November 4, 1950. Toward the end of December, Jim Beck called.

"Lefty, do you want to work the Opry?"

"You mean the Grand Ole Opry in Nashville?" Lefty asked.

Beck laughed. "Son, there's only one. Look, we're leaving for Nashville on Friday. We're on our way, boy. This is it, the Grand Ole Opry."

Lefty was excited. He thought that maybe he really was on his way. He called our mother. "Hey, Momma, guess what? I'm gonna play the Grand Ole Opry in Nashville, Tennessee."

Momma was happy for her boy. "Sonny, oh my, when?"

"This coming Saturday."

"I'll have everyone here sitting by the radio, we won't miss it." She could tell how excited he was.

"Momma, you know they don't let just anybody sing on the Opry," Lefty said. "You got to be special."

"There's no one more special than you," Momma told him. "Oh, and don't forget, you move around up there now. Remember what I told you, those girls love to see you move, don't stand there like a statue."

"I know, Momma, I know. Hey, I gotta go, I love you and I'll see you on the radio."

Lefty and Jim Beck arrived at the Ryman Auditorium at the end of December 1950. Lefty had his guitar and clothes for the show. Jim asked someone where the dressing rooms were, and they both went to put away Lefty's things. Then Lefty wanted to meet with the band and maybe go over the songs for the show. On the way to the stage he recognized one of his idols, Ernest Tubb. He said hello and shook Tubb's hand.

Lefty said, "I've sang your songs about as much as you have, I'm a big fan."

Ernest smiled real big. "Welcome to the Opry, son. I've heard your songs, actually only two of 'em, but I like 'em both."

Lefty smiled back. "Well, that's all I have out right now. I've just recorded another session, but I don't know when they will be released."

Ernest wished him good luck, and then he nodded. "The band is good tonight. Go on out and rehearse and I'll see you later."

Lefty had a chance to meet a lot of the Opry stars that night, but Ernest was the one he talked about the most. Red Foley hosted the segment that Lefty was on, and after talking about Prince Albert smoking tobacco, which was sponsoring the segment, he introduced Lefty.

"Ladies and gentleman, this next fella' is kind of new around here, but I've got a feeling you're gonna hear a whole lot more about him. Please welcome to The Grand Ole Opry stage Lefty Frizzell."

Lefty half jogged, half walked out and shook hands with Red. Then he walked over to the microphone and said, "Thanks, my name is Lefty." With that the Opry band started playing the intro to "If You've Got the Money, I've Got the Time." Everyone in the audience got out of their chairs. When Lefty finished his song he bowed three times to the audience and at least once more

Clockwise from top: William Orville Frizzell; the Frizzell children (*left to right*) Johnnie Lee, Ola Mae, Betty Jo, Sonny "Lefty," Bill, and Lesley (Eldorado, Arizona); school picture— Lefty is second from the left in the back row.

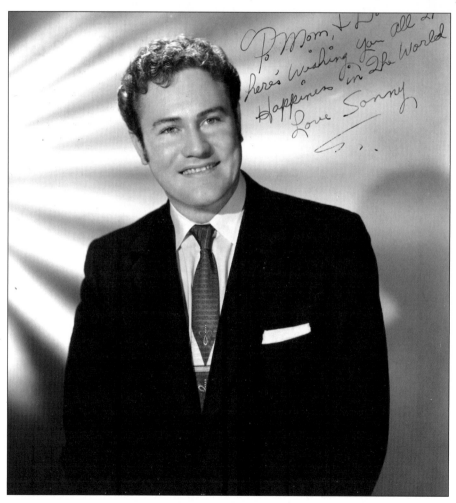

Clockwise from top: **Lefty with his mother, AD;** *(left to right)* **Bill, AD, Betty, Lefty** (*with guitar*), **Lesley, Johnnie Lee, David, and Mae; promotional photo of Lefty, signed "To Mom & Dad, Here's wishing you all the happiness in the world, Love Sonny."**

Top to bottom: Lefty's booking photos, Chaves County Jail, Roswell, New Mexico; young Lefty in his first stage suit, made in Dallas, Texas.

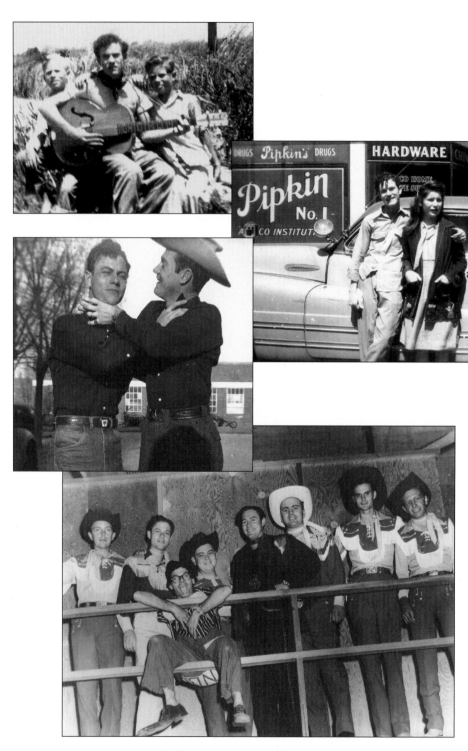

Top to bottom: Lesley, Lefty, and Bill; Lefty and Alice; Bill and Lefty; (*left to right*) Jack Youngblood, Bill, Lum York, Tommy Perkins, Lefty, Lou Millet, Ernie Harvey, and band member.

Clockwise from top: Max Bear and Lefty "carryin' on"; Lefty and his manager, Jack Starnes; Bill and Lefty.

Clockwise from top: the *Billboard* Best Selling Retail Folk (Country & Western) chart, showing three Lefty Frizzell songs in the top five and one on the way up; Lefty with his famous J-200 Gibson guitar; Lefty with one of his Martin guitars.

Clockwise from top: Bill and Lefty, wearing his breakaway fringe shirt; David with his guitar, in the backyard in Tipton, California; promotional photo of Lefty with his customized Gibson J-200 guitar with Bigsby neck.

Top to bottom: Lefty on stage with Jack Skipworth (*right*); Lefty wearing a custom-made shirt of his own design; (*left to right*) Jack and Neva Starnes, Max Bear, Alice, and Lefty.

Top to bottom: Jack Skipworth and Lefty in Juarez, Mexico, with some local kids; (*left to right*) Jack Youngblood, Lefty, and Lou Millet.

Clockwise from top: Lefty on stage; Lefty with his portrait and album cover; Lefty with his Cadillac, at home in Granada Hills, California; Eddie Miller and Lefty.

Clockwise from top: Lefty's thank you to NARAS for the nomination of "Saginaw, Michigan" as Best Country and Western Record of 1963; poster from the Trianon Ballroom, Oklahoma City, Oklahoma; Lefty in the tropics.

Clockwise from top: **Lefty and David in Loco Hills, New Mexico; Lefty and Jack Skipworth in Mexico; (***left to right***) Naamon, AD, David, Alice, Lesley, and Lefty.**

Clockwise from top: Lefty with Alice and their children, Rickey and Lois, in Sulfur Springs, Texas; Buddy Tatum and Lefty after the gun incident; Ferlin Husky and Lefty.

Clockwise from top: Country Music's Who's Who full-page ad and tour poster of Lefty and David; Hank Snow and Lefty; Lefty with AD and Naamon.

Clockwise from top: Lefty on Old Hickory Lake with his sons; David and Lefty; Lefty taking a moment before a show; double exposure photograph of Lefty in Roy, Washington.

Top to bottom: Merle Haggard (*left*), the current owner of Lefty's J200 guitar, and David; Naamon, AD, Alice, and a representative of the Country Music Hall of Fame.

to the screaming girls. He was so happy that he probably could have floated off the stage.

Lefty was surprised to almost run into Ernest, who had watched the entire performance from backstage.

"Boy, that was something." Ernest said in amazement. "I haven't seen the audience get that riled up in I don't know when." Ernest shook Lefty's hand and put his arm around his shoulder. Lefty could have died right then and there; everything he had ever hoped and dreamed had just happened.

Red Foley introduced Ernest next. "And now, please welcome the Texas Troubadour himself, Ernest Tubb."

Lefty watched as Ernest walked out to the middle of the stage to thunderous applause. Ernest stood there for a moment looking out over the crowd, a big smile on his face, and then he grabbed his guitar and flipped it over. On the back of his guitar were letters that spelled out the word, 'thanks.' The crowd went wild again, and then Ernest said something that almost made Lefty faint.

"Whatda ya' think about that Lefty boy?" The crowd once again came to their feet. Lefty felt his knees go weak. Ernest looked back over his shoulder at Lefty and waved for him to come back out and take another bow. Lefty did, and when the applause died down a little Ernest said, "Folks, this is Lefty's night..." he paused, "but bein's I'm here . . . " Ernest paused again, and then sang "I'm Walking the Floor over You."

On January 2, 1951, Columbia Records released Lefty's second record, "Shine, Shave and Shower (It's Saturday)" and "Look What Thoughts Will Do." Both songs took off like a shot. "Look What Thoughts Will Do" became the third hit for Lefty, peaking at number four on the *Billboard* charts. Once again the flip side,

"Shine, Shave and Shower," went to number eight. These songs pulled the listening audience even more into the Lefty singing style. The tone of his voice and the slurring of the words were unlike anything they had ever heard before.

Don Law called for Lefty's third session to be recorded at Jim Beck's studio on January 11, 1951. Once again, Lefty was ready with hit songs. The songs recorded on that session were another version of "My Baby's Just Like Money," "I Want to Be with You Always," "You Want Everything But Me," and "Give Me More, More, More (Of Your Kisses)" written by Lefty and Ray Price. (Of course, Jim Beck's name is on it, too.) Ray had been doing some work at Jim Beck's studio, and had also shown Lefty around the Big D Jamboree during the time this song was written. After the session, Lefty went back on tour throughout Texas and New Mexico.

While Lefty was on tour, Alice and Lois had rented a house in Sulphur Springs. Our family was living in Snyder, but for a short time we had moved just outside of Big Springs while Daddy worked a drilling job. When that job was done we moved right back to Snyder. It was the end of April when Lefty dropped by for a visit.

One evening during his stay, Lefty was sitting in his car playing his guitar and Sister Betty was standing outside of the car, listening as Lefty wrote a new song. All the other kids were playing in the yard.

Lefty told Betty, "I got this idea for a new song about Momma, but as I was writing it I thought maybe I'd better put Daddy in it, too. I don't want to make him mad."

It had started to get dark and Lefty opened his glove compartment and wrote by its light. "What do you think of this?" Lefty asked Betty. He sang a couple of lines of what was to become a country music classic.

Betty nodded. "I like it a lot, sing me some more."

"Okay, let's see," Lefty started playing his guitar again.

He finished writing his classic song "Mom and Dad's Waltz" that night.

Meanwhile, Jim Beck was sitting in his studio, booking dates, and they were coming in fast. Lefty was becoming more and more irritated each time he had to give twenty-five percent of the money he earned from these dates to Jim.

Lefty would later complain. "He just sat there with a phone in his hand while I went and did all the work. He actually liked for me to bring him the money. I know he had to be thinking, 'Look at this idiot working and bringing me the money, what a stupid country boy I've got here.' And you know what, he was right. I was so ignorant; I even gave the old thief my damn songs. Man, every time I think about that I kick my own ass."

Lefty was right. In his mind he had every reason to feel bad. He was convinced these people were taking advantage of him. All he wanted to do was write and play his songs. Lefty said many times that he wished he had finished school. Maybe, if he had, this never would have happened, but it did, and he was damn mad about it. Something was about to happen that would change all that, though; something that would be like going from the frying pan to the fire. He was about to meet Jack Starnes from Beaumont, Texas.

Neva Starnes owned a nightclub in Beaumont and she wanted to book some acts. After checking around, she heard that Lefty Frizzell was one of the hottest country singers in the business. Some of her friends at KTRC radio in Beaumont convinced her that Lefty was the right choice. Ken Ritter from the station gave her Jim Beck's phone number, and she called and booked Lefty for January 20, 1951.

Lefty hit the stage singing "If You've Got the Money, I've

Got the Time." The audience did not stop screaming and hollering for the entire show. Lefty was carrying a big band, mostly all Dallas players who really knew how to turn on a crowd, and they did that night. After the show the booze really started flowing. Lefty was having a great time and it was then that Lefty met Jack Starnes, Neva's husband. The talk eventually came around to the business side of Lefty's career. Jack was curious as to whom was handling Lefty. Lefty was in the right frame of mind to unload on Jack, and told him all about Jim Beck and the deal Jim and Art Satherley had cooked up. Anyway, it was just talk and Lefty wanted to have fun, and right then, standing over by the bar, was a brown haired, brown eyed beauty waiting to make sure that the rest of the night went just fine.

The next morning Lefty went to the office to check out and found Jack waiting for him. "Lefty, last night you told me a few things that I wanted to ask you about. It's obvious you've been taken advantage of and I believe I can do a much better job of handling your career. I know I can make you more money."

"Look, Jack, I'm very unhappy with what's going on," Lefty admitted. "But they've got me tied up pretty good, especially the Uncle Art contract. They're doing nothing for their part. I wouldn't mind so much if they at least did something for the money."

Jack thought for a moment. "Art, you told me, is a big wig at Columbia right?" Lefty nodded. "All right, I think I can get you out of that one. Tell it to me again, everything."

Lefty went over the whole mess again. Jack didn't interrupt, he let Lefty get it off his chest. Lefty actually felt better telling someone he thought might understand. Jack did understand, he really did, and he understood that opportunity was knocking. Jack was definitely not one to question where good fortune might fall.

"Lefty, if you'll sign with me, I'll make you more money. Plus, I'll get you out of this mess you're in."

Lefty asked, "Jack, what's this gonna cost me? If I've learned one thing, it's that it will cost me!"

"Lefty, believe me," Jack reached over and put his hand on Lefty's shoulder. "I'm gonna save you money. Plus, I'm gonna make you more money then you've ever seen. Don't worry about those other guys, they're not gonna mess with me, I promise you." Lefty sat there for a while, and then asked again, "Jack, what kind of a deal do you have in mind?"

"Lefty, look, I know I'm gonna have to put some money out for you. There are a lot of things you need, another car for example. You guys can't travel without the right kind of transportation. What happens if your records stopped being played? I could lose a lot of money. I say, let's split fifty-fifty right down the middle. I'm the one taking the chance, what do you think?"

Lefty was quiet. He didn't say anything for a long time. Finally he said, "I've gotta go now. I'll think about it and let you know."

Jack Starnes went with Lefty to his next show in Lake Charles, Louisiana. The little place was packed with people, but the show couldn't start because there was no public address system. Jack called around and found one and the show went off without another hitch. This impressed Lefty. He wasn't accustomed to someone stepping in and making things work. That was when he decided to work with Jack. Lefty needed help and he knew it. He needed someone who would, and could, take over and make things happen. Contracts were drawn up giving Jack Starnes fifty percent of all monies Lefty made from record sales, publishing, bookings, and any other money that might come Lefty's way. When the contracts were signed, Lefty called Jim Beck and told him their deal was over.

Jim argued with Lefty. "You can't do that, we've got a contract. Besides, you owe me some money."

"I don't owe you nothing. You conned me into signing those contracts. As far as I'm concerned, you owe me plenty.

You took half my songs that you never wrote a word of, and that damn thing I signed with you and Uncle Art, I'm taking that to an attorney. You're nothing but a thief. I've got another manager that I believe will handle things a lot better than you ever could. You don't even know how to book a date; all of them are falling apart. You may as well cancel them all because I'm not gonna show up for any of 'em."

Beck calmed down a little. "Lefty, listen to me, we're having a little bit of success right now but that could stop. One word from me to the right people and your whole career could end before you even really get started. Lefty, where are you right now? I think we should talk face to face."

Lefty told Jim that he was still in Beaumont and was planning to stay a few more days, and that it wouldn't do any good for Jim to come all the way down there, because his mind was made up. Lefty told Jim that he'd already signed a new contract with Jack Starnes, and he would be represented by Starnes' attorney for anything legal from then on.

Beck wouldn't listen. "Lefty, I'm on my way down. We'll make everything right when I get there." Jim Beck got to Beaumont as soon as he could drive down. Lefty and Jim talked, hollered, and screamed at each other, but the end result was the same.

Lefty said to Jim, "I told you twenty-five percent is too much, so this is it."

Jack took over in earnest. He bought matching stage clothes for the boys in the band. He paid Lefty's motel bill and picked up another car for transportation. He was getting things done. He was manager to the hottest act in country music, and it was time to make things happen.

Five weekends a year the Louisiana Hayride would leave its home at the Municipal Auditorium in Shreveport and go on the road. During the week Jack and Lefty were making their new business deal, the show of "almost stars" was getting ready for an appearance at Beaumont's City Auditorium. This was too good an opportunity for Jack to pass up. It was another way of showing Lefty what he could do.

Jack went to see the man in charge, Horace Logan, and told him that Lefty was available that weekend and asked if he could make room for Lefty. Logan said he would make room. Even though Lefty had just worked Neva's the weekend before, he still brought the house down.

"Please welcome Lefty Frizzell." The audience went wild. This was Lefty's first appearance on The Louisiana Hayride, and he wanted to make an impression. He remembered when he was turned down for the show, but tonight was no audition. He was not going to be turned down tonight. *No, not tonight*, he thought.

Lefty hit the stage in a new pair of handmade boots. His matching shirt and pants were covered with fancy stitching, and his dark brown scarf made the whole outfit special, but not any more special than the man himself. When the audience heard that incredible voice and saw the striking young man with the long, curly, dark hair whose head and neck swaying all around the microphone, while his legs were dancing and shaking, they could not stay in their seats. They rushed the stage, all trying to get as close as possible. Young girls screamed his name and reached out their arms to him as he sang, "If You've Got the Money, I've Got the Time." When he sang "I Love You a Thousand Ways," each girl thought he was singing right to them, and he was. Lefty would slur the notes, curl them, and play with them before letting them go. "I love you and I'll prove it in days to come."

CHAPTER NINE

HANK AND LEFTY

efty, Alice, and Lois were still living in Sulphur Springs. Lefty had been home all week and was trying to get ready to leave for Shreveport to play the Hayride that Saturday. He planned to leave Thursday morning, drive the hundred and fifty miles or so, and get a motel room because he had a bunch of interviews on Friday before the show, and he was supposed to meet Jack and some of the band Friday night.

The whole Frizzell clan had, by this time, moved to Sulphur Springs. Our sister, Johnnie Lee, had married a boy from there named Frankie Lee Melton. Lefty teased them about their names: Frankie and Johnnie. Just like the song, "Frankie and Johnny were lovers. . . ."

Lefty asked Frankie if he wanted to go with him to the Hayride that weekend. Frankie said he would really like to go, so they headed out the next morning. Lefty had just bought a new Cadillac limousine and Frankie couldn't wait to drive it.

"Lefty, you just sit back and relax and I'll have you there before you know it."

Lefty had already stocked the limo. His guitar and clothes for the show were packed, plus quite a few bottles of whiskey were hidden in several secret compartments throughout the car. Lefty started drinking as soon as the car pulled out of Sulphur Springs. He would not let Frankie have a drink since he was driving.

They were not even half-way to Louisiana when Lefty pulled a little .22 pistol from one of the cubby holes and started shooting at road signs. They were both laughing and talking, Frankie driving and Lefty drinking and shooting out of the window of that big old limousine.

"Frankie, pull this thing over first chance you get. Tell you the truth I need to find a restroom, find me a gas station." They passed a sign that said Shreveport 52 miles and Lefty put a bullet through it.

After the rest stop Lefty said, "I'll drive, Frankie, you sit over there and act like you're somebody. I'll show you how to get us there." Lefty drove across the border into Louisiana.

Frankie asked Lefty, "How does it feel to have a hit record, Lefty? I'll bet it's just great, isn't it?"

Lefty was trying to slow the big car down. They were coming into the town of Flournoy, Louisiana, speed limit 35 MPH.

"Man, I can't tell you how great it feels. I've nothing to compare it to." The entire time Lefty was trying to explain he was lightly tapping Frankie on the arm or shoulder, or waving his arm in Frankie's direction. "There's no way to describe . . ."

At that moment the road turned sharply to the left and Lefty drove straight through a fence, across a yard, and ran into a parked car in the driveway. Frankie was badly shaken and just sat there. Lefty told him to get in the back and hide all the whiskey. Frankie continued to sit there.

"Frankie, snap out of it, jump in the back and hide those bottles, hide everything!" Once again Frankie didn't move.

Lefty reached over and literally threw Frankie into the back seat, and then got out and started walking toward the front of the car—his head hurt a little and he felt a knot on his forehead. About this time an older man came out the front door of the house, and walked up to Lefty shaking his head.

"What in the hell has happened here?" the man asked.

Lefty was looking for possible damage. He didn't see much wrong with his Cadillac, maybe a little scratch and a small dent, but the man's Chevrolet was caved in pretty good.

Lefty said very calmly, "I'm sorry, sir. I just didn't see that curve in time and . . . "

The man didn't give Lefty time to finish. "You weren't paying any attention, obviously. There's a sign right down the road with great big red letters showing the curve. Look what you've done to my car."

Lefty was still pretty calm. He smiled as he said, "I realize there's some damage to your little car, but look at mine." Lefty pointed to the little scratch on the bumper. "It'll cost more to fix the dent in my Cadillac than to replace the whole back end of your cheap ass Chevrolet."

The man stared at Lefty. He was so mad he was trembling. He ran back into the house. Frankie walked up and stood with Lefty watching the guy. He wasn't gone but a minute, and when he came back he had a pencil and a piece of paper. "What's your name and where did you come from?"

Lefty was starting to get a little irritated by this time. He reached in his shirt pocket and found a piece of paper. He said to Frankie, "Give me your pen. Okay, old partner, what's your name and what are you doing living on such a dangerous street?"

Then the police pulled up behind Lefty's limo. They walked over and talked to the old man. Once in awhile they would glance at Lefty. They walked over, looked at the cars, and wrote something on a pad. Finally, one of the cops said to Lefty, "We're gonna have to take you both downtown. You'll be staying with us tonight, boys."

Frankie was so nervous that he paced back and forth in the little cell. "Lefty, what do you think is gonna happen? Shit, they could keep us here as long as they want to, and besides that I'm hungry."

Lefty was stretched out on the cot. "Frankie, why don't you calm down, hell, they're not gonna do anything to you. It's not your car, you weren't driving, you didn't do nothing, so just relax. It's almost suppertime, somebody will be here any minute." Lefty had barely gotten the words out when the jailer opened the cell door and brought in two trays of food.

Lefty said, "Man, you probably saved our lives, we were starving. We hadn't planned on being here this long and we haven't had anything to eat."

The jailer smiled and sat the food down. "You know, you're not the first guy to drive through that fence. You've made the old man mighty mad though. What did you say to old Judge Monroe to make him so damn mad?"

Frankie was about to take a bite of pork chop. "What did you call him? Did you say judge?"

The jailer looked at Frankie. "That's old Judge Monroe. He's been the judge around here for so long I don't even remember anyone else."

Lefty asked, "Do you mean to say I ran through the judge's fence and wrecked his car?"

"Well, you sure did," the jailer replied. "But like I said, that's all happened before. What else did you do? 'Cause he's madder 'n a bag full of hornets!"

Lefty thought for a moment. "Hell, I don't know, maybe he got mad when I told him he had a cheap car."

Early the next morning, after a jail house breakfast, Frankie and Lefty were taken upstairs to a courtroom. They were sitting when the judge came in. Lefty couldn't believe his luck. Here was the same guy who owned the fence he had run through, who owned the car he had run into, and who was now probably going to run him under the jail.

"Mr. Frizzell, we've done some checking on you and found out who you are. I just want to tell you, you're my wife's favorite singer. I wish I hadn't gotten so mad at you yesterday.

When my wife found out it was you who hit my car, she was so excited."

Lefty couldn't believe what he was hearing. He couldn't stop a smile from creeping onto his face. Frankie's legs gave out from under him and he fell into a chair. The judge kept talking. "Someone is always missing that corner. This is the sixth or seventh time it has happened. So I tell you what, you pay for the damage to my fence and car and give my wife an autographed picture, and then you and your friend are free to go."

Frankie never went on another trip with Lefty.

Lefty had a habit of talking and pecking at you at the same time. He would squeeze your hand, arm, shoulder or knee; anything to be sure he had your complete attention. He would literally wear you out if you were around him for any length of time. If he was telling you a story, he would tap or squeeze you on every word to emphasize a point. Maybe on the punch line of a joke he would double slap you. He would just wear you out.

Gene Autry said a few years later, "It isn't that he hits you so hard, it's that continual peck."

Tex Ritter agreed. "The boy will peck you to death."

Lefty would bring a copy of his sessions by and everyone would gather around to listen. If anyone talked, moved, or in any way didn't pay complete attention, he would stop the music and wouldn't play it again until he was sure you were listening to everything on the tape.

Lefty also loved to pull pranks; always some joke or another. He would go to magic stores and buy tricks, or some kind of magic game. One time he came by to see the family and he called over Sister Betty. "Hey, I want you to see something I just bought."

Betty asked, "What is it?"

Lefty tossed a small silver book over to her. Betty read the title, *All You Need to Know About Sex.* She opened the book and threw it across the room. The little book had two small batteries in it and she had received quite a shock. Lefty laughed and laughed.

He went over to Betty. "I'm sorry, here let me make it up to you, have a piece of gum."

Lefty handed Betty a stick of gum. She unwrapped the gum and put it in her mouth. "Boy, Sonny, that almost scared me to death," Betty said as she chewed that gum, and pretty soon the gum started getting hotter and hotter. Betty finally spit the gum out and ran to the sink to wash her mouth out with water.

Lefty walked over and put his arm around her. "Betty, I was just having fun with you, I hope you're not mad."

Betty started laughing. "I'm not mad, you really surprised me, that's all."

All of a sudden Betty started itching around the neck and shoulders. Lefty had sprinkled some itching powder on her while she was rinsing her mouth. Laughing, he went out to find the other kids.

Lefty also had a fiery temper. He had a great personality ordinarily, but if something or somebody got on his bad side the fight was on. Lefty was playing a show in Carlsbad, New Mexico, when he and Brother Bill got into it after the show. Bill was supposed to look after the guitars, but instead he went out back with a girl that he met. He left his and Lefty's guitars backstage, the cases still open, and the guitars lying in plain view. Lefty saw this and asked one of the boys in the band where Brother Bill was. He told Lefty that Bill went out the back stage door with some girl. Lefty didn't hesitate. He went right out that back door and found Brother Bill in the backseat of the limousine. Lefty nearly ripped the door off. He reached in and pulled Bill out of the car. Bill probably outweighed Lefty no more then ten pounds, so the fight was pretty even, except that Lefty had surprised Bill and had him on the ground before he knew what was going on.

Bill still had on his stage clothes. His shirt had long fringe and Lefty had a handful of it. "The guitars you left are both mine; the car you're doing who knows what in is mine, too; this shirt you're wearing belongs to me, too. Right now I'm taking back everything that's mine, because you can't be trusted anymore with anything that's mine." Lefty ripped the shirt right off Brother Bill's back. The girl scrambled out of the limo and ran back inside the club.

"Aw, Sonny, quit it," Bill said. "I'm sorry about the guitars. I won't let that happen again. Man, come on, Sonny, look what you've done. Look at this shirt; you've ruined this beautiful shirt."

"Bill, you'd better get your ass in there and get those guitars. If someone has stolen 'em, I'm gonna whip your ass all the way home. Why can't you take care of business before you run off with some girl? Damn, Bill, those guitars cost money which you, of course, have none. You're gonna put me plum' out of business."

"All right, Sonny," Bill said as he headed toward the back door, "but you just cost me a piece of ass and that really makes me madder'n hell." Bill's voice trailed off as he went to find the guitars. He was still grumbling.

Two days later Lefty and the boys were in El Paso and once again Brother Bill was missing after the show. Lefty came out the back.

This time, he thought, *I'm really gonna kick his ass; not only that, but I'm gonna fire him, too.*

When Lefty opened the back door and stepped out, he saw Bill standing between two guys. Lefty could see an argument was heating up. He didn't slow down. He walked right through those two fellows, gave them one lick each with his left fist, and both men were down. They didn't get up either. Bill said later that he never saw Lefty hit either one of the guys. He said that all he saw were the two guys falling down around him. Lefty and

Bill stood looking down at the guys on the ground.

Bill looked at Lefty. "Sonny, ah, I'll go get the guitars now. I'll fix 'em up real nice, maybe tune 'em and wipe 'em off."

Bill started walking back toward the club. He looked back and saw Lefty still staring at the two boys on the ground. Bill continued walking, saying under his breath, "Maybe I'd better change the strings, too."

About a week later, Lefty and Bill left Dallas to go to Houston. Bill was driving.

"Bill, I don't know why I let you drive. You're the worst driver in the world. You know I've got to be in Houston tonight, and I doubt if you can get me anywhere near there by then."

Bill smiled. "Sonny, why don't you take a nap and let me drive, and when you wake up, hell, we'll be there. Besides that, you're getting on my nerves."

"Bill! I've tried that before, but it's hard to sleep when I'm just trying to hang on to something. You're so reckless, you're about to hit that truck now. Damn! Why don't you watch out?"

Bill passed the truck smooth and easy. "Now, see there, take a lesson. That's how it's done!" Bill was still smiling.

Lefty was smiling now too. "Bill, you're driving me to drink; you're just driving me to drink, Brother."

On the outskirts of Huntsville my brothers passed a young woman hitchhiking. "Sonny, did you see that?" Bill asked. "Damn, she's about my age. Should we stop and pick her up?"

Lefty sat up in his seat. "Are you kidding, boy, stop this car. She needs someone to look after her. There's a lot of meanness going on out here on the road these days. Man, turn this car around, I'm gonna look after her personally." The boys pulled up alongside the girl.

Lefty leaned out the window. "Where you going, young lady? Maybe we can help get you there?"

She told them she was on her way to Houston and would appreciate a ride. Lefty jumped out of the car and opened the back door.

"It will be my pleasure, I'm sure." Lefty told her. "This is my brother, Bill, and please don't talk to him too much, because he's driving and he needs to keep his mind on the road. I've been trying to teach him how to be a safe driver, but some people are hard learners you know."

The girl laughed. "My name is Ruby. It's nice to meet you guys, and thanks for the ride." Somewhere in the conversation Lefty asked Ruby if she liked country music, she said she did.

Lefty told her, "I play music and, uh, me and my brother here, we're doing a show tonight, and if you want to go with us I'll get you a room where we're staying and you can come to the show with us. You'll have fun, I promise!"

The morning after the show, Lefty walked out of his motel room and saw Brother Bill coming from the girl's room.

"Bill, what in the world are you doing?" Lefty said as he grabbed Bill's arm. "She's our guest; you didn't take advantage of her, did you?"

Bill kind of stuttered. "Well, uh, yes, I guess I did. Man, is she great, what a time."

Lefty interrupted. "Was she really? Aw, man, I wanted to do that. Bill, you're supposed to be looking out for me, you should be helping me. I turn my back and look what you did. Okay, okay, I'm going up there. You wait here 'cause we've got to go back to Dallas, so I won't be long."

Bill said Sonny was right, he wasn't gone long, and he seemed real happy when he returned. "Okay, we've got to go."

"Sonny, you're not gonna want to just jump in the car. You need to get a little protection. You should wash up and disinfect yourself."

Lefty thought for a minute. "Okay, what do I need to do?"

Bill cleared his throat. "Go back in the room; wash with hot water and soap. You might want to scrub yourself real good and then put this on you." Bill reached into his bag and pulled out a little bottle of Campho-Phenique. "Put a lot of this oil all over yourself." Bill handed Lefty the bottle. "Rub it in, you know, all over."

Lefty went back into his room. Bill waited there with a little smile on his face. After he heard the first of many screams, he heard Lefty shout, "I'm gonna kill you, Brother Bill."

When they were finally ready to leave, Bill walked to the car, laughing as he got in the driver's seat, and said to Lefty, "I got you, I really got you this time, maybe you'd like to drive now?"

Lefty was in the early development stages of two deadly habits, one was women. He had already gone to jail because of one. Now, he had hit records playing on the radio, he was traveling all over the country in his limousine, dressed up in his fringed and rhinestone suits, running out onto stages singing "If You've Got the Money, I've Got the Time." Yes, every woman wanted this curly haired, curly voiced, smiling, guitar playing, honky-tonk singing Texas boy. Lefty took full advantage of his stardom, making sure that as many of them as humanly possible got a chance to know him personally.

The other deadly habit was whiskey. Lefty had been drinking a little for the past few years, but nothing like what was going on now. He bought his whiskey by the case. He never went on stage without a drink, and one was always waiting for him when he got off. At first he would drink with other people. Later, when he was, as he put it, "carrying on," he would drink whether anyone was there or not.

One night, Lefty was showing Bill how to drink for the effect, not for the taste.

"Bill, look, you take a sip of your chaser, kinda roll it around in your mouth, then you swallow it. Next, take a sip of your chaser again, but this time hold it in your mouth. Now hold your breath and start drinking the whiskey. You can drink as long as you can hold your breath. Still holding your breath, drink your chaser again. After you have swallowed your chaser you can take a breath. This way you never taste the booze, you only get the effect. Just remember, if you drink too much too fast it'll knock you on your ass."

Bill was a quick learner. He learned that booze would help him forget all the things he wanted to accomplish with his life, but never did. Lefty hardly ever drank socially. He drank for effect. In later years he switched to vodka because he believed it was harder to smell on his breath than whiskey.

It wasn't long before the bookings came rolling in. Lefty bought another show suit and, before long, had a few more made. With Lefty's new Cadillac limousine the show was on the road nearly nonstop. Jack planned on keeping his new property very busy.

Lefty's songs were doing great on the national charts. "I Love You a Thousand Ways" was still in the top ten, and "Look What Thoughts Will Do" was climbing the charts rapidly. Lefty had lost a few members of his band to the Army, one of which was Brother Bill. Lefty was getting tired of the band anyway, so he left it up to Jack to hire new players. Jack found guitarist Blackie Crawford, bassist Pee Wee Reid, and Curly Chalker—who was probably one of the finest steel guitar players around—all working in Paris, Texas. They started playing with Lefty in March 1951, playing dates on the Hayride. Jack had convinced Lefty to go in with him and buy a tour bus, so now the Frizzell tour was traveling in style. Royalties were rolling in from Lefty's songs, so Lefty treated himself to a beautiful ring with his initials, L.F., spelled out in diamonds. He bought a new, custom built Gibson J200 guitar with a Bigsby neck with "Lefty Frizzell" written across the pick guard.

Lefty worked the Hayride on March 31, 1951. It was his twenty-third birthday. He celebrated by signing a new two-year publishing contract with Hill and Range Music. He received a normal percentage plus a $7,000 signing bonus.

In April 1951, promoter A. V. Bamford organized and promoted the dream tour of all time: a six day tour starring Hank Williams and Lefty Frizzell, undeniably the two biggest stars in country music. The tour started out in Little Rock, Arkansas, with dates in Monroe, Baton Rouge, and Shreveport, Louisiana; and Corpus Christi, Texas, and ending in New Orleans.

In Little Rock there were two shows, a three o'clock matinee and another show at eight. After the matinee everyone went back to the hotel. Lefty and Hank were settled in Lefty's room swapping song ideas when there was a knock on the door. Lefty opened it, and standing there was a very pretty young girl. Lefty talked to her for a moment and then she came into the room.

Lefty took her by the hand. "Say hello to Hank."

Hank got up from his chair, nodded to the young girl and said, "Lefty, I'll see you later. I've got to be somewhere else, I'll bet." With that he left the room. Lefty wasn't seen again until just before show time.

Daddy's recollection of Hank and Lefty switching songs went something like this:

Hank came into Lefty's room and said, "Lefty, have you ever written a song you didn't like?"

"Yeah, Hank, there's probably some, why?"

"I have, too. Why don't you give me one that you absolutely hate and I'll give you one of mine. We'll both treat 'em like our own. Let's not tell anyone which songs they are and we'll see what happens. What ya think?"

Hank and Lefty did switch songs and it is a mystery to this day which songs they were. Lefty told me the story in 1956. He didn't give a time or a place, he just said that he and Hank locked themselves in a hotel room for three days and wouldn't let anyone in. They had food and whiskey delivered to the door. Lefty said they each wrote a song during this time and they traded. Later, they were both taken to the airport at separate times. Lefty bought a ticket to Dallas, where Alice picked him up and drove him home to Sulphur Springs, and Lefty believed that Hank flew to Nashville.

Lefty laughed. "I found out later Hank had left his car at the hotel."

Whichever story is right really doesn't matter, I guess. The important thing is which songs were written and traded and that's something we'll never know.

Lefty had hired Daddy to drive the tour bus, which got him out of the oilfields, but he nearly killed everyone trying to drive that bus. Lefty finally had to send him home because, one, the band refused to ride with him, and two, our mother was pregnant again.

Momma had so many problems with the last pregnancy that this time Lefty didn't want to take any chances. The best hospital was in Paris, Texas, some thirty-five miles away, so Lefty rented a small apartment within walking distance. The baby was born on July 1, 1951, Alice's birthday. Lefty named him Allen Doyle after our mother, AD. Allen had to have a blood transfusion. All the kids, including Lefty and Alice, gathered on the lawn outside the hospital and they swear to this day they could hear Baby Allen screaming. The doctors all agreed that Allen probably wouldn't live past his seventh birthday. Allen celebrated his fifty-ninth birthday on July 1, 2010.

While playing a date, Lefty met a beautiful young lady by the name of Judy Baker (neé Burkhart) the first time he played Corpus Christi, and was looking forward to seeing her again on this trip through. Judy was friends with most of the stars coming into town doing shows. Her house parties were well known, and a list of country music's who's-who could be found at Judy's house at any given time. All the Hanks were there at one time or another, some at the same time—Williams, Snow, Thompson—even Johnny Cash, but Lefty was her favorite.

When Hank and Lefty came to town for their fifth show, Judy was there. "Lefty did his show and I went backstage to see him," she related. "Lefty took me by the hand and said, 'Come on you've got to see Hank,' so he and I stood off to the side of the stage, Lefty even lifted me up so I could see Hank better. They both played Lefty's Gibson guitar. I don't guess there's ever been a better show, at least none I've ever seen."

One of the greatest weeks in country music history ended on Friday night at the Municipal Auditorium in New Orleans. Lefty always spoke highly of Hank and talked often of that tour.

Three of Lefty's songs were now on *Billboard's* top ten list. "I Want To Be with You Always" hit the number ten spot, "Look What Thoughts Will Do" was number five, and "I Love You a Thousand Ways" was holding down the number six position. It had been on the charts for twenty-three weeks.

Lefty's career was skyrocketing.

CHAPTER TEN

ALWAYS LATE

hen Jack Starnes booked Lefty in The Palm Isle Club in Longview, Texas, Jack went with him. Jack liked the club so much that he made an offer to buy the place from the owner, Mattie Castleberry. Jack bought the club and everything in it for the price of $18,900, and he took possession on April 10, 1951. Lefty now had three different places he could work, the Hayride in Shreveport, Neva's in Beaumont, and now the Palm Isle in Longview. Later the name was changed to the Reo Palm Isle. All of these places were within easy driving distance of each other. Lefty's band, the Tune Toppers, relocated to Longview, and changed their name to the Western Cherokees. Jack was still trying to make Lefty a permanent member of the Hayride, but that arrangement hadn't come together yet. However, Lefty still played many dates on the Hayride with fellow artists like Faron Young and Webb Pierce, to name a couple.

Lefty was not only original in his singing and songwriting, but was becoming more and more original in his everyday style, like changing the English language around. For instance, if Lefty was going with someone to the show he might say, "I'm going wit'chew," or, "I'm going either." At the same time he would squeeze your arm or tap your shoulder, or maybe wave his hands around. He was very theatrical in all his movements. If he was walking down the street with someone and noticed that they were walking in the same way he was, he would start dragging one foot. He just refused to be like anyone else.

It was also becoming increasingly harder to get Lefty anywhere on time. It became a major problem. People had to start telling him that he had to be somewhere at least two hours before he was actually supposed to be there so he would be on time. If Lefty had an appointment at one o'clock in the afternoon, he might either figure out a way to cancel it, or he might not even start getting ready until one o'clock. Many times Lefty would actually arrive on time, but not let anyone know he was there until he was late. This didn't bother him at all. He took pride in the fact that he could be late and still make everything all right. I believe he enjoyed seeing how people responded to his showing up late. There were even times he didn't show up at all.

Daddy recalled a tour when he was driving Lefty's Cadillac. Lefty was riding in the back, Blackie Crawford was on the passenger side, and the band bus was following behind. Of course, they were late. Daddy won't take the credit for getting them lost, but it seems that's what happened.

Daddy said, "It doesn't seem to matter, Sonny, if it's your fault or not, you're always late."

Blackie noted, "That's a song title, Lefty."

Lefty started waving at Blackie. "Reach in that there glove compartment, Blackie, and find something to write on. We might as well get something out of this trip; let's write us a hit." Blackie got a pencil and paper and wrote "Always Late" at the top of the page.

Lefty said, "Let's say 'all-wa-ays la-ate with your kisses, come on over here and ah . . .'"

Blackie chimed in. "Won't you come over here and love me before it's too late."

Lefty thought for a moment. "Oh no, something like

'Awl-wa-ays late with your kisses, won't you come to my arms sweet da-ar-arlin' and stay-ya-ya.'"

"Always Late with Your Kisses" was written that night on the way to a show in Shreveport.

Lefty's fourth session for Columbia Records was booked for May 24, 1951. The songs recorded were songs Lefty had written: "How Long Will It Take (To Stop Loving You)," "Always Late with Your Kisses," written with Blackie Crawford, "Mom and Dad's Waltz," and "You Can Go on Your Way Now." As was Lefty's custom when he had a new song, all the musicians would gather round and Lefty would play it for them.

"All right, guys, ah, this song goes like this." Lefty started singing, "All . . . wa . . . ays la . . . ate . . ."

Lefty stopped singing and said, "Guys, there are two verses. What ya think? I'll sing a verse; you play a verse. I'll sing another; you play another. At the end of the second verse, just hit a chord and let it ring out, and I'll end it vocally. Something like that, all right?"

From the control room Don Law asked, "Lefty, are we ready to try one?"

"I believe so, Don. Okay, boys, when Don says go, Jimmy, you count it off." Jimmy Dennis was playing drums for the session.

Don said, "Okay, 016JB40, 'Always Late,' take one."

On the song "Always Late," Harold L. "Curly" Chalker played one of the most famous steel guitar intros in country music.

Lefty recorded two of the biggest songs of his career on this session; "Always Late" and "Mom and Dad's Waltz" provided Lefty with another two-sided hit.

Lefty and his band arrived in Nashville on June 16, 1951, to make his second Grand Ole Opry appearance. The band was excited, but when they arrived for sound check they were told that drums where not allowed on the Opry.

"Jimmy, I've just been told we can't bring your drums in. The Opry don't allow drums, can you imagine that? I didn't know it. Nobody told me anything about it at all." Lefty felt really bad when he told Jimmy he couldn't play. "You're gonna have to sit this one out. Now I'll pay you anyway so don't worry about that." Lefty smiled then. "You'll get paid and you won't even have to pick up a stick."

"Lefty, it isn't about getting paid, this is the Grand Ole Opry, man. I'd play it for free." Like most musicians Jimmy Dennis' dream was to play the Opry, and when he learned he'd have to sit this one out he was devastated.

Red Foley, the host, introduced Lefty as a "fine singer of homey songs" and mentioned that Lefty might join the Opry as a regular before long.

Lefty sang "I Want To Be with You Always" and the incredible "I Love You a Thousand Ways."

After the Opry appearance, Lefty and his band hit the road and headed for the West, with a few stops in the Midwest. Lefty played the Rainbow Gardens in Bakersfield, California, to a sellout crowd of over three thousand screaming fans.

A fifteen-year-old teenager was waiting, like everyone else, to see his idol. Many years later Merle Haggard said of this night, "Lefty stepped out on stage dressed all in white, most heroes usually are. I had never seen or heard anyone like him before. The influence Lefty had on me and country music at that time was not even measurable."

Everyone was standing during the show and folks in the back were complaining that they couldn't see Lefty. Someone put a kitchen chair on stage and Lefty stood on it so everyone could see him. The microphone was then raised so Lefty could sing. He sang a Jimmie Rodgers song and received four encores. Then Lefty said he had a couple of new songs he wanted to play, and that he had written one for our mom and dad and that all the royalties were going to them. Merle said that when he sang

"Mom and Dad's Waltz," Lefty had made a fan for life. Merle also said this was the inspiration for his song, "Mama Tried." Later on, because of our father's drinking problem and his inability to handle money, Lefty had to keep the royalties and give them to our mother when our parents needed money.

Lefty officially joined the Grand Ole Opry on July 21, 1951. He was thrilled to be on the same stage as his hero, Ernest Tubb, and to see a little more often his newest friend, Hank Williams. Things were good for Lefty. He had number one hits, he was traveling all over the country singing and playing his songs, and now he was a member of the Grand Ole Opry. These were great times for a young man who only a few years ago was sitting in a lonely jail cell in Roswell, New Mexico, writing songs to someone who had every right to walk as far away from him as possible. The world sure could make some incredible turns.

Yes indeed, these were some great times.

Sometimes the things a person does in his life will come back around and bite him right in the backside. Such was the case when Lefty played the Opry again in August 1951. Two policemen met Lefty backstage with a warrant for his arrest. They allowed Lefty to finish his part of the show, and then they took him downtown. Lefty was being arrested for "contributory delinquency." The young girl who had come to Lefty's door in Little Rock was a minor; Lefty had been caught again. Jack got Lefty out on bail.

The only thing Lefty could say was, "Please, don't let Alice find out."

Jack took care of the situation. He simply paid everyone off, but he wasn't able to keep the news from Alice. When she found out, the fat hit the fire. What may have made matters worse was the fact that Alice was pregnant again with their second child, Rickey. This time Alice had taken enough. This time she was leaving for sure and for good. Nothing Lefty could do or say would change her mind this time.

Lefty promised her everything. It's hard to remember all the things he did promise, but Alice had heard it all before, nothing new, same old promises just like before. Somehow Lefty convinced Alice that this time he had learned his lesson. He would take her and Lois on all the tours so they could be a family again. He wanted to spend more quality time at home with Lois and her, eating Alice's home cooking.

Lefty told her, "You know what let's do, we'll find us a real home. Let's buy us a new house where we can start all over again with our family. We're gonna have another baby soon, and we're making enough money to have us a real good life now, a new home to take our new baby to. Alice, where would you like to live?"

They bought their first home in Beaumont, Texas, at 2214 East Drive, in a very nice upper-class neighborhood next door to a doctor. The house was two-stories with a large front yard and a small back yard. It was their first home and they were both very proud of it. Alice furnished it with brand new furniture, a washer and dryer, and custom made curtains. Alice made it look really nice. When she ran out of things to buy she hired a maid to keep it all clean. Alice was getting good at this thing called "having money." She could shop right along with the best; she knew as well as Lefty did that she deserved it.

After they had settled in, Alice and Lefty heard from some of the neighbors that a few of the houses down the street had been vandalized and that some on one of the other blocks had been broken into. They didn't think it would happen to them until one night, as they were driving in after seeing a movie, Lefty thought he saw someone, or something, going from the side of the house into the backyard. He saw just a glimpse in his headlights as he pulled in the drive.

"Alice, did you see that?"

"What, see what?" she answered.

Lefty reached under the seat for his gun. "A man or something just ran around into the backyard. Damn, you and the kids stay here, don't get out until I get back."

He didn't need to worry. He had just scared the life out of Alice, and she was not going anywhere. Lefty was out of the car like a shot. Alice could see him in the headlights until he got to the back of the house, then he vanished from sight. Alice sat staring after him. Her whole body went rigid when she heard the first shot. Alice didn't know whether to jump out of the car and run, or to get farther down into the car seat. Bam! Another shot rang out. Bam! Bam! Two more shots rang out in quick succession.

Alice couldn't stay in the car any longer. She jumped out and came running to the spot she saw Lefty disappear, hollering, "Sonny, Sonny, are you all right?" She was almost to the back of the house, but still in the headlights, when Lefty stepped out of the dark into the light. He walked right past Alice.

"Son-of-a-bitch got away."

Betty recalls being in the house baby sitting one night while Alice and Lefty had gone out to dinner and a movie.

"I walked into the kitchen and looked out of the window. I saw a man looking back at me. It scared me so bad I'm surprised I was able to move at all. I knew that all the doors in the house were unlocked. I ran throughout the house locking doors knowing that at any minute he might just come on in. I told Sonny when they got home and he showed me where he kept his extra gun. He told me to get the gun and use it."

Another time when Lefty and Alice were in the house, and Lefty heard something in the attic. He grabbed his gun and fired three times into the ceiling.

Lefty was touring almost nonstop, crisscrossing the country, playing the Opry as many Saturday nights as possible, and spending what little time he had left over with his family in Beaumont. "I Want To Be with You Always" hit number one on the *Billboard* charts in June 1951. "I Love You a Thousand Ways" had been in the top ten for thirty-three weeks.

Lefty always wanted to do a tribute album to Jimmie Rodgers, the man who had influenced him the most. Lefty recorded eight of Jimmie's songs with producer Don Law at Jim Beck's studio in Dallas on June 1, 1951. The songs were: "Treasure Untold," "Blue Yodel #6," "Traveling Blues," "My Old Pal," "Blue Yodel #2," "Lullaby Yodel," "Brakeman Blues," and "My Rough and Rowdy Ways." Don used the same great musicians he did on the "Always Late" session. Every song turned out incredible.

Once again Lefty was feeling that he was doing all the work and his manager was taking half the money. Somehow he just couldn't get it in his head that Jack was working as hard as he was. Lefty knew something had to change.

Jack easily booked the Opry on Saturday nights. He would then book Lefty anywhere else after that—California, New York, it didn't matter—then right back to the Opry the next Saturday. Lefty was getting tired of this kind of life. There just wasn't any thought given to scheduling, no pattern to go by. Also, Jack was just sitting in his office while Lefty was traveling all over creation. It was getting the best of Lefty, and another thing Lefty didn't want to bother with was the band. He loved to travel light, and had only one guy on his payroll, Abe Manual, his fiddle player.

Lefty became friends with a rough and tough, colorful character he met in Clovis, New Mexico, by the name of Jack Skipworth. Jack ran a nightclub called the Cattlemen's Club. He was also a champion calf roper who traveled the rodeo circuit. Jack stood about six one or two, and was thin and wiry. He loved drinking, partying, and fighting—in that order. Jack was wild and crazy and so was Lefty. They made a good team.

Lefty was booked in El Paso for a concert on July 19, 1951 and he brought Jack with him. While the band was setting up for the show, Jack and Lefty decided to go across the border. It was about two o'clock in the afternoon when they started across the bridge leading into Juarez. Jack had taken a little bag full of change with him. Lefty didn't know why, but he was soon to find out. There were twenty to thirty kids walking around on the bridge. Jack dropped a little of his change out of the bag. A few of the kids ran for it and scooped it up. Lefty saw this and smiled. Every now and then Jack would drop a little more. The kids would scramble to pick up the money. By the time Jack and Lefty walked into town, all the kids were following them.

Some of the store owners would come out onto the sidewalk and talk to people passing by. Some even offered a drink of cognac to come inside.

Lefty said, "Yeah, I'll have a drink, what ya got in the store?"

"Amigo, I've got the best deals, nobody beats my deals," the store owner said as he passed around the bottle of cognac. Jack and Lefty took a long pull from the bottle. Jack tossed a few coins onto the sidewalk; the kids went scrambling for the change.

"Lefty, what do ya think? Let's go across the street," Jack said as he nodded in that direction.

"Well, I don't know."

The store owner gave up the bottle again. "No, señor, come inside and see. I make best deals on the street."

This went on until the cognac was gone. Jack took the last drink from the bottle. He reached in his bag, got a handful of change, and tossed it all right through the front door of the store. The change went everywhere and so did those kids, thirty little boys and girls trying to get through the door at the same time. As Lefty and Jack crossed the street they could hear the store owner screaming above the sound of all those happy kids tearing through his store.

The club was packed in El Paso that night. After the first show Lefty and Jack were sitting in his limo having a drink with a couple of local beauties when Lefty heard someone knocking on his window. Lefty pushed the button and the window came down. Lefty stared into the barrel of a gun.

A man said, "I believe you have something that belongs to me."

Lefty didn't say anything for what seem to be a long time. Finally he said, "What would that be?"

The man moved a little closer to the window. "You've got my woman in there."

Lefty casually replied, "Well sir, there are indeed some lovely people here, but I don't see a one with your name on 'em. So why don't you calm down, look around, and tell me if she's here."

It was dark inside the limo. The man pulled the gun away from Lefty's face and put his head inside the window. Jack grabbed a handful of the guy's hair and yanked hard, pulling his head down and wedging his shoulders in the window frame. From out of nowhere Lefty's little gun was pressed underneath the man's chin.

Lefty said softly, "Go ahead and drop your gun, fella; it won't do you any good now."

Jack tightened his grip on the man's head. "I think I'll break your neck, you son-of a-bitch. Drop the gun."

The frightened man dropped the gun. "All right, all right," he cried. "The gun's gone; let me go."

Lefty cocked the gun he was holding. He looked the man right in the eye. "You've got two choices, mister. One is, I blow your head off like you were planning to do to me, or second, you act like a man and get in here and have a drink."

The man replied meekly, "All right, I'll have a drink."

Lefty lowered the gun and let the guy in. "Sit over there and, you know, it might be better if you don't say anything, you've probably talked enough for now." With that they all had a drink, or several, then Lefty went in for his second show.

Lefty was tired. His records were selling as fast as they could be pressed. Wherever he played it would be packed; a thousand-seat Texas night club or a twenty thousand-seat auditorium, it didn't matter whether he was working alone or with other Opry acts like Ernest Tubb or Hank Snow. People would jam in to see Lefty. It seemed like Lefty was everywhere at once; it seemed like that to Lefty as well.

Once again, he called his manager, Jack Starnes. "Jack, man, listen, I need a break. You've got me coming and going in all directions at the same time. You're wearing me out. We've got to do something."

"Lefty, we've got to take advantage of your popularity, you know, make it while you can, who knows how long this will last," Jack insisted.

You could hear the exhaustion in Lefty's voice. "I know how long; I'm about ready to drop. It won't last much longer, I promise you. Isn't there something you can do about scheduling a less killing tour? You know, book the dates maybe two, three hundred miles apart, a week or two at a time. Take a few days or even a week off, and then start again in another area. That's the way other artists do it."

Jack pushed. "Lefty, the other artists are not as hot as you are. You must realize everyone wants you now, and they may not later. Look, I've been thinking about it, I believe if we had our own airplane we could go anywhere, anytime. You could get there faster, make all the dates, and end up with more time for yourself. I believe instead of slowing down we should speed up."

In September 1951, Lefty and Jack went in as partners on a twin engine, eight-seater Cessna airplane.

Before starting an October tour of California, Lefty had his pilot fly him to Sulphur Springs to show off the new plane to our folks. He took Momma and Daddy up first. They were so excited; neither one had ever flown before. Momma held back, though. "Sonny, I don't know, your plane is so small and...."

Lefty took her by the arm. "Momma, it's all right, I wouldn't let nothing hurt you. Look at me, I've flown everywhere and I'm in great shape. This will be the best time you've ever hadYou'll be wanting Daddy to buy you one, come on." Lefty pulled her into the plane and sat her down. She grabbed me and pulled me into the plane with her. Lefty showed us how to put on our seat belts.

"Momma, you're gonna love this," Lefty told her. "We're gonna fly right over town; you'll be able to see for miles in all directions."

"I don't want to see in all directions, I see all I want to see right here on the ground." Momma informed.

Lefty just laughed. "Momma, you need a little spice in your life. All you've got is Daddy over there, and believe me, you need all the spice you can get." Everyone laughed as the plane taxied down the runway. During liftoff Momma was holding on to me and the arm rest with her left hand, and gripped Lefty's hand with her right. She was squeezing his hand so hard Lefty had to loosen her grip.

"As soon as we get up in the air it'll smooth out and you'll love it," Lefty promised. Mom didn't respond; she was holding her breath.

When we landed Lefty helped our mother from the plane. "I'll never get on another airplane as long as I live," Momma declared. "They liked to have scared me to death. It wasn't Sonny; it was the guy flying that thing. He turned us almost over."

Lefty was holding Momma trying to steady her. "Are you gonna be all right? Here sit down in the car. You were doing just fine until the plane rolled up on its side."

"He tried to turn that plane over with me in it." Momma accused as she climbed in the car.

"Momma," Lefty explained, "the pilot was trying to turn around so we could come back and land. He wasn't trying to scare you. Now sit here and relax; you'll be fine." Then he grabbed me and said, "Okay, kids, are you ready to go?"

The next morning Lefty had just finished packing his suitcase and was getting ready to leave when I came in with a friend. "Where are you going, Sonny?" I asked.

Lefty grinned. "Well, I'm gonna go play some music. Say, who's your partner there?"

I nodded at my friend. "This is Lonnie. He lives around the corner."

Lefty reached out and shook Lonnie's hand. "Nice to meet you, Lonnie. Say, how old are you, son?"

"I'm almost ten." Lonnie answered. Then he asked, "Did David really help you write your songs, you know, the ones we hear all the time on the radio?"

A big old grin came across Lefty's face as I fell to the floor crying out, "You weren't supposed to say nothin', oh my God."

Lefty tried to hold back a laugh. "Did David really say that?"

Lonnie was watching me squirm around on the floor. "Yes, he did, he told me he liked writing songs with you. He said you were the best songwriter in the world."

Lefty, still smiling said, "Well, I may not be the best song-writer in the world, but I'm glad he thinks so, and, yes, he did help me write all those songs. One day he may be the best song-writer in the world, who knows. I've gotta go. David, get up off that floor and help me get my suitcase in the car. See you later there, Lonnie."

While Lefty was playing the Riverside Rancho in California, the owner, Marty Landau, introduced him to Nudie, the Rodeo Tailor. Lefty had been designing his own stage outfits for awhile. Detachable fringe was one of his innovations. The idea was that when the girls grabbed for his shirt the fringe would pull away and his shirt wouldn't tear. Nudie made Lefty a white suit with the letters L and F spelled out in blue rhinestones. This was the first time rhinestones were used on a country star's clothing.

CHAPTER ELEVEN

LEFTY MEETS MERLE

In October 1951, Lefty accomplished one of the most incredible feats in country music history. *Billboard Magazine* listed Lefty as having four songs in the top ten at the same time. "Always Late" was number one; "Mom and Dad's Waltz" was number two; "I Want To Be with You Always" came in at number five; and "Traveling Blues," a Jimmie Rodgers song Lefty had recorded was the number seven song. There was no doubt Lefty's star was blazing across the country music sky.

Lefty went back into the studio October 19, 1951, to cut four more sides. This time Don booked the ACW Studio in Houston. Some of the musicians were different, too. Blackie Crawford and Bill Callahan were added to the session. It could have been the change of studio or the different players, but whatever the reason, the session went poorly.

Lefty brought in four new songs that he had written with the help of friends. The songs were: "I Love You (Though You're No Good)," "It's Just You (I Could Love Always)," "(Darling Now) You're Here So Everything's All Right," and "I've Got Reasons to Hate You."

Jack booked Lefty on a Canadian tour that started at the last of November and ended two weeks before Christmas. This was the tour that, as far as Lefty was concerned, was the end. The tour was so badly put together that some of the dates didn't come off at all. Others had no promotion, and some had no equipment to speak of. Also it was cold, I mean really cold. Lefty didn't have the comfort of his limo. He didn't have his newly purchased airplane. He had nothing but some whiskey to keep him warm. This was the last straw.

Lefty called Jack and told him, "Jack, you're sitting there in Beaumont in the eighty degree sunshine. I'm here in Canada and it's sixty degrees below zero, ice and snow everywhere. You're driving around in a Cadillac I bought you. I'm riding with who knows who in a wreck that, most of the time, the heater don't work; or it's probably too cold for their heater to make any difference. I had to charter a plane to fly me somewhere to a show. There wasn't even a runway; we had to land on the icy damn road. My plane is sitting there with you doing nothing, just like you. I want to make it perfectly clear, I'm through, I quit." With that he hung up, he didn't talk to Jack again until he arrived back in Beaumont just before Christmas.

In the meantime, "Give Me More, More, More (Of Your Kisses)" was released December, 12, 1951, and first showed up on the *Billboard* charts the middle of the month. It went to number one during the first week of March.

Lefty and Jack Starnes' face off came just before Christmas at Jack's house. Lefty thought his contract with Jack was over after the first of the year, but Jack argued that the contract they both had signed provided him with a two year option.

Lefty disagreed. "Jack, I never signed a contract like that. We agreed to just one year, and that year will be up after the first."

"Well, Lefty, let me tell you, son," Jack said smugly. "I've got the contract at my lawyer's office. I'll be more than glad to show it to you if it'll help to jog your memory."

Lefty grew concerned. "All right, let's go see it right now." Lefty headed for the door.

When they drove up to the attorney's office no one was there. "Lefty, they're all gone until after Christmas," Jack was talking fast. "We'll see it then, okay? Lefty, what's important now is that I've got some great things happening in the spring."

Lefty didn't say a word; he just sat there. Jack pulled away from the curb still talking. "I've got two major tours booked already, one on the East Coast and one in California and up into the Northwest, and Lefty, I've saved the best for last," Jack stopped talking enough to catch his breath. "I've got you on the Perry Como show in New York City."

These bookings were too good to turn down and way too much money to say no to, so Lefty didn't. It was agreed that they would wait until after the tours to settle their differences. Lefty told himself, *What a year this has been, four songs on the charts at the same time. What a Christmas this is gonna be!*

Don Law and Lefty both agreed that the magic was there in Jim Beck's studio in Dallas, and they wanted to keep the magic going, so on January 8, 1952, they went back into the Dallas studio and re-cut three of the songs they had recorded in Houston the previous October, "I Love You (Though You're No Good)," "It's Just You (I Could Love Always)," and "(Darling Now) You're Here So Everything's All Right," plus another song Lefty wrote called "Don't Stay Away (Till Love Grows Cold)".

"**P**lease welcome my next guest," Perry Como said to the audience the night of March 19, 1952, "Lefty Frizzell!" The camera panned over to Lefty.

He smiled, walked up to the microphone and started to sing, "I'd walk for miles…"

Lefty sang his heart out to all the hundreds of people in the studio and to the millions of fans watching on television.

For the next few minutes Lefty owned the world. He kept it going with "I Love You a Thousand Ways," and ended his part of the show with "If You Got the Money, I've Got the Time." Lefty walked over to Perry Como after he finished.

"Mr. Como, thanks for having me on the show, I've had a great time."

"Lefty, it could be you're the best country singer I've ever heard, and thank you for coming."

L efty made it back to Beaumont for a few days before heading to Dallas for his next recording session at Jim Beck's studio. Again, Don Law was the producer. The musicians working with Lefty were Jimmy Rollin, lead guitar; Joe Knight, rhythm guitar; George McCoy, steel guitar; Artie Glenn, bass; Johnny Gimble, fiddle; and Harold Carmack, piano. Lefty brought four new songs, and out of these, one really stands out.

Lefty picked up his guitar and spoke to the band. "Okay, guys, I think we have some good songs for this session. Let's start with this one," and he began singing "Forever and Always."

"Forever and Always" is as good a song as any Lefty ever wrote, and the session went great. Two other songs recorded that day were "If You Can Spare the Time (I Won't Miss the Money)" and "A King without a Queen," co-written by Martha Dean Moore, Bob Wills, and Billy J. Wills. The final song recorded was another written by Lefty, "I Know You're Lonesome (While Waiting for Me)."

A few days later, Lefty was on his way to the West Coast to begin one of the longest and hardest tours he had done so far. This tour started after the April 4, 1952, session in Dallas and was to run through June. Starnes had contacted the Americana Corporation, which was run by Steve Stebbins, to book the tour.

Stebbins was a big, heavy, cigar smoking ex-cop. The tour started in the Los Angeles area, went on down to San Diego, and then back up into Bakersfield. Lefty played the Rainbow Gardens again to a sold out crowd. The evening of the show Lefty was backstage with Alice, and Wayne Raney and his wife, when a man approached Lefty.

"Lefty, I'm Bob Teague and I've got a young friend who wants to meet you real bad. Would you have time do you think to say hi? He sings just like you."

"I'll take the time, bring him on in." Lefty was great about listening and helping young artists. (To note a few, Freddie Hart, Ray Price, and me.)

A young boy of about sixteen walked up and shook Lefty's hand. "Hi, my name is Merle Haggard."

Lefty could tell the boy was nervous so he said, "Pick up my guitar and sing me something."

Merle sang a couple of song, and Lefty thought, *Dang, he does sound a lot like me.*

Joe Snead, the club owner, came over to get Lefty. "Lefty, it's about time. Everything's ready. It's a packed house. Those people are going nuts waiting for you."

Lefty nodded. "Listen, I'll go on right after the kid sings a few."

The club owner argued. "Lefty, there are over three thousand people here to see you, not some kid. Please, let's go."

Lefty looked at Joe and drawled, "Ah…I'll go, and I'm ready to go, right after the kid."

Joe headed back to the stage muttering to himself, "Damn, these stars are…." From the stage Joe calmed the crowd. "Ladies and gentlemen Lefty is just about ready to sing, but first please welcome a talented young man from right here in Bakersfield, Merle Haggard."

Merle came to the microphone carrying Lefty's guitar. "Thanks. I know you're all here to see Lefty, but while he's getting ready I hope you'll like this song."

> "For years and years I've rambled,
> Drank my wine and gambled,"

That boy sure the hell can sing, Lefty thought as he watched from back stage. Merle went on singing "My Rough and Rowdy Ways" and a couple more songs. He got a good reception.

Steve Stebbins had sent Al Flores, one of his agents, on the road with Lefty to handle the business end of the tour. Murphy's Law was in full effect. Everything that could go wrong did go wrong. The biggest problem was Lefty's voice gave out. They were playing five, or sometimes six, nights a week and that was just too much. As the months and the miles rolled past, Lefty got worse. He could hardly speak let alone sing. Al Flores called Steve Stebbins and told him that he didn't believe Lefty would be able to hold out for the rest of the tour. They still had about ten more dates when Lefty called his manager and told him he was quitting.

"Jack, I can't do this anymore. Cancel the rest of the tour. My voice will not hold out; it's over. I will never work like this again; it's too much. When I say I'm through, I mean I'm through with working with you. When I get home, I'm gonna book myself with agents who I'll only have to pay fifteen percent of what I make. Our deal has gone on way to long."

Lefty went back to Beaumont for a much needed rest, knowing he'd have to face Jack again at some point. That time came when he didn't receive his royalty checks from Columbia for record sales or from Hill and Range for song publishing. Lefty and his band leader, Blackie Crawford, went over to Jack Starnes house.

"Jack, where are my royalty checks?" Lefty asked.

"Lefty, they've been delayed until we can come to an agreement on what our deal is." Jack stalled.

Lefty was getting irritated. "Jack, our deal is over. That's the only agreement I know. Once again, Jack, where are my checks? Go get 'em and we'll come to an agreement right now."

"Lefty, half of that money is mine. My lawyer is holding the checks until that fact is understood."

"Jack, I've got a lawyer of my own. We might as well get this over with."

There was a lot of tension between Lefty and Jack in those days, and Lefty finally let it all out one evening while playing a show at Neva's in Beaumont.

Lefty took the stage with "If You've Got the Money" and followed with "I Love You a Thousand Ways."

He said to the sellout crowd, "Hello, everybody, I'm glad to be back at Neva's. We always play some mighty fine music here. I hope y'all are having a great time here tonight. I'm gonna play you all my hit songs, and thanks to you for making them my hit songs." The crowd was laughing and applauding. "Tonight is very special for me. I want to introduce my manager who has just joined us. Please give him a round of applause. Jack, would you stand up so everyone can see you." Jack got up from his table and smiled and waved at the crowd.

Lefty went on. "Jack, I'm so glad you came tonight. I've got something to tell you. Remember about a year ago when I called you and told you that I had just made a thousand dollars. I was so happy until you said, 'Lefty, don't you remember we signed a fifty-fifty contract, whatever you make I get half.' Remember that, Jack? A little while later I called you again and said, 'Hey, Jack! Man, I just made twelve hundred and fifty dollars tonight.' You didn't waste any breath saying, 'We, partner, we made twelve hundred and fifty dollars tonight, and please send me my half.' Well, buddy, I must tell you, and I'm glad you're here so I can, a little while back, partner, we went out with this beautiful woman. We got this beautiful woman in the family way. She had twins and mine died. What do you want to do with your half?" The only person not laughing and applauding was Jack.

Lefty went into "Always Late" and the crowd went crazy.

Within a few days Jack's lawyer had filed an injunctive suit against Lefty. The petition outlined the terms of the contract originally signed and spelled out how important Jack had been to Lefty's career. It said that Lefty was really only a regional artist until Jack took over as manager. Jack didn't say anything about Lefty having had two nationwide, number one records before they had even met. Jack also showed the two year options that Lefty claimed weren't there on the original contract. All assets were held until a court date could be set. Jack's lawyers tried to get the court to stop Lefty from playing concerts or making any money from recordings until this matter could be settled. The courts denied this request, stating that Lefty had a right to make a living for his family.

One of the first calls Lefty made after walking away from Jack Starnes was to J. D. Miller, a friend who lived in Crowley, Louisiana. Miller owned a small recording studio and ran a couple of independent record labels. One was called Feature and dealt with country artists, and the other was Fais Do Do specializing in Cajun music.

"I ain't working with Jack anymore. I want you to manage me. I'll pay you twenty-five percent, what ya say?"

Miller had done a lot of traveling as a musician and didn't want to give up his home life. "Aw, Lefty, man, I can't run around all over the country like you do. I'm a homebody."

"Come on, I need you." Lefty coaxed, "Besides, you can use the money, can't you?"

Miller thought about it a moment. "Okay, I don't know if I'm good enough, but if you think I can help you, then I'll try."

One of the first things Lefty and his new manager did

was write a few songs together. Lefty was so impressed with Miller's writing that he called Troy Martin, a Peer International music representative in Nashville, and told him about Miller's songs. Troy came down to Louisiana and met with Miller. He took back to Nashville what was to become a country classic, "It Wasn't God Who Made Honky Tonk Angels."

Miller was heard to say about Lefty, "I love Lefty for his almost child-like devotion to laughter and having fun." However, he did not care for the way Lefty handled business. Lefty had gotten worse about not showing up to shows on time, and his drinking was way past anyone's ability to handle.

One time Miller and Lefty were driving through Dallas and Lefty spotted a black limo at a car dealership. "Hey, turn this thing around, that's the prettiest car I've ever seen."

"Lefty, we don't have time to see any car," Miller said. "I've got to get home. Besides, you don't have any money, at least not enough to buy that car."

Lefty insisted. "Turn around anyhow. I want to see that car now, J.D."

Lefty walked around the limo and ran his hand along the fender. "What a beautiful car, it has everything, J.D."

Miller went looking for someone to help them. "Hey, is there any one here; someone wants to see this limo. Hello."

A man from the service department came out. "Maybe I can find someone to help you. I don't know where everyone is."

"Well, do you think they want to sell this car?"

The man nodded. "I don't see why not. It's been sitting there a long time. Hold on, one of the salesmen is coming now."

The salesman walked over and apologized. "Man, what a day this has been, sorry, I didn't know you were here. What can I show you?"

"Do you see that guy standing over by the limo?" Miller pointed to Lefty.

"Yes."

"That's the country singer, Lefty Frizzell, and he wants to see that car." Then Miller walked over to where Lefty was standing.

The salesman got very excited. He said something to the man from the service department, then hurried over and greeted Lefty. A minute later the owner of the dealership came over to help and to meet Lefty. Moments later four guys came out and started wiping the car down. The salesman asked Lefty if he wanted to take a test drive.

"Yes, I'd love to take it around the block." Lefty was convinced he wanted that car. "J.D., I've got to have this car. What can we do to get the money?"

Lefty had no concept of money or money management. If he needed money, he just expected his manager to find it. Unfortunately, his lack of money savvy contributed to his being taken advantage of by many people.

Miller was already calculating. "Well, Starnes has all your royalties tied up. Let me think, I remember your publishing contract is just about up. You know what, let me call Hill and Range and see what I can work out."

Miller called and worked out a new contract and got an advance of ten thousand dollars, and had the money wired to them in Dallas. Miller and Lefty went back to the dealership and bought the limo. The price was $9,000, but Miller got the price down to $7,500, which left $2,500 for the party they threw that night.

Lefty did a session at Miller's studio on July 10, 1952. The musicians on the session were Woody Guidry, lead guitar; Herdy Hall, steel guitar; Bob Henderson, fiddle; and Benny Fruge, piano. The songs recorded were "Lost Love Blues" and "Send Her Here To Be Mine," both written by Lefty; and "That's Me without You," written by Miller. Four days later Don Law called for a session to be done at Jim Beck's studio. Only two songs were recorded that day, "That's Me without You" and Lefty's "Lost Love Blues."

For several months Miller tried to work as manager for Lefty, but Lefty was already unmanageable, showing up late for shows or not at all. He was also drinking more than ever. After a time Miller threw up his hands.

"Man, this just isn't gonna work, so, Lefty, I'm done." With that Lefty had no one to even try to keep things rolling along. He was completely on his own.

His attorney, Harry Rovenger, accompanied him to Starnes lawyer's office. Mr. John G. Tucker took Lefty's deposition. After 146 pages of testimony, Lefty came out looking and feeling none too well. Lefty stuck to his guns when it came down to believing that the two year option had been added to the contract after the original had been signed. This was really all he had and he had no real proof.

Mr. Tucker asked Lefty, "Would you swear something has been put in the contract since you signed it?"

"I will swear that it is not the same."

"What do you mean, not the same?" Mr. Tucker pressed.

Lefty stood firm. "I mean the part about the two year option."

Three days before, Lefty had been with his producer, Don Law, recording yet another session at Jim Beck's studio. Again Lefty had written four more great songs: "I Won't Be Good For Nothin'," "If I Lose You (I'll Lose My World)," "I'm an Old, Old Man (Tryin' to Live While I Can)," and "You're Just Mine (Only in My Dreams)."

Lefty pulled up a chair and grabbed his guitar in his usual manner. "Guys, this next number is kind of up tempo. Ah, I believe a D chord would work, any way it goes like this."

Lefty started strumming his guitar. "Said an old man…"

"I'm an Old, Old Man" would be Lefty's next single. Although it never made it to number one, *Billboard* charted it at number five on January 3, 1953.

Lefty never wrote a song that didn't have heart. When he sang his songs you could feel that Lefty had put everything he had into his vocals. He was writing more great songs than ever. These songs may have or may not have been as great as the songs he'd written before, but still, they were Lefty through and through. The songs were: "I'll Try," "(Honey, Baby, Hurry!) Bring Your Sweet Self Back to Me," "Time Changes Everything," and "All of Me Loves All of You."

On February 6, 1953, Lefty was back at Jim Beck's studio in Dallas recording his new songs. Don booked some great musicians for this session, like Jimmy Rollins, lead guitar; Joe Knight, guitar; Paul Blunt, steel guitar; Eddie Duncan, bass; Jack Youngblood, fiddle; Fred Cantu, drums; and Harold Carmack, piano.

A few months earlier, on the Grand Ole Opry, Lefty had met a very talented harmonica player by the name of Wayne Raney. They became instant friends, and started running together and playing some dates. Lefty told Don Law about Wayne and Don invited him to Lefty's recording session on February 7, 1953. Some of the players were changed from the day before. Roy Nichols was on lead guitar, with Lou Millet on guitar; Ernie Harvey was on the steel guitar; Lum York on bass; Jack Youngblood on fiddle; Wayne Raney on harmonica; and Tommy Perkins on drums. Lefty recorded two songs of the great Jimmie Rodgers, "California Blues (Blue Yodel #4)" and "Never No Mo' Blues," as well as two of his own songs, "We Crucified Our Jesus" and "When It Comes To Measuring Love."

Lefty told the band before starting, "This, I think, is my first religious song. I like it a lot; it's real slow, key of C, I think." Lefty cleared his throat and sang, "We cru . . . ci . . . fied our Jesus . . ."

That winter Lefty was in Phoenix staying at the Adams Hotel. Steve Stebbins was with him when the phone rang. Lefty answered, "Lefty her . . . ah."

A man's voice on the line said, "Lefty, this is Freddie Hart. I'm a friend of Wayne Raney. He told me you were coming to town. I sing and write songs."

Lefty was slurring his words. "So-o-o," Lefty said, "You know Ra . . . aney, huh."

"Yes, I do. Would you have time to listen to any of my songs while you're in town?"

"Why don't you come on by the hotel and sing me something?"

Freddie couldn't believe what he'd just heard. "Sure, when would be a good time for you?"

"How's now?" Lefty drawled.

Freddie was there before Lefty got out of the shower. Steve answered when Freddie knocked on the door.

"Come on in, young fella," Steve said and motioned to the couch. "Sit down, my name is Steve. Lefty will be out in a minute." Freddie sat down and Lefty stepped into the room wrapped in a towel.

"Hey, Freddie, any friend of Raney's is a friend of mine. Here!" Lefty picked up his guitar and handed it to Freddie. "Play me something."

Freddie played Lefty several songs he had written, and Lefty was so impressed he offered Freddie a job right then and there. "You want to go with me on this tour? You can help me with my guitar and sing a few songs to open the show."

Freddie was in shock. "You mean now, go with you now?"

Lefty put the guitar back on the bed. "Of course, I mean now, I'm leaving as soon as I can get dressed."

"Will I have enough time to go pack a few things, you know, maybe tell my wife goodbye."

Lefty smiled. "Yeah, I know all right, don't take too long and I'll wait for you."

A few short months later, Freddie signed a recording contract with Capitol Records, plus a long term booking agreement with Steve Stebbins of the Americana Corporation. Freddie Hart is one of the Frizzell family's closest friends to this day.

Lefty's tours were almost non-stop. He would come by Beaumont long enough to kiss Alice, hug the babies, and get some clean clothes, then he would go back on the road. The recording sessions were the only thing that broke up this routine. Somewhere in all this mess he found time to write more songs.

On March 9, 1953, Lefty was back in the studio with Jim Beck and Don Law in Dallas.

They used the same musicians as the session before. Lefty recorded two more Jimmie Rodgers songs, "Sleep Baby Sleep" and "(I'm) Lonely and Blue."

Lefty told the band, "You know, since we're all here and some of us are in tune, why don't we go ahead and cut a hit." Everyone laughed, and Lefty started singing "Lonely and Blue."

This song was released by Don as a single on May 1, 1953, just in time for the biggest event of the year, The First Annual Jimmie Rodgers Memorial Day. Ernest Tubb and Hank Snow, and several of the area's high rollers, organized this show. Everyone was there. Lefty took Alice with him to the event, and in 1982, Freddie Hart and I had the pleasure and honor of playing this show together.

"Before You Go, Make Sure You Know," "Two Friends of Mine," "Hopeless Love," and "Then I'll Come Back to You" were recorded on June 4, 1953, at Jim Beck's studio. After the session Lefty went home to Beaumont just in time for his civil suit. The court was ready to hear both sides; the judge was ready; the jury had been selected. An out of court settlement was reached at the last minute.

Betty was waiting in the car with the kids when Lefty and Alice got in. Lefty slid behind the wheel, but didn't start the car. He just sat there. Finally, he looked at Alice, "We've lost everything because I was too trusting. I just trusted everyone; I won't do that again. If I'd 'a had an education, you know, this never would have happened to me."

Alice sat quietly for a moment. "At least you're done with Jack, and that's something."

Lefty spoke with a little more enthusiasm. "That's right. We didn't need him in the beginning and we don't need him now. I don't mind starting over, how about you?"

Lefty sat at the kitchen table. He poured out a little salt and crushed it with his thumbnail. He thought, *Damn, that thing hurts, bet I'm gonna have to see a doctor about it.*

Alice walked into the room. "Are you feeling, all right? You want me to call the doctor for you?"

Lefty crushed a few more granules of salt before answering. "No, I'll call him. Boy, I hate to, but it's bothering me so much I guess I'm gonna have to."

Lefty called the doctor and made an appointment for the next morning. He suffered throughout the night and the next morning.

"Lefty, how long has this been bothering you?" The doctor asked the next day.

Lefty thought about it for a minute. "I don't know, about a month now, I guess." The doctor continued his exam. He finally said, "Well, here's what we'll do, I want you to keep the area very clean and use a little Vaseline to soften the skin. I'll give you a prescription to take care of any infection. We'll be able to operate in about a week. Set it up with my secretary and we'll see you then."

Lefty went home and informed Alice. "Okay, the doctor told me he'd have to operate next week. Boy, I hope I can hold off that long."

"Just do like the doctor says, and you'll be all right." Alice encouraged him.

Lefty grumbled as he left the room. "Easy for you to say."

The day of the operation Lefty arrived at the hospital. The nurse took him into a little room. "Take off your clothes and put this gown on. Lie down on the bed and try to relax; we'll be ready in a moment."

Lefty got undressed, put on the gown, and said to himself, "How am I suppose to relax, I wonder? I need some medicine for that."

The doctor came in. "Lefty, how are you today? Are you ready?"

Lefty responded as calmly as he could. "Yeah, Doc, under the circumstances I'm doing okay."

The doctor pulled up a chair. "Lefty, here's what we're gonna do. This procedure is done all the time. There's really nothing to worry about."

Lefty tried to joke. "Really, man, I wish you were doing this on someone else; it's got me worried all the way to hell and back."

The doctor laughed. "Now, Lefty, this won't take long. Nurse, take Mr. Frizzell into the operating room."

The nurse rolled Lefty into the operating room, and she tried to reassure him. "Lefty, you won't feel a thing. I'm going to give you something to make you sleep and when you wake up the circumcision will be over." Lefty wasn't so sure it would be all right.

After the procedure our mother called to check on Lefty. "Momma, yes, it hurts. Come on down here; I'd love to see you. I could use some of your great home cooking. . . .Yes, I got the little pillow you sent and it works just fine. . . . I am using ice, Momma. . . . Yeah, and a peach cobbler would make me feel a lot better." Lefty was quiet, listening. "Well, Momma, you know, if I could wish for one good thing to come out of all this, I'd wish for the swelling to stay."

J ack Starnes had taken most of Lefty's money and now the IRS wanted the rest of it. The only way out for Lefty and Alice was to sell the house, so the house went on the market. Lefty was still touring as much as possible, and thanks to Steve Stebbins, Lefty worked a lot, especially in California. Steve was partners with Cliffie Stone who ran a TV show called The Hometown Jamboree. Lefty played it many times and always packed the house. The television part of the show was from seven to eight every Saturday night. Then the chairs were moved out of the way and the crowd would dance until one in the morning. A lot of country television shows cropped up in California during this time, such as Cal's Corral and a variety show called The Town Hall Party. Lefty became a regular on the 'Party' along with his pal, Freddie Hart.

In 1953, Lefty recorded eight more songs he had written. On November 14th he recorded "The Tragic Letter (The Letter That You Left)," and three more songs were recorded on November 15th, "Two Hearts Broken Now," "You Can Always Count on Me," and "I've Been Away Way Too Long." Everyone gathered at Jim Beck's again on November 17th to record "Run 'Em Off," "The Darkest Moment (Is Just Before the Light of Day)," "You're Too Late," and "My Little Her and Him." Lefty didn't record again for almost a year. The next session was booked at Jim Beck's on October 5, 1954.

Betty had come to stay with Lefty and Alice to help look after the kids. One afternoon Betty and the kids were home alone when the door bell rang. Betty went to open the door and saw two men standing there.

One of the men introduced himself. "Hello, young lady, my name is Don Law. I'm here to see Lefty."

"Well, they're not here right now, but come on in. Ah, would you like something to drink?"

"You know, that would be real nice," Don said. The two men came in and Don asked, "What's your name?"

"I'm Lefty's sister. My name is Betty. Have a seat and I'll bring you some iced tea." The two men sat down and Betty brought the drinks.

Don introduced the other man to Betty. "Betty, this is my friend Troy. The other day when I spoke to Lefty I told him we'd be here tomorrow. We just came down early and took a chance that he'd be home."

"They'll be home tonight kinda late I think, but are you hungry?" Betty offered. "I'm cooking right now and it's about done; I'm ready to set the table. The kids are hungry, and if you want to have dinner with us it's just a matter of setting out two more plates."

Don stood up. "Betty, I'm starving and I know Troy is, thank you very much. Can I help you with anything?"

Betty shook her head. "Well, no, I believe I've got everything, y'all come on."

Lefty and Alice came in around ten that night, and Betty told them that Don Law and Troy Martin had come by.

Lefty said, "They're supposed to be here tomorrow. Did Don say where they were staying?"

"No, they didn't, Sonny, they only said to tell you they'd see you tomorrow. They sure are nice guys; they stayed and had dinner with us."

"They had dinner here?" Lefty raised his voice, "Don and Troy had dinner here?"

"Why yes, and he liked it, they both ate a lot, and they were so nice."

"Betty, Don Law is from England, and I know he's pretty finicky about what he eats. What could you possibly have fixed for 'em?"

Betty shrugged. "Well, we had red beans, corn bread, fried potatoes and . . ."

Lefty stood there staring at our sister in total disbelief as she continued to rattle off the menu. He threw both hands in the air, shook his head, and left the room.

The next afternoon Lefty was saying goodbye to Don and Troy when Betty came in.

"Sonny, I'm going to the store can I get you anything?"

"No, I don't need a thing, but hold on a minute."

Lefty turned from Betty and walked Don and Troy to the door. He said to Don, "It's great seeing you again, especially out of the studio. Troy, thanks for coming; it's always nice to see you."

"Lefty, I'll see you in Dallas, and tell your lovely sister thanks for a great dinner," said Don.

Lefty walked back inside. "Betty, when you see I'm talking to important people don't call me Sonny, call me Lefty."

Betty looked at our brother. "I thought Sonny was who you were." She turned and started to walk out of the room.

"Oh, ah, hey, Betty. You, ah, hold on a minute." Betty stopped and turned to face him. "Ah, look, hon, it's all right, you can call me Sonny anytime you want to."

Lefty and Alice's fights were famous. We could fill up the pages of this book with the many arguments and a blow-by-blow description of who won what round. It didn't matter who was there or where they were when the fight broke out. The only way you could get away from it was to leave town, but if you came back within a week they would probably still be at it.

Momma, Brother Bill, and Betty were in the living room with Lefty and Alice watching television when one really good argument broke out between them. It quickly turned to hand-to-hand combat. Momma, Bill, and Betty paid no attention, they just kept watching television. Alice pushed Lefty to the floor and tried to kick him. They rolled around on the floor. Lefty was just trying to keep from getting hurt. He knew that if he hurt her she would really get mad, so he just held her down. The rest of the family still paid no attention, they moved their legs if the battle ran into them. All of a sudden Alice cried out, and Lefty loosened his hold. Alice jumped up and ran to their bedroom. She was gone for a moment then returned with Lefty's handgun. Lefty was still on the floor. When Momma saw the gun, she got up and walked over to Alice.

"Alice, give me the gun."

Alice looked at Momma and handed her the gun. Alice turned and walked back to her bedroom. She was crying and upset for days because this was the first time their arguments had ever gone that far. She was shocked that she had grabbed a gun. How could the thought have ever entered her mind? Then she realized she hadn't been thinking at all. She just reacted, and that was the scariest part of all.

The house in Beaumont finally sold in February 1954, and Lefty, Alice, and the kids moved back to Sulphur Springs for a while.

One day Lefty said to Alice, "You know what? I'm doing so much work in California maybe we should move out there. There's a lot of TV shows; I like working with Steve. Who knows, I might even get in the movies." Then Lefty did his best Rhett Butler: "'Frankly, Scarlett, my dear, I don't give a damn.' See there, Alice, maybe they need another Clark Gable out there."

Alice laughed. "I'll bet they could use another Gable, but I doubt if it could be you 'cause Gable had big ears and yours are small. And you know something else, a few months ago when the doctor took the scissors and went snip, snip, your ears ain't the only thing small." Alice ran from the room laughing.

CHAPTER TWELVE

CALIFORNIA BLUES

Plans were made to move out to California, but first Lefty had a tremendous amount of bills to pay, so he called on Steve Stebbins. Steve once again came through. Lefty said that he needed to work and Steve put together a tour that would help Lefty with his money problems. The only trouble was this tour was almost four months long, starting in March 1954, and going into July. The previous year Steve had booked a three month tour and it almost killed Lefty, and everyone else. Lefty had a different reason for the tour this time. He had obligations; he was a man of his word; he paid his bills. The tour would bring in enough money to pay those obligations; even if it was four months long.

A great band was put together for the tour. Floyd Cramer was picked as bandleader, and given the job of finding the other players. Cramer chose D. J. Fontana on drums, Chuck Wiginton on bass, Bill Peters on fiddle, Jimmy Day on steel guitar, and Van Howard on rhythm guitar and as front man. The band was named The Drifting Cowboys and was probably one of the best bands ever to back Lefty. This tour took Lefty and the Cowboys all over the Southwest, through California, and up into the Northwest.

With the money Lefty made from this tour he and Alice

were able to clear up their many debts and move to California. First they rented a small place in Pasadena, and then another in Granada Hills in the San Fernando Valley. It wasn't long before they were able to purchase a nice ranch-type home with a pool in the back yard. Lefty liked appearing on television, and Steve kept him busy playing clubs around California, and every once in awhile, a longer tour out of state. Lefty thought he could go on like this forever. He was still recording, but not cutting any hits. At least Columbia Records didn't think so. Lefty didn't receive promotion on anything during this time.

Lefty was back in Dallas on October 5, 1954, for yet another session. Once again Don Law assembled several great musicians including Jimmy Rollins, Joe Knight, Paul Blunt, Grundy "Slim" Harbert, Johnny Gimble, Fred Cantu, and William "Bill" Simmons. The songs recorded were "I Love You Mostly," "You're There, I'm Here," "Let It Be So," and "Mama." The song "I Love You Mostly" was credited as being written by Lefty and Bob Adams, but for years the family has believed that Brother Bill, not Lefty, had a hand in writing this song.

Lefty enjoyed working The Town Hall Party television show with its cast of talented performers. His long time friend, Freddie Hart, was a regular. Joe and Rose Lee Maphis performed, as did Fiddling Kate, Les "Carrot Top" Anderson, Johnny Bond, Tex Carman, and Skeets McDonald. Tex Ritter was a frequent guest as were two very talented young entertainers, The Collins Kids. Larry and Lorrie were just dynamic. They would explode on the stage, and the crowd would go wild. Lorrie would stand there and sing while Larry danced all around her, up and down the stage, playing his guitar. Joe Maphis was one of the finest guitarists in the business. He played a double neck Gibson and Larry learned to play from him. The show was great, it had so many performers with different styles, no wonder it was a hit. Jay Stewart was the host of this most entertaining show, and later became an announcer on *Let's Make a Deal*, which starred Monty Hall.

Lefty lived in Granada Hills on Superior Street only a few miles from the Devonshire Downs, a horse racing track, and many nights at Lefty's house the cast of Town Hall Party would drown out the noise of the track. Lefty's backyard was famous for these all-nighters, and many hot stars cooled off in Lefty's pool.

Lefty just couldn't seem to get a hit, even though country music was selling more then ever. He was working as much as he wanted, and it didn't seem to bother Lefty. With all the TV exposure, he seemed to be doing just fine.

Don Law took Lefty back to Jim Beck's studio four more times in 1955: January 19th, June 18th, and December 6th and 7th. They cut fifteen songs during this time, but still a hit eluded them.

Steve Stebbins called Lefty in May of 1955. "Lefty, I've got something that might interest you."

"What's going on, Steve?"

"Well, I'm involved in putting together talent for a country music show at the Hollywood Bowl. Man, this will be the first one ever at that place. You wanna be a part of it?"

"Well sure, Steve," Lefty said. "When is it and who all's gonna be there?"

"August 6th is when they want to have the show, and I believe Hank Snow is guesting on the Town Hall Party on August 7th. Maybe you and Hank can headline the show and we'll put some of our other people on with you, such as Freddie, The Collins Kids, you know, round out the package, put on a hell'va show for 'em. We'll see how them high society folks gets along with us hillbillies."

The Hollywood Bowl was packed. There were about as many country fans as there were high society season ticket holders. Lefty had played a lot of big shows, but the Hollywood Bowl was practically in his backyard. Lefty walked out to the applause of over 17,000 country music fans.

"If you've got the money, I've got the time,

We'll go honky-tonkin', and we'll have a time . . ."

The show was a huge success and one that Lefty was proud to have been a part of.

It was during this time that Lefty's name was enshrined on the Walkway of Stars in Hollywood. It is just below that of another one-of-a-kind superstar: Michael Jackson, and can be found right in front of Grauman's Chinese Theatre.

Tragedy struck in May 1956. Jim Beck had been working on some radio equipment and cleaning parts with carbon tetrachloride. Later that evening he became ill. His wife called the doctor and Jim was admitted into the hospital. He slipped into a coma and never came out.

Lefty's last session recorded at Beck's studio had been December 6 and 7, 1955. The songs recorded were: "These Hands," "You Can't Divorce My Heart," "Treat Her Right," "Promises (Promises, Promises)," "My Love and Baby's Gone," "Today Is That Tomorrow (I Dreamed of Yesterday)," and "First To Have a Second Chance." This last song was written by Teddy Wilburn and Webb Pierce.

Don Law had already planned Lefty's next session for May 1956. With the passing of Jim Beck, Don had to find another place to record. Lefty and Don had cut so many great records at Beck's studio, at least in the early days, that they both had thought it was just a matter of time before the hits would come again, but now Jim Beck was gone.

Lefty had never recorded in Nashville. This was his chance to give it a try. The session was booked for May 22, 1956, at Music City Recorders, at 804 16th Avenue South. Lefty was excited to work with some of the best studio players around: Loren Otis "Jack" Shook, guitar; Samuel Pruett, guitar; Donald Helms, steel guitar; (Don Helms is one of the greatest steel guitar players in country music history. He worked with Hank Williams throughout his career.) Ray Edenton, bass; Jerry Rivers, fiddle; and Farris Coursey, drums. The songs recorded were: "Heart's Highway," "I'm a Boy Left Alone," "Just Can't Live That Fast Anymore," and a great waltz, "The Waltz of the Angels." All of these songs came off well, but Lefty still could not get a hit.

I had been touring with Lefty on and off for about a year. I would do some of the driving, make sure the guitars were tuned, anything it took to keep the show on the road. Steve liked me and felt good when he knew I would be out there with Lefty to kind of look after everything. Steve and Lefty started letting me collect the money from the dates and hang onto the money throughout the tour. I would pay expenses such as motels, gas, and food. At first Lefty would bring me out to do a song or two, but later I started opening the show. I would do fifteen minutes or so then bring the star out.

Lefty recorded in Nashville again with Don on November 7 and 8, 1956, at the same studio. This time the musicians were different,: on guitar was Grady Martin, steel guitar was Johnny Sibert, bass was Bob Moore, drums were Walter Lenk, and Marvin Hughes was on piano. Lefty had written "Glad I Found You" with Joe Johnson, and the other songs recorded were "Lullaby Waltz," "Now That You Are Gone," and "From an Angel to a Devil." All good songs, but again, no hits.

At the end of the year Lefty became a father for the third time. Marlon Jaray Frizzell was born in Northridge, California, in December 1956.

Daddy and Momma were now living in Ojai, California, a few miles northeast of Ventura. Mae, Allen, and I were still living at home. Betty was there off and on, and Brother Bill would stop by every now and then. Our sister, Johnnie Lee, was married and living in Sulphur Springs, Texas. Lesley was in the Army stationed in Korea. Lefty and Alice lived two or three hours away and would come by often.

One time when Lefty and Alice came by, Betty, Bill, and his wife, Marge, were there, too. After dinner everyone went into the living room and Lefty starting talking.

"I've thought about writing a short story. You know, something like a thriller, a whodunit kind of story. Now, who all wants a part?"

Well, everyone wanted to play, especially Marge. She fancied herself an actress and was excited when Lefty asked her to play a detective along with him. The two of them were going to solve the crime. Bill got the part of the butler and Betty was the victim. Lefty told her all she had to do was lie still and not move. Betty acted this part really well, only every so often Lefty would have remind her to lie still.

"You're supposed to be dead," he would say.

She would rise up on occasion and say, "Sonny, maybe I'm really not dead, I'm just acting."

"Okay, but right now you're dead, so be still."

Lefty made up everyone's part. Mae was the ditsy, blonde teenager who couldn't be still—Lefty had her moving all around the room. Sometimes when she moved around too much, he would move her out of the room. I was the killer and had hidden the weapon, a knife, in a flower pot. The stage was set; the actors were in place.

Lefty hollered, "Action."

Lefty and Marge, his assistant, entered the room. Everyone was sitting in chairs or on the couch, except Betty, who was on the floor acting dead.

Lefty turned to Marge. "As you can see, my pretty little assistant, we have a dead person on the floor. Now, one of these people is guilty, and it's our job to find out who the murderer is." Lefty would ask Marge a question, but before she could answer he would answer it for her. "Now, my pretty little assistant, who do you think could have done such a dastardly deed? I know they all look guilty, but probably only one is the murderer. You have a question. I know what you're gonna say, and yes, the butler is mighty suspicious looking." Lefty never let Marge say a word. "Right now, my pretty little assistant, you're thinking we should question David, right? And right you are."

"David, why are you looking so guilty, and where did you hide the knife, ah huh?"

Before I could say anything Lefty continued. "I'll bet you hid it in the flower pot." Lefty picked up the pot. "See here, the murder weapon, I thought so." Without pausing Lefty kept right on talking. "Who's the little ditsy blonde dancing everywhere? Little girl, I'll bet you know who murdered this lady on the floor, don't you?" Before Mae could say a word, Lefty said, "You may have stabbed her as you were dancing by. Don't try and deny it. Now hold still, my pretty little assistant wants to ask you, where were you when the lights went out?"

The whole play went like that. No one got a chance to talk except Lefty, but we all had fun. Everyone did when Lefty was home.

Later that evening Betty told Lefty that she needed to talk to him, so for privacy they went into the bathroom. Lefty sat down on the commode, and Betty started, "I'm just unhappy. Russell and I have been married for almost five years and I just don't think I love him. I'm not sure that I loved him when I married him."

Lefty sat there a moment before saying, "You know, I use to think I loved someone a long time ago. Betty, you should probably remember Margaret."

"Well, yes, I do, kinda."

"She was the love of my life; no one came close. She was the one I used to gauge everyone else by. As you know, we couldn't be together and the strangest thing happened awhile back. I was in Dallas recording and something happened to my car. Somebody at the studio told me about a garage that could fix it, so I drove it over there and pulled the car inside. I walked into the office and, what do you think, there was Margaret sitting behind a desk. It turns out that her husband owned the garage. I looked at her and she looked at me and you won't believe how big that girl was. I thought to myself, '*How in the world could my beloved Margaret look so bad in only a few short years?*' Damn, I'm glad I didn't get stuck with her. Listen," Lefty took her hand, "Russell is a good man, but if you don't really love him you're not doing yourself or him justice. Think about it real hard and go with your heart."

Lefty and Daddy had been drinking most of the day and now it was time, like every time before, to start arguing about religion. Daddy seemed to know quite a bit about the Bible. Lefty knew not much of anything on the subject, but that didn't stop the arguing. Alice would try to stop them saying they had to go home, but neither one of them paid her any mind. The drinking continued; the arguing got louder. They both stood up a time or two trying to make a point. One would push the other one down. After a while it seemed like they would take turns pushing each other down. Finally, they got quiet. Lefty seemed to pass out, you could hear a soft snore coming from him. Alice took this opportunity to ask the family to help her get him in the car. Brother Bill got Lefty by one shoulder, and Daddy staggered over and took the other shoulder. I grabbed one leg, and Alice, Betty, and Marge took the other.

"On the count of three we'll all lift." Alice instructed. "Mom, if you'll open the doors, we'll get him into the back seat. Okay, one, two, three, lift."

Off we went, each one struggling to hold on, keep up, and not drop him. Out the front door we went. I dropped his leg, but grabbed it back up. Lefty moaned. The girls dropped the leg they were carrying and I dropped mine again. Bill and Daddy dragged Lefty four or five feet before everyone regained their position. Momma had the door to the back seat open. Daddy was walking backward, and ran right into the door and dropped Lefty's shoulder. He reached down to pick him back up, got off balance, and fell down beside him. There came a loud moan from Lefty, but it didn't seem to wake him. What a time we had getting Lefty into the car, but finally it was done. Alice said her goodbyes and got in behind the wheel and started the car.

Everyone was standing, waiting for Daddy to get Lefty's foot safely in the car before he shut the door. Lefty's foot moved; Daddy shut the door. Lefty rose up and said, "Thanks."

The family stood watching as Alice drove away.

Lefty recorded in California again on March 13, 1957. He did a duet with Johnny Bond on a song called "Sick, Sober and Sorry." Johnny had realized great success with the songs, "Ten Little Bottles" and "The Hot Rod Lincoln."

Lefty recorded in Nashville again on May 10, 1957. Once again the songs were okay, and the musicians were great, but still there were no hits .

Lefty was home watching television one afternoon after he'd gotten back from Nashville. He stood and walked over to the picture window. He could see down the road a piece and saw me walking up to the house.

Lefty thought, *I wonder how he got clear over here; there's no one else with him.* I was a long way off still so Lefty just stood and watched as I made my way to the door. Just as I reached to ring the bell, Lefty opened the door. We just looked at each other; neither of us said a word.

Finally, Lefty moved to let me in. "Okay, you're with me now."

I lived with Lefty and Alice and worked with Lefty until I joined the Air Force. I think about these times often. I learned everything from Lefty; how to walk on and off a stage, how to handle myself in any given situation. I was privileged to work closely with one of the most talented human beings ever to be born, a man different from anyone else, incredibly honest, sincere and humble, but tremendously strong at the same time. I've never seen anyone be so creative, positive, and funny, then in a flash be impossible to deal with. Someone asked me once if I could pick five people in the history of mankind I would most like to meet, who would they be. My answer was Jesus Christ, John Wayne, Johnny Cash, Elvis Presley and my brother, Lefty, and not necessarily in that order.

Lefty was in Nashville again on May 10, 1957, recording three more songs, "No One To Talk to But the Blues," "Is It Only That You're Lonely," and "Mailman Bring Me No More Blues."

Added to this session was another great guitar player, "Sugarfoot" Hank Garland. Add Grady Martin to the mix and you've got a tremendous recording session. Sadly, there still were no hits.

Everyone was gathered around the pool table at Lefty's house one day. Lefty, Betty, and I were playing cutthroat pool when the phone rang. Alice called to Lefty saying it was for him. Lefty went to the living room to answer the phone, and he was back in a minute.

"That was Steve and he wants to know if anyone wants to

go with him this evening to meet Elvis. He says he's got to meet with the Colonel, and Elvis is filming a movie. Who wants to go?"

I was, and still am, a great Elvis fan so I stepped right up. "You know I've got to go. I'll even let you beat me playing pool if I can go."

Betty was excited, too. "Sonny, we really should go. Do you think we're dressed good enough?"

Lefty laughed. "I believe we're fine. Steve said he was to meet the Colonel and Elvis on the set of *Jailhouse Rock*. We should go; I need to meet him myself."

Steve came by a little while later, but we were having so much fun playing pool that Steve left without any of us.

Steve booked Lefty at the Riverside Rancho and came by the house to pick him up. I was in Ojai with our folks for a few days. When Steve got there they got in Lefty's Cadillac and headed out. About three quarters of the way there, a car side-swiped them. Steve slammed on the brakes, and the car started sliding around in a big circle. Steve's door opened, and since he didn't have a seat belt on he began to slide out. Lefty raised his right arm and it broke the windshield, leaving him with a badly cut wrist. With his other hand Lefty grabbed Steve and held on to him until the car stopped. The police came, an ambulance was called, and Lefty was taken to the hospital where the doctor stitched up his arm.

Steve rented another car and they made it to the show. Meanwhile, Lefty's car was towed away, and an old Plymouth station wagon was given to him as a loaner.

The following Wednesday night Lefty, Alice, the kids, and I went to the drive-in theater for a double feature. We sat through the first movie and during intermission Alice said she wanted to go get some popcorn and drinks.

Lefty said, "Alice you go and take the kids to the restroom. You know I can't go up there."

Alice came back with, "Aw, Sonny, ain't nobody gonna recognize you."

"Alice, you know someone always does," Lefty moaned. "And I don't want to go through that tonight."

"All right, I'll take the kids. David, stay with Sonny and we'll bring back enough snacks for everyone."

Lefty was sitting on the passenger side of the car and I was behind the wheel. After Alice and the kids left, Lefty said, "You know, I need to go to the restroom myself, but I'm not goin' up there." Even though the lights were on all over the drive-in Lefty decided to open the door a little and relieve himself.

To try and stop him I suggested, "Sonny, maybe you should go on up to the concession stand. I'll go with you and keep everyone away from you."

"No, I can do this. Look." Lefty opened his door and the light came on. "Damn. All right, I can open the door and I'll hold the light button down and the light will go off." Lefty opened the door a little and the light came on. He reached out his left hand and pushed the button with his thumb, and the light went out. With the other hand he got everything ready and relieved himself right out that door. When he finished, he shut the door on his thumb. He screamed and pulled his thumb away. I couldn't stop laughing; my head was hitting the steering wheel as I cracked up. Lefty was laughing too, and holding his thumb. He opened his hand, and his thumb from the thumbnail to the joint was as thin as a dime. We stopped laughing long enough to say, "My God."

Alice and the kids came back, and Lefty told her what had happened and showed her his thumb.

"Sonny, I told you to come with us. Now look, you've broke your thumb."

"Aw, Alice. It'll be all right. I want to watch this movie about Al Capone. Man, I've been waiting for this movie for weeks."

Al Capone came on, and so did the feeling in Lefty's

thumb. He was squeezing his thumb and could hardly eat his popcorn. He started to moan a little, at first, then the pain got worse and he got louder.

Alice said, "Sonny, you can't keep this up. David, stop laughing and get us home."

About one in the morning Lefty went to the emergency room and the doctor x-rayed his hand. Lefty had crushed the bone in his thumb. He came back from the hospital with his thumb in splints. The next day we discovered that Lefty's door was the only one whose light would come on. All the other door lights were broken. That weekend Lefty and I played in San Diego. I laughed all night at Lefty playing the guitar with his thumb sticking straight up.

One morning Steve phoned Lefty. "Hey, Lefty, there's a little get together over by Columbia Studios in Hollywood Wednesday night. I wanted to see if you would go with me. It's nothing serious, just a few people and some other artists. It should be fun."

"Steve, you know I hate having fun. You know I'm married. Damn, aw well, what time is this little gathering and is it casual? I don't feel like dressing up, especially not on Wednesday."

"Nah, Lefty. You won't need to dress up. I think it's just some other promoters in town. Who knows, maybe we'll get a tour out of it or something."

"Steve, you know my little brother, David, is here. Is this the kinda thing that he could come with us? I don't wanna leave him here, you know, I like having him with me."

Steve laughed. "Sure he can. Hell, he'll probably get more out of it than we will anyway."

Wednesday evening Steve picked us up at Lefty's home in Granada Hills and drove us over to Hollywood. There were probably between thirty and thirty-five people at the party and I had the chance to meet Steve's partner, Cliffie Stone. Lefty had done a lot of television and concerts with Cliffie and they were big friends. Everyone went about the room shaking hands with each other. They all seemed to know Lefty and he would introduce me.

"David, oh, he's working with me now. He's singing rock and roll and stealing all the shows. I'm gonna send him back home if he keeps it up." Everyone laughed. "We've been doing some things here in California, but we're getting ready to go on his first major tour and it'll be good, you know."

One of the men shook my hand. "You been singing some rock and roll, huh?" Still holding onto my hand he said, "Maybe you'd like to meet a couple of rock and rollers." The man pulled me around toward two other young men. "David, meet Ricky Nelson and Gene Vincent."

Even though the man kept talking to me, I didn't hear a word he was saying. I knew that Ricky Nelson was enjoying a huge multi-million selling record called *I'm Walking*. Any given week millions of people watched him on *The Ozzie and Harriet Show* on television. Gene Vincent had just come off of a huge song called "Be-Bop-A-Lula," and had recently been on *The Ed Sullivan Show*. I was a huge fan of both these guys, and I still am. I remember being so stunned I couldn't even say hello. Lefty stepped up and of course, both the young rockers knew him. That made it a lot easier. Finally, I was able to tell them that I was opening Lefty's shows and trying to get started. They both wished me well and we spent most of the time at the party together. I was later on many shows with Rick and I never knew anyone I liked better. I've met his brother, David, a few times and I've always enjoyed being around him as well. I never saw Gene again, but I'll never forget the night I met those two rock and rollers.

Lefty was booked on a new television show called Country America; Freddie Hart was also on the show. It was filmed at Paramount Studios. Alice had fixed some hard boiled eggs for Lefty, and I was trying to prepare them while Lefty was driving to the studio.

Lefty said, "Boy, you're gonna have a time today. There's a guy on the show that is unbelievable; he is a wild man."

I handed Lefty an egg. "Who is it?"

Lefty thought for a minute. "I can't think of his name right now, but I met him sometime back and he's crazy." Then he laughed., "He's right up your alley, wait'll you get a load of him."

Lefty was right, I was held spellbound when Jerry Lee Lewis did his part of the show. I'd always been an Elvis fan, but I was so knocked out by Jerry that I added him to my list. We also had a chance to say hello to Jim Reeves, who was taping another show at Paramount, and on our way out of the studio we were introduced to a very talented actor by the name of John Derek.

Lefty traveled back to Nashville again on October 25, 1957, and recorded five more songs: "You've Still Got It," "Tell Me Dear," "To Stop Loving You (Means Cry)"—which Lefty wrote—"Time Out for the Blues," and a Freddie Hart song called "The Torch within My Heart."

One day, the mailman brought a huge box to Lefty's home from Columbia Records. Lefty put it on the dining room table and it sat there about a week. Finally, Lefty said, "I wonder what Columbia sent me, let's open that box!" It was a Sony reel to reel tape recorder. With my help, Lefty put it together. This gave Lefty an excuse to listen to some tapes of songs that had been sent to him. Lefty had a small Wollensak tape recorder, which was really easy to operate, but didn't sound nearly as good as the Sony. The two of us played tape after tape, and after each song we would share our opinion.

Lefty would say, "How could a song that bad be allowed to come through the mail? Why I oughta sue the post office!"

After hearing another song, one worse then the ones before, Lefty joked, "Someone should take the guy who wrote this and string him up. There's gotta be a law against this kinda song." We would laugh and put on another song. The two of us sat there all afternoon playing songs and laughing. There were a few good ones and Lefty would put these aside and play them again every so often. He ended up with a bunch of pretty good songs. One such song I kept putting back on the machine and replaying.

Lefty told me, "If you play that song one more time, I'm gonna have you arrested. That's a brand new machine. If Columbia knew you were playing that song on it, they'd take their tape recorder back and throw it away, 'cause that's all it'll be good for. Now quit it, you hear me."

I begged, "Just one more time. This is the best song we've heard all day, come on one more time."

"Where'd we get that tape and who sent it?"

I looked on the tape box. "Steve sent it."

"I'm gonna call him and chew him out. I'll tell him don't ever send me anything like that again. I told him a long time ago to send me only hits. What's the matter with him?" We both laughed and then Lefty said, "I was just kidding, I kinda like that. What's the name of it?"

I looked at the box. "'That'll Be the Day,' and the singer and writer it says here is Buddy Holly."

"Okay, put it here with the good songs, and you know what, I don't even like that Sony recording machine. It's too hard to work with. Pack it up and we'll send it back, I like my little Wollensax." Lefty got up went to the kitchen and got himself a cold beer, walked back to the living room, and turned on the television.

One morning, around nine o'clock, the doorbell rang. Alice went to the door and said hello to a man who had driven up in a pickup truck with a horse trailer. The man told her he was delivering a horse for Lefty. Alice stepped out through the door to get a better look. It was obvious Lefty had told her nothing about a horse. Alice, by now, was used to strange things happening when Lefty was involved in any way, but surely not a horse. He had brought home a boxer puppy once that had grown into a monster. Lefty called him Duke. Duke killed everything in sight if he got out of the backyard. Alice was the only one who could control him. She did so by opening the car door, Duke thought he was going somewhere, and he would jump into the back seat.

Alice stuck her head back into the house. "Sonny, you better come out here!"

Lefty walked to the door. "Alice, don't be hollering at me like that, the neighbors will hear you, then I'll have to come out and kick some ass." By that time Lefty saw the man taking the horse out of the trailer. "Alice, what in the hell have you done now, this place is nothing but a circus."

As it turned out some friends had given Lefty a horse sometime back and were now bringing it to him. Lefty had forgotten about it, but now the horse was there. Lefty went outside to say hello to the man.

They do seem to know each other, Alice thought.

Lefty found out the horse was a mare, around three years old, and had been trained for pleasure riding. Lefty's daughter, Lois, was turning twelve and was extremely excited; she learned to ride very well that year.

Across the street lived a family with a young girl around sixteen who raised and trained horses. Lefty was able to stable Lois' mare there until a fence could be built in the backyard. So there they were in the backyard, the mare Lois named Lady and Duke, the monster dog.

Eddie Acreage was a champion rodeo rider and a sometime country singer. Eddie was also a friend of Lefty's. Eddie loved country music and, like most everyone else, Lefty was his hero. Eddie lived in beautiful Apple Valley. He told Lefty, "Why don't you bring your mare up to my place, Lefty, and we'll get her bred. I've got a friend who has a champion stud, and boy, is he something. He is probably one of the most famous studs in the country. A friend of mine, his name is Buck Abbott, owns him."

"What would it cost me?"

"Lefty, I'll get it done for nothing. He's a friend of mine and a great fan of yours. You don't want to pass this up."

Lefty told Alice about the opportunity. "I'm taking Lady up to Apple Valley and get her bred. My friend, Eddie, says he'll take care of everything."

Alice looked at Lefty with that look he had seen most of their life together. "Sonny, we can't even take care of the one horse we've got. What in the world would we do with another one?"

Lefty scowled at her. "Alice, one thing about you I can always count on is you to be negative about everything. Alice, we don't have to even bring the baby back here. We can just leave it there, you know, maybe sell it. Damn, Alice, at least one of us has to try and make some money. I realize your part is to spend it."

"Aw, Sonny, shut up," Alice said as she walked out of the room. Lady was taken to Apple Valley to Buck Abbott's ranch.

Sometime later Lefty said to me. "Let's drive up and see the horse. You know, see what's going on. I'll call Eddie and have him meet us."

Lefty and I arrived in Apple Valley and went straight to Buck's ranch. Eddie and Buck showed us around. Buck said, "Lefty, wanna see the stud we're gonna use for your mare?"

"Sure." They walked toward the stables and I brought up the rear.

"This is a beautiful place. How many horses do you have here?" I asked Buck.

"Well, let's see. There's probably over two hundred. Most are boarded, around fifty are mine, our main guy here is our stallion. He's the reason we're in business. People from all over the country bring their mares to breed with him."

Lefty spotted a very pregnant mare standing in a small corral. "What a beautiful horse, Buck, how far along is she?"

"Lefty, she's ready almost anytime. Isn't she something?" Lefty asked Buck if he could pet her.

"Sure, she's gentle."

Lefty climbed through the railed fence and started walking over to the mare saying in a very gentle voice, "Look at yourself, young lady, ah now, just look at yourself. How many times have I told you to quit parading around in front of the boys." The mare was eating, but now she stopped and looked in Lefty's direction. Lefty kept talking ever so gently. "If I've told you once, I've told you a hundred times what would happen if you turned your back to the wrong man. Sure I know you said you'd be careful, but just look at you now. What'll I tell your mama? This will just break her heart." Lefty walked up to the mare, put his hand on her neck, and started rubbing her. The mare looked at Lefty and nodded her head up and down and blinked her eyes a few times. She was very calm. Lefty picked up a handful of feed, and she ate it from his hand. "All right, look, don't worry, I'll take care of everything." Lefty was still speaking very softly. "I'll look after you, but please pay a little more attention to me in the future. I'm only thinking of you. Imagine how the boys around this place are talking; you don't want them to think you're that kind of girl, do ya? Okay, well, look, I've got to go, but just remember I love you and I'll be back later to see how you're doing."

Lady never got pregnant. "Well, she's just not that kind of girl." Lefty joked.

CHAPTER THIRTEEN

THE LONG BLACK VEIL

Four of Lefty's biggest hits were re-cut in early 1958. The session was held at Radio Recorders in Hollywood on February 19th. The songs were: "I Love You a Thousand Ways," "If You've Got the Money, I've Got the Time," "I Want To Be with You Always," and "Mom and Dad's Waltz." This session was never released by Columbia. Lefty recorded these songs again the following December. Nine more songs were recorded in the same studio on February 24, 1959. Four of these nine songs were never released, and the other five did nothing to help Lefty's career. At this point Don Law was the only reason Lefty was still on the label. He believed there was still a hit in Lefty, and Don was a man not used to being wrong. Don was right, of course, he was only a year off.

In the summer of 1958, Steve booked a package tour starring Lefty, Freddie Hart, and introducing me, Little David, "the rock and roll sensation of the nation." I was really into Elvis, Ray Charles, and Little Richard, and could rock and roll with the best of them. The band for the tour came out of Oklahoma, and was called Hershel Clothier and The Oklahoma Travelers. Steve came along on this tour, driving Lefty's Cadillac with Lefty riding in the back most of the time. Hershel had an old bus that carried the band, equipment, and sometimes me and Freddie. This was my first real tour and I was excited.

Elvis was the biggest thing in music at the time and I would do a song or two of his on the show. I danced all over the stage, jumped out into the audience, picked out a girl and danced with her, jumped back on the stage, and didn't miss a beat. Steve and Lefty never missed my part of the show. At first the show started out with Hershel and the band doing a few numbers, then Hershel would bring me out. I would rock and roll the crowd, next Freddie was introduced, and Lefty would close the show. Before the tour ended Freddie and I changed places. I would sell pictures of Lefty, Freddie, and myself for fifty cents each. I didn't make much money on this tour, but the experience was invaluable. Freddie and I have remained best friends throughout the years.

Steve was booking Lefty on just about every kind of show imaginable, anyplace, anytime, and for any occasion, but one show was really different and special. The Johnny Otis Show was a very popular television show filmed in Los Angeles. The format was mostly rhythm and blues, blues, and early rock and roll, so do you think Lefty fit in? You bet your life he did! When Lefty, Steve, and I arrived at the studio we were taken to a small dressing room. The lady told Lefty that Johnny was excited to have him on the show and would be here in a moment to say hello. She said she was arranging for a band rehearsal. Lefty said, "Thanks," and then set his guitar down. I was hanging up Lefty's show clothes when Johnny came in.

"I'm a big fan and thanks, man, for doing the show."

Lefty smiled. "Well, I'm glad to be here. Hey, say hello to my manager, Steve, and my little brotha.'"

Lefty went and rehearsed his song, Steve and I watched from the side of the stage. I told Steve, "God, man, this ain't no band, this is an orchestra. See if you can talk Sonny into taking them on tour." Steve just laughed.

After the rehearsal Lefty and Johnny walked back toward the dressing room. Johnny told Lefty, "This is going to be a fun show tonight, they'll start lettin' the people in pretty soon and we'll get the show going." As Johnny walked away he said over his shoulder, "This is going to be great!" The show opened to about four or five hundred people. Johnny went out, did a song, and welcomed everyone.

"Tonight, my friends, you will not believe what we got going on. Please welcome my first guest, a man who's had so many hit records it'd take the rest of the show to tell you the names of 'em, so I'm not gonna do that. I'm just going to ask you to welcome Lefty Frizzell."

The band kicked off "If You've Got the Money, I've Got the Time," and Lefty walked out wearing his rhinestone fringe, orange and tan suit with a green rhinestone scarf. The people went crazy and they hadn't even heard him sing yet.

I had never heard Lefty sing "Money" with an orchestra. It was incredible with the organ and the horns blasting. In all that fringe Lefty looked like he was moving every way at once. It was an amazing sight. After Lefty's song, he came backstage and talked to a heavy set man who had been watching Lefty's every move. He grabbed Lefty and hugged him.

They were talking still when Johnny Otis said, "This gentleman has the biggest song in the nation today. Please give a big welcome to the Big Bopper."

The big man went out on stage and proceeded to bring the house down with "Chantilly Lace." After the show Lefty introduced the Big Bopper to Steve and me.

The Big Bopper said, "Lefty, it's great to see you again. When you lived in Beaumont, I lived probably no more'n nah couple of miles from you. I betcha I've played your songs on KTRM radio about as many times as you've sung 'em."

We learned the Big Bopper's real name that night. J.P. Richardson had been a disc jockey and program director in

Beaumont, Texas, before having a huge hit with "Chantilly Lace." The Big Bopper also wrote "White Lightning," a George Jones hit, and "Running Bear," a number one song for Sonny James.

When Steve booked a tour of Texas, Oklahoma, and Kansas, Alice thought this might be a good time to visit her family in Sulphur Springs. Lefty and I dropped her off and went on up to Kansas City. The show went well, but Lefty's voice was fading. The next day, his throat was so sore he could hardly swallow. I drove to the next venue, which was about two hundred miles west. The town was so small it only had one motel. I checked in and told Lefty that I would try to find the club while he took a nap. I found the club ten miles from where we were staying.

Lefty was having a tough time getting ready for the show. He would take a drink of vodka and then throw it up. His throat was already sore and this could not have helped. This went on for quite some time, Lefty taking a drink and throwing up. I was ready, and had been for an hour, but I knew we would be going nowhere until Lefty could keep one down. Finally, Lefty was ready, and; we drove the ten miles to the gig. The band was great and they did a good job of backing Lefty and me for the first show. After Lefty's first show there was a thirty-minute break and then everything would start again.

Lefty said to me, "I've got to go back to the room. I'm not feeling too good and I think I'll be able to rest better there." I drove Lefty back to the room. Lefty was lying on the bed when I said, "Sonny, it's time to go."

Lefty groaned "I'm not able to go. I'm feeling real bad. Listen, you go and do your second show and then tell them I'm not gonna be there."

I thought, *Oh boy, here we go.* I drove back to the club; the band was just finishing their set and they called me on. I did a much longer show, then took a break. I motioned for the bandleader to come over. "Lefty can't make the show; here's what we'll do." I told him to make sure the lights were low. I explained that I had brought Lefty's hat and fringed jacket. I told him that rather than disappoint the audience I was going to do a little impersonation. I asked him to please just play along.

"Hell," I argued, "by now everyone's drunk anyway."

I had Lefty's show down; his moves, everything. Most of the crowd didn't know the difference or care, and the show went fine.

After the show I talked to the club owner. "I'm sorry Lefty couldn't do the last show. He's so sick. He's been coming down with something for the last few days, but his first show was great."

The club owner looked at me. "My contract with Lefty calls for two shows, he only did one."

"Yeah, I know, but I'm not joking. He's very sick and I think he did you a good show. Nobody came and asked for their money back, so I need to collect our money."

"Well, my good man, I have no complaints about you, the band, or the fact that nobody asked for their money back. It's the principal of the thing. Lefty did not perform the second show so I can't help you." The owner turned to walk away.

"I'm gonna ask you one more time. For the sake of all concerned, please pay the money." The club owner walked on into the back.

I drove back to the motel, and found Lefty still lying on the bed. "The club owner wouldn't pay." I hardly had the words out of my mouth, and Lefty jumped out of bed and pulled on his pants and boots.

"I'll betcha he'll pay me," Lefty said as he grabbed the car keys.

I got in the car as Lefty drove out, spinning the wheels. Ten miles goes by in a hurry when someone is driving that fast. Lefty drove up in front of the club and jumped from the car while it was still moving. By the time I stopped the car, Lefty was climbing the front stairs to the club's front doors.

A policeman was standing at the top of the stairs and took a step toward Lefty. "We're closed, you can't go in there."

Lefty grabbed him by the front of his uniform and threw him down the stairs and went through the doors. I helped the man up before going in.

"Why don't you stay out here? It'll be okay." I suggested. I opened the front door and went in.

Lefty had the club owner up against the wall with his right forearm across the guy's neck. "I want my money, you bastard, and I want it…now!"

The owner's feet were not touching the floor. He was trying to say something, but Lefty's forearm was cutting off his air. "I've paid . . . your . . . money . . . to . . . the band leader . . . go get it from him."

Lefty slapped him across the face and dropped him. As Lefty walked past me he said, "He's all right. Wait for me in the car."

I walked over to the club owner, bent down, and said, "Would've been easier to have paid me." I stood up and before walking away I said, "Good night." Lefty collected his money and I drove us back to the motel.

Afterwards, Lefty said, "Let's go to Texas and find Alice."

The next stop on the tour was Lubbock, Texas. The show was to be at The Old Cotton Club outside of town. The Cotton Club booked a different act almost every week. The week before Lefty's appearance Chuck Berry had been the special guest and people were still talking about it. Our Uncle Andy and his family still lived there and that was the first place Lefty and I went. A few years earlier Andy had given me my first guitar, a Stella. The strings were so high off the neck that it was very hard to play, but I learned to play it anyway, and I kept the guitar for years.

The night of the show the club was packed with rowdy people. By the time the second show came around everybody was drunk and ready to fight. I took the stage and was almost through with my set, Lefty was standing backstage ready to come out, when the fight started right in front of the stage. Chairs were flying through the air; people were hitting each other; some were on the floor; some were standing on other people. I looked over at Lefty and caught his eye.

Lefty shook his head and said something that might have been, "No reason to come out now."

I was still standing at the microphone. I had been about to call big brother out, but instead I started calling rounds. "In this corner from the cotton fields of south Lubbock is Big Sally and it looks like she's ready to fight. I pity anyone trying to stand up to her. As you can see she has a weapon, I believe it is a chair, yes, it is a chair. She has just hit the gentleman in the red shirt, the one with his back to her, and, oh yes, that was a white shirt, but it's red now."

Chairs, tables, bottles, glasses, and people were flying through the air. I made a hasty exit from the stage when stuff started hitting the bandstand.

"Gotta go folks, show's over," I shouted over my shoulder. And it was.

The police came and arrested about half the crowd. A lot of the shows were like that in Texas and Oklahoma during those days. People came to fight as much as they came to dance. Most of the clubs didn't sell hard drinks. They sold set ups, soft drinks and ice, and people would bring booze in paper sacks or they'd drink outside in the car. Anyway, it worked because by the end of the night fights would break out all over the place; inside of the club, outside of the club. One of the reasons a fight would start was most men, and some women, wore cowboy hats, and if someone knocked someone else's hat off, or maybe sat on it, the fight was on. This happened more often than anyone could recall.

Lefty and I arrived in Dallas two days before the show that was scheduled there. Lefty heard about the movie, *I Want to Live*, starring Susan Hayward. We both loved Susan and decided to take in the movie. The theater was packed that afternoon, but we managed to get two good seats up near the back.

Lefty said before the movie started, "David, I heard this is gonna be a sad movie, so control yourself, don't get choked up on all that popcorn."

The movie started. Susan was great. The movie was especially sad when Susan was being prepared to go to the gas chamber. The whole theater was quiet; I mean there wasn't a sound. Then the officer got a phone call and she was given a reprieve. Some people were crying.

We were sitting so engrossed in the movie and completely taken in by Susan, that people even quit eating their popcorn and candy. Susan was readied for the gas chamber for the second time. I could hear people holding their breath, because I was, then the officer got a call and she got another stay of execution. Finally, when Susan was led to the gas chamber she asked, "Could I have a mask? I don't want to see all those people staring at me?" Everyone knew this was it. There wouldn't be another call from the Governor saving her this time. The theater was deathly quiet, the silence was long and still.

The only sound that could be heard was Lefty when he said, "I'd be asking for a gas mask." At first there was a little sound of laughter that came from me, and then someone sitting close to us who was trying to smother a laugh. I looked over at Lefty and he was desperately trying to hold back. Someone else started snickering. Finally, I couldn't hold it any longer, and laughter exploded out of me. Two or three people on each side of us were howling with laughter. People all over the theater were turning around trying to hush us. They were irritated because we were laughing during the saddest part of the movie. Lefty was laughing so hard tears were streaming down his face. We had to get up and leave the theater. He told me later he didn't mean to say it so loud.

"It's just that the theater was so quiet. You could've cut the silence with a knife. I was only gonna whisper it to you. At first I was embarrassed, but after that I was laughing too hard to care."

On September 12, 1959, Lefty was in Nashville to record another session. One of the more memorable songs he recorded was written by Marty Robbins, "Cigarettes and Coffee Blues." The other three songs were "You're Humbuggin' Me," "She's Gone, Gone, Gone," and "I Need Your Love."

Lefty said, "Hey, boys, you're not going to believe this song and probably no one else either. I hope the sax player shows up." With guitar in hand Lefty sang "You're Humbuggin' Me."

This song was later recorded by some of the biggest blues and rock players in the business, such as Johnny Winters. Then in December, Lefty recorded five of his biggest hits plus two more great songs: Hank Williams' "My Bucket's Got a Hole in It" and a real Lefty treasure, "If You're Ever Lonely, Darling." The new version of the hits "I Love You a Thousand Ways," "If You've Got the Money, I've Got the Time," "Mom and Dad's Waltz," "I Want To Be with You Always," and "Always Late with Your Kisses" received the new Nashville treatment, with lots of background voices and more instrumentation.

We were working a strip joint called the El Maurice Club in Hobbs, New Mexico, on February 6 and 7, 1959. Lefty told the club owner, "Listen, I've been in this business a long time and I've found out there are two things you don't do, one is follow a kid act and the other is never follow strippers. Now the way I see it, the strippers go on, then David, then me. What ya' think? David's no kid and he's following the strippers, not me."

"Lefty, anyway you want to play it is okay with me."

What a time Lefty and I had. There were four beautiful strippers and everyone used the same dressing room. This was the first time Lefty ever got to a job on time, and it wasn't exactly easy getting him out of there that night.

Later Lefty told Daddy, "Hell, Daddy, David was just as wild on stage as those girls were, man, what a showman."

A few years later, Lefty said, "I've found out there are two more things you don't do in this business besides follow kids or strippers, and that's follow George Jones when he's singing or David when he's entertaining."

The next evening before the show Lefty received a call from Steve. After the call Lefty found me. "Man, something's happened and we need to talk about it. Come on over here and sit down." Lefty had never talked like this before, so I knew he was serious, so I sat down and didn't say a word. "Just talked to Steve and something real bad has happened. It seems there was a plane crash and several big stars were killed. One was Buddy Holly . . . now here's the deal, Steve tells me he thinks he can get you on the rest of that tour if you want it. He say's he knows the people real well and he believes it would be a big break for you, what do you think?"

I sat there shaking my head. "I can't believe this. How do you think it could have happened?"

"I don't know what happened at all, but we've got to act fast if you want to take advantage of the situation." Lefty stopped talking for a moment, and then he said, "Let's think this thing through. We're on our way to Nashville after a few more shows. I've got to record the first week in March. You can come on and go with me, or . . . David, I've got a good feeling about this trip to Nashville, I think something great is about to happen, not just for me, I mean for both of us. I can't say for sure, but it's an over-whelming feeling. Look, you make up your own mind, I'll back you either way."

I was still in shock over the news of the crash so I just sat there. Finally, I spoke up, "Steve says he can get me on the tour?"

"That's what he says. He doesn't say something like that if

he can't do it. Hell, you know Steve." Lefty reassured me.

"Yeah," I responded thoughtfully. "If he says he can I won't doubt him, but Sonny, I wouldn't leave you. I think something will happen for me at some point. I'm learning an awful lot from you. I've got a lot more to learn, so I'm just gonna stay with you, okay?"

"I'll call Steve back and tell him thanks. David, you've made the right decision. Let's get ready, it's almost time to go see the strippers." On my show that night I sang several Buddy Holly songs and dedicated them all to him.

After the show that night I walked from my motel room to get something from the car. I turned around when I heard my brother's voice. "David, come here I want to show you something." I went into Lefty's room. It was really dark with just a little light coming from the bathroom. "Sit there in that chair. I want you to witness the most incredible work of art that I've ever seen."

About that time a beautiful woman came out of the bathroom. I recognized her from the club. She was one of the dancers and she was magnificent. She moved over to the bed and jumped up on it. She was humming some tune that she alone had heard before. She moved, she danced, to her own rhythm, and she took off what little clothes she had on. All the while Lefty kept saying, "Boy, have you ever seen anything as beautiful as she is? Watch how she completely keeps your eyes on her. You couldn't look away if you wanted to." Lefty could plainly see I had no intention of looking away. I could plainly see there was a lot to learn about this business, and Lefty was going to be a great teacher.

Lefty and I drove into Nashville a week before his recording session on March 3, 1959. Lefty had a friend from California who had rented a small house just outside of town and that's where we stayed while in Nashville. When we got to Nashville we stopped at a gas station where Lefty made a call, and then we drove to his friend's house. I believe her name was Gloria, I can't be sure, but I do remember she had a '57 Chevy hardtop. You have to remember I was seventeen years old.

One afternoon, Troy Martin came to the house and talked to Lefty in the front room. I was in the den watching television, but I could still hear them.

Lefty said to Troy, "I've got two songs I can give you, but I need an advance on 'em."

"Okay, let me hear what you've got. Lefty, it's good to see you again. I think your session this time will produce a hit for you. You know Don believes in you so much, he tells his bosses he will get another hit song with you. Lefty, he really believes it, he's not just telling them that."

"I know. Don has always believed in me and I hate to keep letting him down. It seems like getting a hit was so easy at first, but now, damn, it's worse then pulling teeth."

"Maybe you're trying too hard. It'll come, in its own good time, it'll come. Let me hear those songs."

Lefty cleared his throat. "Troy, my throat is a little sore. Would you mind if I call my brother in and let him sing the songs for you?"

Troy nodded. "Fine with me."

Lefty cleared his throat again and called out, "David, grab my guitar and come here, please." I brought Lefty's Martin in and said hello.

Lefty introduced me. "Troy, this is my brother, David, and he knows the songs as well as I do. David, I need for you to sing Troy those two songs I wrote the other day, you remember."

I sang them. Then I told Troy and Lefty, "Those are two of my favorites, otherwise I probably wouldn't have learned them." After that, I left the room.

When Troy left, Lefty came in where I was. "Troy liked

your voice and said he was going to talk to Don about you."

The next day, Troy called Lefty and asked him to bring me to meet Don. The meeting took place in Don's room at the Andrew Jackson Hotel in downtown Nashville. When I met Don he asked me to sing something. I took Lefty's Martin from the case and sang "That'll Be the Day" and "I Love You a Thousand Ways." Don signed me to a one year contract, and Troy signed me to a one year management contract. Part of Lefty's premonition had come true. Now if only the second part would.

The morning of the session Don called Lefty and asked him to come down to the hotel and listen to some songs. Don had put out the word that he and Lefty were looking for songs, and it wasn't long before the room was filled with songwriters and songpluggers. A young lady from Oklahoma came to the suite with a song that would fulfill Lefty's premonition, "The Long Black Veil." Marijohn Wilkin didn't even have a taped demo of the song. She and Danny Dill had finished writing it that morning. Marijohn sang "The Long Black Veil" for Don and Lefty a capella, and they both loved it. Lefty's last single, "Cigarettes and Coffee Blues," had done pretty well across the country and just was beginning to fade off the charts when Don and Lefty found "The Long Black Veil." This was the song they had both been waiting for.

Later that day at the studio, the musicians set up their instruments: Grady Martin was on lead guitar, Harold Bradley was on rhythm guitar, the great Don Helms was on steel guitar, Joe Zinkan was on bass, Buddy Harman was on drums; and Marijohn Wilkin played piano. The session started out with "Sin Will Be the Chaser for the Wine" and "Knock Again True Love." It finished with "One Has Been to Another." While the band took a break, Lefty sat in a corner of the studio with his guitar trying to learn "The Long Back Veil."

When Don Helms played that eerie steel guitar lick on "The Long Black Veil," everyone knew the song was going to be a hit. Lefty's vocals hit the listener right between the eyes. You could hear Lefty breathing the words to the song. The feeling was overpowering. Lefty dug down into his soul and came out with a masterful performance. To think that Lefty had only heard the song for the first time that afternoon is still unbelievable to me. What a lesson I was learning.

Lefty had to leave the next evening, but he wanted to see Jim Denny about some future bookings, so a meeting was set up for the next day. I went with Lefty to meet Jim. We arrived at Jim's office, and after the pleasantries, Jim told Lefty that it would be a little hard at first to get the big jobs, but he could do it.

Then Jim asked Lefty, "When are you planning on moving back?"

I was stunned, that was the first time anything about moving had been mentioned. Lefty told him he had been thinking about it for some time. He just wanted to make all the right arrangements first. Jim told Lefty to keep him informed and he would help him in everyway he could. Outside Lefty told me not to say anything because after he had made up his mind for sure he would have to tell Alice. If I didn't learn anything else working with Lefty, I learned very well the "don't say anything to Alice" lesson.

After the meeting, Lefty and I drove down toward Birmingham on the way to the next date in Shreveport. Lefty was sitting on the passenger side, leaning against the door. We were both quiet, each wrapped up in our own thoughts.

Finally, Lefty said, "Man, can you believe it? Isn't it something, everything that's happened the last few days? Who would've thought you'd get a Columbia recording contract? You know what, I told you big things were gonna happen, I'm a regular prophet." We laughed. "Boy, I wish I could do that all the time."

"It sure is amazing how you called it. Somehow you knew it. I'm gonna hang out with you because you know everything, oh Swammie, and can you believe that song? I get cold chills just thinking about it, let alone hearing it."

Lefty became serious. "That's the song that's gonna bring me back, gonna put me right back on the top of the charts again. I'm gonna predict that it will. David, you watch, we've both just started to take over the world."

I could see it, hit songs, top of the charts. Well, I could at least see it for Lefty, my success, on the other hand, was another thing entirely.

About mid-morning Lefty took over driving. I was about asleep when Lefty, while passing a bread truck, ran his front wheel off the pavement. The car went flying off the road, down a steep embankment, into a cotton patch. When I woke up enough to realize what was going on I could see people running in every direction. The car finally stopped and Lefty and I got out to see what the damage was and discovered the a-frame was broken. A farmer came over with his tractor and, after recognizing Lefty, pulled the Cadillac about four or five miles into town. It took the rest of the day to get the car fixed.

Lefty grumbled, "Some prophet I turned out to be."

L efty wanted to stop in Juarez, Mexico, so we found a parking place at the border and walked across the bridge into town. We had a great time. Lefty and I bought gifts for the family. We spent a few hours there shopping and when we walked back over the bridge, Lefty had all his gifts plus two gallons of vodka. We walked up to customs and the officer asked what we were declaring. We showed everything plus the two gallons of vodka. The fellow asked what nationality we were and I said American. Lefty said Chinese. Well, that's when things started to happen. Lefty was taken inside a small room. I don't know exactly what happened while he was in there, but whatever it was took a long time. When he finally came out, everyone was laughing.

Lefty said, "Boys, I'll never say the word Chinese again."

We made it back to the car and left for Los Angeles. I had been driving, it seemed like, for days with Lefty riding in the back.

Finally, Lefty ordered, "Stop this car. You're never gonna get us there. You've been driving forever and we're not home yet. I'll show you how it's done." I stopped the car. Lefty drove around the block into his driveway. "Now, see there, we're home." I had driven from El Paso to within one block of the house, and when we got there Lefty only had one gallon of vodka left.

Lefty and I went back to Nashville in July not only for Lefty to record, but me as well. Lefty recorded "Farther Than My Eyes Can See," "My Blues Will Pass," and "Ballad of the Blue and Gray." The last song was written by Harlen Howard, hoping to cash in on the popularity of Johnny Horton's "Battle of New Orleans." It only missed by a country mile.

After the session, Lefty wanted to go to the Opry. I had never been to the Opry so I was excited. When we got there Lefty got us in backstage. I was introduced to some of the biggest names in country music: Hank Snow, Ernest Tubb, Marty Robbins and Don Gibson, just to name a few. Ernest invited Lefty over to his record shop for a radio show that was broadcast every Saturday night over WSM called The Midnight Jamboree. Don Gibson had asked Lefty to take him somewhere, so we all headed for Lefty's Cadillac.

When we reached the car, Don got in the back seat, Lefty drove, and I got in on the passenger side. Don told Lefty how bad the Nashville establishment was, how badly he felt he was being treated.

Lefty said, "I've been invited to Ernest's radio show and I told him I'd be there. Now, Don, you don't have to go in if you don't want to. I'll only be a minute. Just wait for me in the car."

Don said he would. Lefty and I went in and Lefty sang

two numbers on the show and all went well. Ernest was so nice, not only to Lefty, but to me, too. I enjoyed every minute. We left and Don was still in the back seat. Lefty asked him where he needed to go and Don said over on 16th Avenue, he was staying there for awhile. Lefty drove from Broadway over to 16th and Don, who was drinking pretty heavily, cursed Nashville and everyone in it all the way. Finally, Don said, "Pull up over there."

Lefty stopped at the curb. He and Don both had a big pull from Lefty's vodka bottle. We sat there for a few minutes and they both had another pull from the bottle. Don got out of the car and asked Lefty to come in for a minute.

Lefty told him, "I'll make sure you get in the house then I've got to go." They started walking up the sidewalk. I got out behind them just in case either one needed help. Don was still bad mouthing Nashville as he climbed the five or six stairs to the entrance of the house and Lefty was right beside him.

"Don, if you say one more thing about Nashville or anybody in it, I'm gonna knock your head off. I don't care that you don't like them; I'm just tired of hearing about it."

"Them sorry sons-of-bitches I oughta get my gun and…"

Lefty grabbed him and threw him hard against the side of the house. Don hit the wall with such force that his toupee fell onto his shoulder. Lefty held him there. "Don, you're the son-of-a-bitch, if you don't like it around here, why don't you leave? Anyway get yourself inside, no one, including me, wants to hear about who you hate anymore tonight."

Don tried apologizing. "Lefty, I'm sorry I didn't . . ."

Lefty interrupted him. "I don't want to hear it. Get in the house, Don." Lefty came back to the car and said, "Some guys shouldn't drink. David, you drive." As he took another pull from his bottle, I drove us back to the hotel.

Back home in California I was out in the front yard when I heard Lefty calling. I rushed into the house just in time to hear one of the songs I had recorded in Nashville playing on the radio.

It was my first time hearing myself on the radio. I looked over at my big brother. Lefty was smiling. He seemed to be so proud of me, his little brother.

Lefty and Alice told me to get ready. They needed to go to town and they wanted me to drive them. We drove over to San Fernando and I followed them into an elite men's store.

Lefty said, "David, I want you to find something real nice to wear. We've been invited to the Columbia Records Convention in Miami, Florida." Then he looked at me, smiled, and asked, "Wanna go?"

Lefty and I flew into the Miami airport and a limo was waiting to take us to the Americana Hotel. When the limo pulled up in front of the hotel, I jumped out. The size and the elegance of the place was awesome. Inside there were more celebrities than I can mention here. Lefty and I were introduced to Mitch Miller and pop singer Johnny Ray. I saw Johnny Cash walk by. I also saw Marty Robbins and Johnny Horton. I was kind of relieved when I saw my old friend, Freddie Hart. At least I felt I could talk to him. Every artist signed to Columbia Records was there, and not just the country acts. We were invited to different shows and a lot of press events. It seemed everyone wanted to talk to Lefty. I didn't really care. I was so nervous and in awe of everything and everybody that I couldn't have given a decent interview anyway.

There was a rehearsal the afternoon of the big show and Lefty, Freddie, and I went together. It seemed like everyone except me was singing big hits. Stonewall Jackson sang "Waterloo;" Marty Robbins knocked everyone out with his huge hit "El Paso;" Johnny Horton belted the "Battle of New Orleans;" Johnny Cash implored "Don't Take Your Guns to Town;" and of course, Lefty tugged at our hearts with "The Long Black Veil." The Jordanaires backed all the acts. When I found out I went on after Marty Robbins, well that about did it. I was worthless the rest of the day.

For the show I didn't wear anything that was bought in San Fernando. Instead, Lefty let me wear a red tuxedo that Nudie had made for him, which he had worn only once for a photo shoot. Lefty and I were both dressed and ready for the show.

Lefty stepped out onto the balcony and what he saw made him holler for me. "David, come here quick!"

I ran to the balcony. Lefty pointed up at a blimp flying overhead. The names of all the artists who were on the show were blinking on and off on the side of the blimp. All of a sudden on the side of the blimp "David Frizzell" appeared. It was all just too much for me. Lefty was excited, too, but it was because of me. You could see it in his eyes; he was just so proud of his little brother. After seeing my name on the blimp, I followed Marty without any hesitation. Why, I could have followed Elvis himself, that's how excited I was. The red tux I wore for that show still hangs in my closet.

Lefty's next recording session was in Nashville at Bradley Film and Recording Studios. Some of the best musicians in the world joined Lefty and Don for what would be Lefty's only session that year. Playing on the session were Grady Martin, "Sugarfoot" Hank Garland, Harold Bradley, Joseph Zinkan, Buddy Harman, the great Floyd Cramer, and one of the great fiddle players, Dale Potter. "That's All I Can Remember" written by Marijohn Wilkin and Mel Tillis was a song as sad as "The Long Black Veil," but it didn't get the airplay and certainly didn't sell as well. The other songs recorded were "So What, Let It Rain" written by Lefty, and a very clever song written by Mel Tillis, "What You Gonna Do, Leroy."

Lefty and Alice went to Hawaii later that year. Lefty only played a few dates, so it was more of a vacation then work. While Alice was there she learned to cook a complete five course Chinese dinner. This was great, because when they got back, Alice practiced what she learned on the rest of the family.

I had recorded another session for Columbia Records and just wasn't having luck with getting any hits either. So all we did was tour up and down California. Finally, I went to Lefty and told him that I had decided to join the military, hoping to better my education.

Lefty asked me, "You mean you're gonna volunteer to get up at four in the morning and march all over the place with some guy hollering in your face and eating off the ground? Boy, you must be crazy."

"Well, I may do some of that, but I'd like to get more of an education. I need to learn more than just running around the country playing these old smoky dives. I think what I want more then anything else right now is to learn to be on my own. I love working with you. It's been the best school anyone could ever hope for, but I need to do something for me, on my own. You know, make a decision and play it out, good, bad, or indifferent. Either reap the benefits or face the consequences. You know that's what you've done all your life. I guess really what I want is to start living my own life."

Lefty laughed. "Oh, you're gonna reap the benefits and face the consequences all right. Wait 'til you've been in the Army about a week." Then Lefty became serious. "I understand what you're saying. I don't know if joining the service is the right move or not, but doing something for yourself, by yourself, I certainly understand. Good luck, my boy."

I joined the Air Force on August 22, 1960, along with two high school buddies.

Betty and her husband, Russell, came to spend the New Year's holiday with Lefty and Alice. They were living about two hours away, just outside of Ojai where our folks were living.

When they arrived, Alice was getting ready for a New Year's Eve party. She was very excited. "We're going over to a friend's house. He's a doctor, and kinda, you know, kinda high fallutin'. Sonny don't wanna go, but I'm gonna have a good time. These are the kind of people we should get to know, so Betty, you and Russell make yourselves at home. We'll be in after the party."

"That sounds like fun," Betty said. "You two have a good time and we'll watch the kids. Besides, Alice, you deserve to go out; you never go and have any fun."

"Well, I'm going to tonight." Alice said as Lefty called for her.

"Alice," Lefty growled. "I've already told you I don't want to go to this damn party. I don't know any of those people, don't wanna know any of those people, and I don't like the way this shirt looks."

"Oh, Sonny, I'll iron it for you. You're gonna look so nice." Alice disappeared into the bedroom."

Betty could hear our brother complaining. "Alice, you're just saying that. You know I don't look good, because you know I don't want anything to do with this."

"Aw Sonny, you're gonna have a good time. You'll probably be the life of the party. Quiet down. Your sister, Betty, and Russell just got here."

"All right, I'll just stay with them and you go to this stupid party."

About ten o'clock Lefty and Alice were walking out the door. Betty said, "You both look real good. Y'all have a great time and we'll be waiting up for you."

"We're only going about two blocks over. If anything goes wrong, Lois knows where we are," Alice told Betty.

"Okay. Everything will be fine. Have a good time and

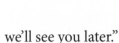

we'll see you later."

Betty and Russell were watching television when, around one o'clock in the morning, Alice burst through the door. Betty and Russell looked up surprised.

"You can go get your brother!" Alice said as she walked into Lois' room.

Betty and Russell went out to the car. Lefty was passed out on the passenger side. Russell opened the car door and caught Lefty before he fell out.

Betty shook her head. "I don't want to see him like this. I'm going in the house." She turned and walked away.

Russell helped Lefty out of the car and half-carried him into his bedroom. Russell laid Lefty on the bed, turned off the lights, and left him alone to sleep it off. Lefty fell off the bed three times and Russell picked him up three times. Finally, Betty told Russell to just leave him on the floor.

The next morning Betty and Russell wanted to leave, but they couldn't get their goodbyes said because of the fight. Alice was cursing Lefty because he embarrassed her.

"You were falling into people, grabbing their drinks, pushing them around. You were drinking everything in sight; you wouldn't let anyone else talk; you grabbed the doctor's wife and tried to dance with her."

"Alice, I did not grab the doctor's wife. I kinda fell into her and I was only trying to hang on."

"Sonny!" Alice didn't slow down. "Now, you know you don't dance, and no one else was dancing, but there you were. You looked pitiful; drunk and pitiful."

"Well, Alice, I told you I didn't want to go. Alice, remember one thing, don't ever make me do that again."

Before Betty and Russell left, Betty got the opportunity to talk to Lefty alone. "Sonny, why did you do that to Alice? She never gets a chance to do anything and you just spoiled the whole night for her. She never gets a chance to be proud of you in front of other people. How could you do this to her?"

"Well, Betty," Lefty put his arm around our sister's shoulders. "Those are not my kind of people. I don't even know how to talk to a doctor except to tell him where I may be hurting. I didn't want to go in the first place. Lord knows, I told her enough times. I can't relate to what these people do and they can't talk to me about singing or writing a song. We're just not on the same level. Anyway, it's over and I'll bet she won't do that again."

When Lefty went to Nashville for his February 7, 1961, session at Owen Bradley's Quonset Hut studio, he recorded two more songs that he'd written, "I Feel Sorry for Me" and "Looking for You," plus a song written by Wayne Walker called "Heaven's Plan." This time while he was in Nashville, Lefty drove around looking at property. A real estate agent took him around Old Hickory Lake. He told Lefty there was good fishing, plus a lot of country music people lived by the lake. Hendersonville was a small community northeast of Nashville situated on Old Hickory Lake and Lefty liked that area at the time.

In the winter of 1961, Columbia Records bought out Owen Bradley's Quonset Hut studio and opened an office in Nashville. Across the street from Columbia, Jim Denny opened his office and started booking Lefty.

Some of those early bookings were for very low money. One contract Lefty received from Jim Denny's agency was for $250, and Lefty had to go to North Carolina to play the show. These small paying jobs continued throughout 1962 and on into 1963.

Later Lefty signed as a writer to Cedarwood Publishing, owned by Jim Denny and Webb Pierce. After signing to Cedarwood as a writer, Lefty got a chance to work with some of

244   I Love You a Thousand Ways

the best writers in the business, such as Mel Tillis and Marijohn Wilkin.

On May 9, 1962, Lefty recorded at what was now Columbia Recording studios. Lefty recorded a great song called "Stranger," co-written by Wayne Walker, and three other songs. The session did not produce a hit, and now Lefty really needed a hit song. This was the only way to get better bookings and more money.

CHAPTER FOURTEEN

SAGINAW, MICHIGAN

Lefty had enjoyed living in California. He loved the climate and he enjoyed working the television shows. He had met and gone fishing with Gene Autry and they had become friends. Tex Ritter was another close friend. Lefty had even met Tarzan's Johnny Weissmuller.

Now the television shows were all canceled; the club gigs dried up. All his recording sessions were in Nashville; he'd started taking dates from the Jim Denny agency. Everything was pointing to Nashville.

Lefty was having a little more luck with his songs. In 1958, "Cigarettes and Coffee Blues" stayed on the charts for eleven weeks. In 1959, "The Long Black Veil" stayed on the charts for thirteen weeks, reaching number six on the *Billboard* charts. It seemed all the good songs were back in Nashville. Lefty wanted to do more writing, and some of his songwriting buddies already lived in Nashville.

Lefty told Alice, "If I'm gonna stay in this business, I'm gonna have to be where the business is, Alice. That's in Nashville." The Frizzells put their belongings in storage, packed two cars, and headed for Nashville in August 1962.

It was hot in Nashville when the Frizzells pulled into

town. With no place in particular to go, they rented a room at Drakes Motel south of Nashville. They eventually found a small cottage in Donelson. Lefty started working the Opry, which paid very little, but somehow they got by. Those early Nashville days were rough. Lefty took whatever dates he could regardless of the money. The Jim Denny agency booked Lefty in Abilene, Texas, on December 13, 1962, for $250 and December 14th in Lawton, Oklahoma, for the amazing price of $200.

Lefty and Alice bought a home at Harbor Hills on Old Hickory Lake in Hendersonville on December 10, 1962. The house had a finished basement where Lefty put his pool table. This room became the playroom for many of Nashville's elite singers and songwriters. Mel Tillis recalls a time Alice kicked him and Lefty out of the house, along with Lefty's old buffalo head. Once, after an all-nighter, Tillis woke up in Lefty's garage looking into the dead eyes of that buffalo. When he left he just took the buffalo head with him. Faron Young was allowed in only if he watched his language. George Jones said he spent about a week in that little den of Lefty's. Wayne Walker became one of Lefty's favorite writers and one of his favorite drinking buddies. Poor long suffering Alice put up with all this. Sometimes she would kick a few of them out, but as soon as she would turn away they would come right back in.

Despite all that, Lefty did start writing again, and that was the important thing. Lefty's drinking was getting worse, though. Alice would check Lefty into Madison Hospital to dry out. Then Lefty would go back on the road playing low paying gigs.

Some of Alice's relatives came out to Nashville to visit. With them was a man who was to become one of Lefty's best friends and almost constant companion. Abe Mulkey was a singer, songwriter, and guitar player. Lefty wasn't around Abe long before he offered him a job. Abe was living in Oklahoma at the time, so he went back to Oklahoma, packed up his family, and moved to Nashville. Abe traveled with Lefty and made sure Lefty got to the shows.

Abe sang harmony with Lefty, wrote songs with him, and played guitar. All these things Abe did for Lefty, but most of all Abe was Lefty's friend. This was what he needed the most. Lefty told of the time he was doing a radio interview over the phone for an upcoming concert.

The disc jockey said, "Lefty, it's great talking to you. Everyone is excited about your coming here this weekend."

"Me, too, it's been awhile since I've seen your part of the country. I'm looking forward to it."

"What can we expect from you this time?"

"Well, I'm gonna sing all my hits, you know, 'Mom and Dad's Waltz,' 'If You've Got the Money,' and my last big hit, 'The Long Black Veil,' and this time I'm bringing Abe Mulkey with me."

The disc jockey was confused. "Did I hear you right, Lefty, you're bringing a monkey with you?"

Lefty laughed. "No, no, I didn't say a monkey. I said Abe Mulkey."

The disc jockey was still confused . "Lefty, so long as you show up, I'm sure it'll be all right with everyone if you want to bring your monkey. See you this weekend."

No one knows if that was a true story or not, but Lefty told it many times.

On June 26, 1963, Lefty was back in the Columbia studios recording four more forgettable songs. They were: "That Reminds Me of You," "Don't Let Her See Me Cry," "Through the Eyes of a Fool," and "James River."

Don Law brought in another producer to help on Lefty's next session recorded on October 1, 1963. Frank Jones was a fine man, and he would take over for Don when the great man retired. They recorded one song called "Preview of Coming Attractions" and two songs written by Lefty called "Lonely Heart" and "What Good Did You Get Out of Breaking My Heart." It was the next session, however, that brought Lefty one of the biggest songs of his long career.

Lefty had a meeting with Buddy Killen of Tree Publishing a week or so before his next session on October 21, 1963. Buddy said he played Lefty a bunch of songs. Finally, he played "Saginaw, Michigan," a song written by Don Wayne and Bill Anderson.

Lefty said, "It sure sounds like a hit record. I only hope it is if I cut it."

This historic session was only Frank Jones' second time to co-produce a Lefty session with Don Law. The session started out with Lefty recording a song he had written called "When It Rains the Blues," next was a Wayne Walker song titled "I'm Not the Man I'm Supposed To Be." Finally, Lefty cut "Saginaw, Michigan," the song that would bring him back to superstardom.

The session went a little rough, with Lefty worrying about how to phrase the words to "Saginaw." There were more words to this song then he was used to singing. In 1963, everything was cut at the same time; all the musicians, Lefty's vocal tracks, backgrounds, everything. If someone hit a bad note, they would stop and start at the top. If the singer was having problems, everyone had to start over. After a few times, the musicians became a bit grumpy. Lefty would mess up and the tape would be run back to the top and they would all start over. About this time Lefty's friend, Merle Kilgore, came in with actor George Hamilton. George was in town filming the movie, "Your Cheating Heart," the story of Hank Williams. They didn't get in the way, but Lefty couldn't concentrate, so they were asked to leave by the session leader, Grady Martin. Lefty felt bad, but he knew it couldn't be helped. He had to give the performance of his life.

"Damn," Lefty said, "Grady play that intro again. Man,

this is a hard song. Let's just try it you and me. Go ahead and hit the intro."

"Saginaw, Michigan" was to be Lefty's biggest song since "Always Late" in 1951. It was released by Columbia in November 1963, and made its first chart appearance January 11, 1964. It stayed on the *Billboard* charts for twenty-six weeks reaching number one in March and holding that position for four weeks. "The Long Black Veil" was a big hit for Lefty but nothing like "Saginaw." This song completely revived Lefty's career. The jobs were bigger, better, and paid a lot more. People wanted to see Lefty again. Package tours were put together with Lefty as the headliner. He was asked to do some television shows in Nashville also: *The Porter Waggoner Show, The Billy Walker Show,* and *The Del Reeves Show.* Lefty's career was back in full swing.

Unfortunately, just as "Saginaw" was about to break, Lefty's health took a turn for the worse. Lefty ended up in the hospital with severe stomach ulcers aggravated by his continual alcohol abuse. A few shows scheduled in December had to be canceled.

When Jim Denny passed away in August, 1963, the agency was renamed the Denny-Moeller Agency. Lefty was added to a very impressive lineup of stars, like Webb Pierce, Faron Young, Billy Walker, and Bill Anderson. Those tours were selling out all over the country, and "Saginaw" was number one when the tour hit St. Louis.

Bill Anderson recalls, "Lefty was on the show and 'Saginaw, Michigan' was number one in St. Louis and everywhere. Lefty went out on the stage that afternoon at the Keil Auditorium and did his great hits, 'Always Late,' 'I Love You a Thousand Ways,' and 'Mom and Dad's Waltz,' all the great songs from the fifties, and he left the stage. The people started shouting "'Saginaw, Michigan,'" "Saginaw, Michigan!'" The emcee brought him back out. The people continued screaming, 'Sing "Saginaw, Michigan!"'"

"Lefty stood there in front of all those fans screaming for the number one record in the country, and he shook his head and said, 'I don't know it.'" Bill Anderson says he came back on stage and stood behind Lefty and mouthed the words to Lefty as Lefty sang the song.

Why Lefty didn't take the time to learn the words to his number one record is hard to say. He had plenty of opportunities to sing "Saginaw" as it was climbing the charts to number one. He did eventually learn the words because he sang "Saginaw" on April 29, 1964, during Derby week in Louisville, Kentucky, on a show with some other big stars, including Johnny Cash.

Lefty appeared in Saginaw, Michigan, on May 23, 1964, at the downtown auditorium with Bobby Bare, Billy Walker, and Hank Snow. He was presented a silver gavel by the mayor.

"Saginaw, Michigan" earned Lefty a Grammy nomination.

Lefty returned to the studio on January 22, 1964. Five songs were recorded on this session. Only one of them was written by Lefty and co-writer Abe Mulkey, "Hello to Him (Goodbye to Me)." Merle Kilgore wrote, "There's No Food in This House." Also recorded was "The Nester" written by Don Wayne, who was a writer on "Saginaw, Michigan." "I Was Coming Home to You" rounded out the session.

Don Law picked "The Nester" to follow the phenomenal success of "Saginaw, Michigan." It hit the charts August 8, 1964, and climbed to number 28 on the *Billboard* charts before stalling.

Lefty was making good money from his tours and the sales from "Saginaw," so he decided to invest in real estate. Lefty bought two vacant lots on Old Hickory Lake, and partnered with Merle Kilgore to buy two old Victorian houses on 18th Avenue, two blocks from Music Row. The idea was to remodel the homes, turn them into offices, and rent them out.

Lefty had been thinking about starting his own music publishing company. He had already chosen a name—Golden Eye. Also, Lefty and Ralph Spicer, another friend, were talking about starting their own record label. These were all good, sound business decisions. There was just one thing wrong; Lefty was no business manager. He couldn't handle day-to-day business of any kind, and the people he chose to work with were worse than he was.

While Lefty was thinking and working on all these new business ideas, he was called in for another recording session. Songs were gathered, and on October 16, 1964, everything was ready. Lefty recorded another song he had written with Abe called "I Can Tell." Freddie Hart contributed "Make That One for the Road a Cup of Coffee." Next was "Gator Hollow," a Mel Tillis song, and last was "It Cost Too Much to Die."

On February 10, 1965, Lefty joined Don Law and Frank Jones at Columbia studios to record four more songs. This time they got lucky with a song written by Harlan Howard called "She's Gone, Gone, Gone." Abe Mulkey's harmony really helped to set up the song.

Lefty said to the band, "This one will be easy for you. It's a Harlan Howard song."

Released as a single, it would reach number twelve on the Billboard charts. Other songs recorded during the February 10th, session were "Running into Memories of You" and "Confused," written by Lefty and Abe Mulkey, and a Harlan Howard song called "How Far Down Can I Go."

Lefty and Abe were together most of the time doing shows and recording, and being together gave them plenty of time to write songs, so it was common to see one or two of their songs on almost every session.

On February 11th, Lefty recorded four more sides. This

time he recorded two songs he and Abe had writen called "It's Bad (When It's Thataway)" and "I Don't Trust You Anymore." To fill out the rest of the session Lefty cut "A Little Unfair" and "Woman, Let Me Sing You a Song."

Frank Jones had a syndicated radio show in Nashville and invited Lefty to be his guest.

"Lefty, welcome to the USA microphone."

"Thank you Frank, it's a pleasure."

"You know Music City, USA, has an air of sorta a dream fantasy world. Of course, it really isn't a fantasy world. It's a world where many, many writers, musicians, and singers spend their efforts in making the many, many thousand of records that originate in the Music City studios. Now, when did you move to Nashville, Lefty?"

"Frank, about a little over two and a half years ago and, when you said fantasy, this is almost like a Disneyland of country music because this is where dreams will come true." Lefty agreed.

"Well, Lefty, as I've said before, being an old friend of yours. . . ."

"Old fan," Lefty interrupted.

Frank corrected himself. "Well, an old fan, so to speak, and, of course, a present fan."

Lefty laughed. "You're not much older then I am."

Frank changed the subject. "You know in our Music City studios at Columbia we meet many of the youngsters that come in and many of them, of course, come in to audition and send in their tapes. They seem to have a very familiar ring and style to their voice and, of course, it's that Lefty Frizzell style. I think you'd probably advise any aspiring vocalist. . . ."

Lefty cut in laughing. "I can advise 'em to cut it out, to

cut it out."

Frank rephrased. "To originate their own style."

"Absolutely."

"Because there's only one Lefty Frizzell."

Lefty laughed again. "And I'm having trouble with him."

Lefty was impressed to have other singers sounding like him, some kind of an honor, perhaps, but he appreciated originality more.

Lefty's last session in 1965 was recorded on March 1st, and only three songs made the cut. "Preparations To Be Blue," a song Lefty had recorded a year earlier called "Stranger" and "Love Looks Good on You."

I was released from the Air Force in August 1964. I played music around the Northwest for several months, then made my way back to Nashville in the early summer of 1965. I brought long-haired Bruce Delaney with me. He was a friend from the Air Force and a good bass player. We hung out with Lefty and Abe through most of the summer.

One afternoon Lefty, Abe, Bruce, and I were in downtown Nashville at an oyster bar eating and drinking beer. The afternoon wore on into evening, and finally we went over to Tootsie's Orchid Lounge. We boys were holding our own until around midnight when Lefty decided it was time to go. Our car was parked across the street. When we reached it, Abe and I got into the back seat. Lefty and Bruce were about to get into the car when an old man ran past with two younger, bigger men chasing him. I recall that night vividly.

Lefty called after them, saying something like, "Ain't he a little old for you to be chasing." The old man was running pretty fast, but Lefty knew the younger men were bound to catch him.

Lefty and Bruce started running after them. By the time Abe and I were able to climb out of the car, they were about a block away. As Abe and I were running I saw one of the young men punch Lefty. Down he went. The other young man pushed Bruce down and they were wrestling on the sidewalk. While I was running I noticed a police car parked on the curb directly across the street from where the big guy was standing over Lefty. I started hollering at them and was surprised to notice they were watching the action, but weren't getting out of their patrol car. I was running so fast that by the time I got there I ran into the man standing over Lefty, and knocked us both off balance. I thought I was never going to stop falling.

Abe managed to untangle Bruce and the other man, and when I finally looked up, two policemen were there. One had Lefty and Bruce, and the other had the two young men. They were putting handcuffs on all of them. I looked around for the old man, but he was nowhere to be found. The policeman had called for backup, I guess, because two more police cars showed up. Lefty, Bruce, and the two young men were loaded into the cars. One of the policemen told me they were taking them to jail.

I asked why they were taking my brother and Bruce when all they were trying to do was help an old man. The policeman asked, "What old man?"

Abe and I followed the police cars to the station and Lefty and Bruce were booked. For some reason none of them would listen to Abe or me. Bail was set and no one had enough money to get them out, so guess what I had to do? I had to call Alice. Boy, was she mad. I tried to tell her it wasn't Lefty's fault, but still she was madder than hell. She had calmed down a little by the time she reached the police station. It was about two in the morning when we all walked out. Because of that night, Lefty and Bruce became good buddies. Lefty had found someone just as rough and ready to rumble as he was.

One morning I got up and went downstairs looking for Lefty, and found him at his little boat dock walking around barefoot. "What's going on?" I asked.

Lefty was looking at his small runabout boat that was partially under water. "Man, how could this happen? It was all right awhile ago."

I walked onto the little dock and saw the half-sunken boat. We just stood looking at the boat.

All of a sudden Lefty said, "Damn, look at that fish." A catfish, about a three-pounder, swam out from under the boat. It didn't leave the area, it just swam around the boat.

Lefty started running back toward the house, or I should say trying to run—he didn't have any shoes on and his feet must have been tender. He was kind of skipping and jumping around going up to the house. I stood on the dock, laughing at him.

Lefty hollered over his shoulder, "Keep an eye on that fish. I'll be right back." He came back with a bow and arrow with a reel on it. He hobbled down to the dock. I was laughing more then ever.

"Don't scare my fish away. Look out, I'll spear the son-of-a gun."

I got out of the way, but couldn't stop laughing.

"You won't laugh when I bring that big'n in, just watch this." Lefty drew that bow back, aimed, and shot at the fish. The arrow went into the water and missed the fish by so much it didn't even try to swim faster.

I laughed so loud that I hardly heard Lefty holler. When I looked at him, he was holding his hand, and I could see blood. The line attached to the arrow had a knot in it, and had taken a piece out of Lefty's hand. He was really hobbling and jumping around trying to get back up to the house. It was hard for me to get back up to the house because I was on the ground laughing.

That summer I convinced Lefty, Alice, and Abe to go water-skiing. Lefty had a really nice eighteen-foot ski boat with

160 horsepower inboard/outboard motor. I had Lefty drive the boat as I demonstrated how to get up on the skis. I showed them how to get in the water, put on the skis, and bring the tip of the skis out of the water.

"When I'm ready, Sonny, I'll tell you. You give the boat all the power it's got. Keep the boat straight; don't run into anything. When you turn, make a big wide circle."

"I got it." Lefty assured me.

He did just fine. I skied for a few minutes, and then dropped the rope and told him it was his turn. That was when the fun started.

"Let Abe go first," said Lefty.

We all laughed because Abe wore a wig and we knew what was going to happen, and it did. We were lucky to find that thing after Abe went under water. Other than that, Abe skied just fine.

Alice was next. She was good, except she couldn't stand up. She skied all over the lake in a squat position looking very much like a momma duck. She had a great time. It was wonderful to see Alice having a good time; she had such a nice laugh.

Then it was Lefty's turn. On the first try Lefty lost the rope. On the second try he lost the skis, but didn't let go of the rope. He swallowed a good deal of water before finally turning loose of the rope. On his third or fourth try he made it up out of the water, but, like Alice, he couldn't stand up. Despite looking like a frog about to leap, Lefty had the best time skiing all over the lake in a squat position.

Lefty had two small paying shows that weekend. One was an outdoor festival on Friday in Pennsylvania with other acts from the Opry: Grandpa Jones and Faron Young. The Saturday show was another outdoor festival out of Morehead, Kentucky, and I believe Jean Sheppard was also on that show. Lefty was doing a lot of shows at that time with Abe Mulkey, but for some reason Abe couldn't go on this trip, so Lefty asked me to go with him to help him drive and keep him company.

"Sure, count on me." I told him.

We left that Thursday around ten in the morning. We made the show in Pennsylvania easily, and it was a great show. This may have been one of the first times I had met Grandpa Jones, and he was great. There were two shows, and in between shows, Grandpa invited everyone over to his camper and cooked a great meal for us.

Lefty and I headed out after the last show for Morehead, Kentucky, so we were pretty wiped out by the time we pulled into the motel early the next morning.

Lefty began complaining that afternoon, just before the first show, about a severe pain in his back. Nevertheless, he did a great first show, and afterward he wanted to see Jean Sheppard's show. She was one of Lefty's favorite female singers and she made a fan out of me that day, too.

After the last show I was helping put away Lefty's guitar when he came up to me and said, "You know, David, we're not too far from home, but I think we're both wore out. We've already got a motel room here so why don't we stay over and get some rest. We'll drive on in tomorrow"

"That suits me fine, I bet I'll sleep good tonight."

I woke up around 10:00 A.M. and walked out of my little room. My intention was to go down to the lobby and get us both some coffee and whatever else I could find. I walked up to Lefty's door and knocked very lightly. "Sonny, it's a little after ten and we'll need to check out by eleven."

It surprised me when I heard Lefty say, "David, come on in, the door is unlocked."

I opened the door and stepped inside. Lefty was sitting on the side of the bed wearing only his boxer shorts. He was staring down at a bloody washcloth in his hand. He had a pretty good grip on himself when he looked up at me, but I'll never forget that look, very helpless and hopeless.

"What am I gonna do with this?"

When I was able to say anything at all I said something like, "Let's get you cleaned up, we're going home."

I helped him into the shower, and then I got him some clean clothes and laid them on the bed. I called Alice and explained to her what was happening. Alice was waiting for us when we drove in, and immediately took Lefty to the hospital in Madison, Tennessee. Lefty was tested and treated for a severe bladder infection.

I left at the end of summer and went back to California. I started working with the Buck Owens group in Bakersfield. Bruce stayed on with Lefty and Abe for awhile, touring and writing songs, before he returned to his home in Montana. It wasn't until 1968 that I was re-signed to Columbia Records.

Unfortunately, once again, Lefty was losing momentum on the charts. His next single following "She's Gone, Gone, Gone" was a song recorded during the February 11th, session called "A Little Unfair." This song was released in October 1965, and spent only five weeks on the charts, peaking at number thirty-six. Another single, "Love Looks Good on You," was released on November 13th and did worse. It spent four weeks on the charts and peaked at number forty-one.

Lefty started off the New Year with a session consisting of four new songs, three of which were published by his new company, Golden Eye. The first song recorded was "Mama," followed by "It's Hard to Please You," written by Lefty and Abe; "You Don't Want Me To Get Well" written by Abe, and "The Writing on the Wall" written by Bruce Delaney. Lefty called Bruce and told him he was recording his song, and asked him if he wanted to come back to Nashville to write and help run the company. With this session Golden Eye Music was formed.

The next session was March 31, 1966, Lefty's birthday. He recorded four more songs, three of which were published by Golden Eye: "I Just Couldn't See the Forest (For the Trees)" written by Lefty and Bruce, "I'm Not Guilty" and "Everything Keeps Coming Back (But You)" written by Abe and Lefty, and "It Couldn't Happen to a Nicer Guy" written by Hank Cochran.

The publishing company was getting a lot of cuts, but no hits, not much air play, and no sales. When Don decided to release "You Can't See the Forest," a Golden Eye song, as Lefty's next single, Lefty had high hopes. The single was released October 15, 1966. It stayed on the charts six weeks without climbing higher than fifty-one. Songs from Golden Eye were pitched to other artists with no success. The company folded after only one year.

Lefty started recording outside songs again, and only occasionally would a Lefty song appear on the sessions.

Lefty's next two sessions, recorded November 11 and 15, 1966, only produced one single. "You Gotta Be Putting Me On" first appeared on the charts on March 25, 1967, and stayed for ten weeks peaking at number forty-nine.

Other songs cut during the sessions were: "Heart (Don't Love Her Anymore)," "You Don't Have To Be Present To Win," "My Feet Are Getting Cold," "If There's Anything I Can Do," "The Old Gang's Gone," "A Song From a Lonely Heart," and "There in the Mirror." Columbia just wasn't pushing Lefty's songs. They were busy with other artists like Johnny Cash and Marty Robbins. Lefty was not getting the airplay an artist needed to stay on the top. After "Saginaw, Michigan" and "She's Gone, Gone, Gone" any single Columbia put out on Lefty was lucky to hit the charts at all, and the ones that did never broke out of the top forties.

Don Law retired from Columbia Records early in 1967, and Frank Jones took over producing Lefty's sessions starting on March 8th that year. A great songwriter from Waco, Texas, A. L. "Doodle" Owens, brought a song to Lefty called "Get This

Stranger Out of Me." Lefty loved the song and recorded it on the March 8th session. Connie Smith had turned down this song earlier, saying she thought the song was dirty. Two other songs were recorded on this session, "Money Tree" and "Hobo's Pride," co-written by Lefty, Abe, and Jack Kirch.

"Get This Stranger Out of Me" was released as a single in September. It was a great song, but it didn't do well. It only stayed on the charts for four weeks and peaked at number sixty-three. However, anyone who has been in the music business for any length of time knows that it is not always how good the song is. Promotion plays a major part in the making of a hit record.

Although Lefty was comfortable with Frank Jones as his producer, he still missed Don Law. After all, everything Lefty had accomplished in the studio was in part due to this good-natured, classy man from England. Don and Lefty had a great love and respect for each other.

Don said of Lefty: "Of all the artists I have worked with in my forty years with Columbia Records, Lefty Frizzell was the most colorful and exhilarating. He was really a unique person, warm, lovable, generous, funny, and extremely talented. . . . He was never on time and sometimes did not show up at all, but once we got organized the sessions were a riot. Thanks to Lefty's exuberance and keen sense of humor everyone had a ball, and we made some darn good records."

Ray Price remarked about Don Law: "He let an artist be an artist, and not what he wanted them to be. That was the beauty of the man."

Sanger D. "Whitey" Shafer, another songwriter from Texas, came to Nashville in 1967. Whitey started writing with Dallas Frazier and Doodle Owens. He later co-wrote with Lefty some of the best songs Lefty was ever to record. The important thing was Lefty wanted to write again, and with the help of these great songwriters the best was yet to come.

Lefty's August 15, 1967, session was incredible, not so

much for the songs but because of the musicians. The session leader was Grady Martin on lead guitar, Ray Edenton on rhythm guitar, Harold Bradley on guitar, Lloyd Green on steel guitar, Joseph Zinkan on bass, Charlie McCoy on harmonica, Buddy Harman on drums, and Hargus "Pig" Robbins on piano. This was as terrific a lineup of top musicians as you could find. The songs recorded were "When the Rooster Leaves the Yard," "Anything You Can Spare," and "Only Way to Fly." Lefty went back into the studio on November 3rd, and recorded four more songs starting with "A Prayer on Your Lips Is Like Freedom in Your Hands," "Little Ole Wine Drinker Me," "A Word or Two to Mary," and "Almost Persuaded." Lefty came back to the studio in December and recorded "Have You Ever Been Untrue" and a remake of his own "If You've Got the Money, I've Got the Time."

Lefty's first session of 1968 was on April 29th, and he recorded "When the Grass Grows Green Again," "I'll Remember You," and "The Marriage Bit."

Lefty grabbed his guitar and said, "All right, guys, listen to this. I'm just learning this one myself." He curled into "The Marriage Bit." After a few phrases he stopped playing, shook his head, and said, "Boy, I'm sure messing these words up."

He tried again, and again stopped playing. "Man, that's a tongue twister."

"The Marriage Bit" was a very clever song and was released as a single in August, but it did nothing. It hit the charts for three weeks, but only went to fifty-nine on *Billboard*.

In 1968, I flew to Nashville to sign contracts with Columbia Records and to find songs. When I got into Nashville I called Lefty. Alice answered and said Sonny was out of town, but that he would be back the next day. She said she would come and pick me up. When we got back to the house I noticed a change in Alice, she had always been great to me, and she still was, but she was different somehow. She asked me if I was saved. I told her I was.

"David, I'm glad for you. Make yourself at home. I've got to go out for awhile; I won't be long. You can take the bed in the back room."

Lefty came in early the next day and we went downtown to his booking agency so he could sign a contract or something. On the way I asked him about Alice. He told me that she had gotten into religion. I said I thought she was a little different just in her asking me if I was saved.

Lefty told me, "This preacher, Jimmy Snow, has put religion into everyone. He's got people giving him money to build him a church, telling people to do all kinds of silly things." I asked who Jimmy Snow was. "He's Hank Snow's son. He wanted to be a singer, but he can't sing so he's preaching. What's so bad is everyone's listening to him. Can you imagine that?"

I told Lefty I had never heard of him. Lefty growled, "Well, you're the lucky one. You know, David, the first time I ever heard of him was when his dad, Hank, took him on tour up into Canada. Jimmy was only maybe eight or nine at the time. One evening after a show Hank called home and talked to his wife. Now, David, you'd have to know Hank to appreciate this, but Hank, after talking to his wife for awhile, asked, 'How's my son, Jimmy?' His wife answered, 'I don't know; he's with you.' Hank said after a pause, 'Oh! Yeah, Jimmy's fine.'" We both laughed, then Lefty got serious again.

"Jimmy's been talking people out of their money to build his church, and Alice was one of them. It made me mad when I found out, so I gave him a call and asked him why he took my money. Jimmy said, 'The Lord told me to.' I told him, 'Well, the Lord told me to get mine back or kick your ass. I'll be there in twenty minutes. You have my money or I'm gonna take it out of your ass.' Me and a friend of mine, Rusty Adams, went over and I got my money."

I asked Lefty how much money, and he said, "A couple a grand; ain't no telling how much everyone else gave him. Man, what a racket. And Alice, there's just no living with her. I love the Lord as much as anyone, but she's pushing me further away. I don't know if I'll ever find my way back."

I knew that Lefty and Alice had lived a rough life together, but they always seemed to find a common ground. With this I didn't know what was going to happen to them. I looked over at my brother while he was driving and he had such sadness on his face. For the first time, I was worried about him, and I'll admit, even a little sorry for him.

Carol Lee of the Carol Lee Singers, Grand Ole Opry background group, was married to Jimmy Snow at the time and she tells the story slightly differently than Lefty. She says that Lefty was on the road a lot in those days and while he was gone Alice started going to Jimmy's church and giving money to Jimmy's building projects. Jimmy told Alice that he didn't believe she could lead a good Christian life living with a sinner like Lefty and that she should leave him.

When Lefty came home after a tour, Alice had his clothes packed and told him that Jimmy said he should leave right away. Lefty asked her how much money she had given Jimmy, and she told him about two thousand dollars. Lefty grabbed a handful of his clothes and walked out.

Carol Lee said that she was in the kitchen when the doorbell rang. Because of the way the house was built she could see the front door while she was cooking. Since she was busy, she asked Jimmy to answer the door. When Jimmy opened it, Lefty asked him what gave him the right to tell Alice to leave him. Jimmy replied that he and the Lord had been talking and the Lord told him to tell Alice that she could not be a good Christian living with a sinner.

Lefty responded with: "You know, me and the Lord has been talking as well and he told me to come over here and whip your meddling ass." With that he hit Jimmy. Carol said if it hadn't been for the far wall Jimmy would still be falling.

"While you're down there, get me my money," Lefty demanded.

Lefty did a tour of Germany in 1968 playing all the military bases. During this tour he came down with a very bad case of the flu and laryngitis. He was ready to get home for a much needed rest before his next recording session.

Lefty and Frank Jones were in the studio again in September 1968, trying to get that elusive hit song. They recorded three songs that day, "Wasted Way of Life," "Keep Them Flowers Watered While I'm Gone," and a song that would be Lefty's first single of 1969, "An Article from Life."

Lefty's daughter, Lois, had toured Vietnam in 1968, and was asked to come back the following year. She convinced Lefty to do this tour with her. The tour was booked for the entire month of March 1969, by Lee Maynard of VIP Shows. He and Lefty were instant friends. Lefty and Lois left a month early and played tourist throughout Saigon.

Lee booked Lefty a room at the Embassy Hotel next to the Presidential Palace in Saigon. Using this as headquarters, they did their gigs from there. Lefty was told not to drink the water and not to go out alone.

One morning, Lefty woke up to a baby crying. He got up and followed the sound to the balcony. Looking down from the second floor, he saw an old man sitting beside the entrance to the hotel. A four or five month old baby was lying beside the old man, and Lefty could hear the baby's cries even louder now. Lefty thought, *How sad*, as he walked back inside.

Later in the day, Lefty could still hear the baby's cries and once again he thought, *How sad to hear a baby crying like this*.

Lee came by late that afternoon, and Lefty told him about

the baby and walked Lee out to the balcony where the baby's cries could still be heard faintly. "That poor baby has been crying all day. I don't understand how someone could just let a baby cry like that."

Lee explained the situation to Lefty. "Lefty, this is a very hard country. Some of its ways are hard to understand, but the reality is that when the baby is crying tourists feel sorry for it and will give money to the old man. When the baby stops crying it's because it's dead. The old man will go and get another baby to cry."

The cries of the baby haunted Lefty for years to come.

A day or two later, Lefty decided to take a walk. He remembered Lee telling him not to wander off alone, but he wasn't going far. He just wanted to move around a bit. Lefty walked out of the hotel and noticed the old man was gone.

People were everywhere going in every direction. Lefty was moving in and out of the crowd when, all of a sudden, a small boy about seven- or eight–years-old jumped onto Lefty. The boy wrapped both his legs around Lefty's legs. At the same time the boy pushed his hands deep into Lefty's pockets and hung there. Lefty could not get the boy off of him. He grabbed the boy's arms and tried to pull him loose. This didn't work. The boy's legs were so tight around Lefty's that he thought he was going to fall. Lefty looked around for help. People went right on by as if nothing were happening. Lefty saw a young girl, a few years older than the boy, standing, just watching him wrestle with the boy.

"Hey! Does this belong to you?" The girl said nothing, she just stared back at him. "Can you help me?" Lefty pleaded. Not knowing if the girl understood any English at all, Lefty kept trying to communicate. "Before I have to knock this little kid's head off, do you think you can get him off me?" The girl walked over a little closer. "Look, I'll give you what money I have in my pockets if you'll get this kid off of me. I don't want to hurt him, but if you don't help I'm gonna knock him out first, then I'm gonna throw him into a ditch, what ya think?" The girl walked over and touched the boy, and he let go. Lefty reached into his pockets and turned them inside out. The young girl and boy were still picking up Lefty's change as he walked back to the hotel.

Lefty joined Lee on the helicopter that was to take them to various military units to perform. One of the pilots told them, "Please stay down; keep your seatbelts on. We'll probably draw fire where we're going and we don't want anyone to get hurt, so stay down."

The flight was pretty smooth. Lefty was trying to get comfortable when he heard something hit the belly of the helicopter.

"What in the world was that?" Lefty shouted.

One of the pilots cautioned. "Someone down below is shooting at us. Stay calm. I'll get us out of here."

Lefty heard more bullets hit the helicopter. *Damn*, Lefty thought, *I've got to see what's going on.*

Lefty stood up and walked up to the open door and looked out. He could see a small boat in the river with two men holding guns pointed up at them. More bullets ricocheted off the helicopter fairly close to Lefty. Everyone was hollering at him to come back and sit down.

Lefty looked around. "Man, this is like some of the shows I did with Hank Williams."

Several months later Lefty visited our folks, and he gave Momma yards and yards of fine silk and a beautiful platinum watch-ring crowned with rubies, which he brought back from Vietnam.

Lefty only recorded one session in 1969. This was also the last session Frank Jones produced for Lefty. The songs recorded on May 15th were "Blind Street Singer" and "Honky Tonk Hill." Doodle Owens and Whitey Shafer wrote both songs.

Whitey had just finished a demo session the night before and drove up to Lefty's house and knocked. Lefty came to the door with a beer in his hand.

Whitey recalls, "I introduced myself and told him I had a song he might like to hear. Lefty must've been in a good mood 'cause he said, 'Come on in. You want a beer?' I said, 'I sure wouldn't mind having one.' We sat down at the table and talked for a few minutes. Then he said, 'Well, let's hear that song, matter of fact let's hear all four of 'em.' He picked out 'You Babe,' then he said, 'I'm recording tomorrow so I'll just record it then.' Then he added, 'If you want to come on down to the session, you can.'

"I went over there [to Lefty's house] one day and ate more then my share of tomatoes and crackers. The next day I came back and Lefty had a plate of beautiful tomatoes and crackers on the table. I was about half hungry and I stabbed a couple of those tomatoes and stuck 'em in my mouth and damn near died. Lefty had soaked 'em in Tabasco.

"I was with Lefty one morning," Whitey continued, "and he said, 'I gave Alice a key to the house and she threw it away.' I told him wouldn't it be nice if someone found that key and brought it back. We wrote 'She Found the Key (That You Threw Away).' We went up to Dallas' cabin one day and I sang, 'I've been throwing horseshoes' and stuff like that. Lefty said, 'That's the way love goes.' I said, 'That's it.' We wrote 'That's the Way Love Goes' and 'I Never Go Around Mirrors' that same day.

"Lefty wrote romantic type words like the second verse of 'Lucky Arms' where he says, 'mister rainy skies, dry your eyes.'" Whitey remembers."

Whitey continued his story. "Haggard came in town, oh I don't know, a few days after that and we went down to his motel room. Lefty said, 'Hey, knucklehead, sing Merle our new song.' So I sang 'That's the Way Love Goes.' Merle said, 'That's my next single.' Lefty said, 'Naw, it's my next single.' Johnny Rodriquez was leaning against the wall. He had his ears out and he loved the song. He recorded it and it went to number one."

CHAPTER FIFTEEN

THAT'S THE WAY LOVE GOES

Lefty recorded three sessions for Columbia Records in 1970 under producer Don Davis. The first session was on February 19th, and only two songs were recorded, "My Baby's a Tramp" written by Harlan Howard, and "She Brought Love Sweet Love" written by Jerry Crutchfield. On May 26th, Lefty recorded "Watermelon Time in Georgia" written by Harlan Howard. (This was one of the family's favorite songs recorded by Lefty that he didn't write.) When the single was released in August of that year, it stayed on the charts for ten weeks, but only went to forty-nine on the charts. If a song stays on the charts for ten weeks or more it means someone out there likes the song. For it to stay that long and not go past the top fifty means it didn't get any serious attention from the promotional department of the record label. The other songs recorded at that session were "I Must Be Getting Over You" and a Dallas Frazier song called "Out of You."

After Lefty's single, "Watermelon Time in Georgia," Columbia didn't issue another single of Lefty's until August 1972. "You Babe," written by Whitey Shafer, another terrific song, stayed on the *Billboard* charts for a total of ten weeks, and peaked at number fifty-nine. Once again radio liked the song, but the promotional department was busy with someone else's record.

Of the songs recorded in the next few sessions it was easy to tell who Lefty's favorite writers were. Harlan Howard had been a favorite as had Dallas Frazier, and now Doodle Owens and Whitey Shafer were. The real stuff was still to come when Lefty and Whitey started writing songs together.

Lefty and Don Davis recorded their last session together on October 19, 1970. The songs were "It's Raining All over the World," "There's Something Lonely in This House," and another Harlan Howard song, "Three Cheers for The Good Guys." Two of these songs were not even released.

Lefty recorded one session in 1971 in which he cut only two songs. Producer Larry Butler gathered together some of the best musicians in the business, but they still didn't come close to the hit that Lefty needed.

Lefty said about "Honky Tonk Stardust Cowboy," "I just couldn't figure out how to sing it, it wasn't my kind of song."

The other song cut, "What Am I Gonna Do," was written by Lefty. Both songs were released on albums at some later date, but not as singles.

After twenty-two years, Lefty and Columbia parted ways. His last session for Columbia Records was scheduled on June 14, 1972, with yet another producer, Glenn Sutton. The songs chosen for this session were "You Babe," "This Just Ain't No Good Day for Leaving," and a remake of Lefty's "Give Me More, More, More (Of Your Kisses)." Lefty's last song to be released by Columbia as a single was "You Babe."

Lefty and his songwriting friends would get together at Doodle Owens' house and just have fun drinking, telling jokes, and writing a few songs. At any given time you could find Lefty,

Doodle, Dallas Frazier, and Whitey laughing, telling stories, and what Lefty called "carrying on." Lefty loved hanging with his buddies where he could have fun away from Alice, who wouldn't allow this kind of behavior at the house anymore.

(One of the Victorian homes on Music Row was sold to Hill & Range in September 1968, and the other was sold to Hill & Range the following year. This put Lefty out of the real estate business.)

Lois bought a little house in Hendersonville in 1968, with money she had made touring Vietnam. It was a cute, little brick house on Cline Court, really close to where Doodle lived. After about a year Lois sold it to Lefty and Alice. Lefty let his oldest son, Rickey, live there for awhile, but when Rickey moved out they didn't try to rent it to anyone. Instead, Lefty started using it for songwriting get-togethers. He was still living at the big house, and he and Alice were getting along somewhat, but life would never be the same. Alice had her religion and Lefty had his "carrying on." The Little House, as everyone called it, became the center of the action. Lefty was spending more and more time at the Little House, and eventually he was there most of the time.

Dallas Frazier recalls the Little House: "We threw knifes over there, big ol' knives, right into the walls making big holes in the wall. I mean big ol' Tarzan knives."

Dallas talks of the time Lefty came by his house to visit, and Lefty started talking about barbershops. "Lefty said, 'You know, I go to a lot of different barbers around the country and every time I tell them, "Before you start cutting my hair, I want you to notice this little mole right here on my neck. Can you see it?" I tell 'em, "What I don't want you to do is run those clippers up in there and cut that, all right? Okay, let's get started now." Inevitably, before they get through, they start fooling around and talking. They always get up in there and cut that little mole. Now the first thing I do is say, "See this little mole right here. Just go ahead and cut it, then you can start on my hair."'

I had signed with Ron Chancey at Cartwheel Records, and I flew back to Nashville from California for the session. I recall clearly what happened when I arrived at the Nashville airport. I called Lefty at the Little House and he said he was sending someone to pick me up. In a few minutes two guys showed up. I can't remember their names, actually, I don't recall if I ever knew their real names because Lefty had nicknames for them. One he named Lubert Lugwrench, and that is all I can remember. Anyway, they drove me over to Hendersonville to the Little House. When I opened the door and walked in, I saw Sonny sitting in a chair talking on the phone.

"Come on in, David, I'll be through here in a minute. " Lefty said to me, then he turned back to the phone. "All right, Alice, this time you've gone far enough. I've had it with you, after all these years. I should've left you long, long ago. What? I'm not kidding here." Lefty covered the mouthpiece and motioned for me to come and sit on the couch. "Alice, you're right. I may be going to hell, but I'll have a lot of company, and one might be you the way you're acting." Alice must have hung up on him because Lefty got really mad, really fast.

"Daddamnit, David, I'm sorry. This crap from Alice is driving me insane. Hey, boy, you're looking good. I'll be through here in a second." Lefty still had the receiver in his hand. He dialed a number. He was silent for a moment then he said, "Hey, uh, this is Lefty. Can I speak to Buddy Lee? . . . okay, I'll hold on."

Lefty looked back to me. "What's going on with you?" I told him I just came to town to do a session with Ron and would be here a few days. About that time Lefty said into the phone, "Buddy, yeah I'm okay, it's Alice again. This time, Buddy, I've had it . . . No, I'm leaving her this time . . . Aw, Buddy, I've tried that. I can't even talk to her anymore . . . Yeah, she's so into that religion I can't reach wherever she is . . . Do you think you can find me an attorney? . . . Oh yeah, I'll probably need a good one . . . Okay, I'll hold on."

Lefty turned back to me. "How's Momma and every-body?" I told him fine and everyone really wanted to see him. He said he was planning to come out soon.

He spoke back to the phone. "Yeah, Buddy, I've got a pen." Lefty wrote a name and phone number on a piece of paper. "Okay, I'll call him, Buddy, tell me, whatda you think? . . . Really? . . . Oh, damn, you mean, oh, mmm, she can do that? . . . Well, hell, mmmm, I'm not gonna give her all that . . . Buddy, yeah I'll be calm . . . I'll call you later."

Lefty still had the receiver in his hand when he turned to me and said, "David, I'm almost done here." He dialed another number. There was a brief moment of silence. "Yeah, it's me, Alice, hon. Aw, come on, we can work this ou . . . u . . . ut, come on Alice . . ." While Sonny was talking I got up and walked back outside. I didn't want him to see me laughing.

That afternoon I asked Lefty if he had any songs I could hear. Lefty pointed at a pile of tapes thrown in the corner of the room. "All the songs in Nashville are laying right over there, help yourself."

I looked through the tapes, most of them hadn't even been opened. There were songs from Willie Nelson, Kris Kristofferson, and Bill Anderson, some of the biggest writers in the world. I found about ten songs that I loved, and when I played them for my brother he said, "Uh, David, this one here is one I've got to do." It was "This Just Ain't No Good Day For Leaving." Another one I picked out was a beautiful song called "Mary in the Morning."

Lefty said, "Okay, you can have that one." I believe this was the first time Lefty had heard either one of them, but we had fun going through all those great songs. We laughed and threw tapes at each other all afternoon.

The next morning we went up to Center Hill Lake, where Lefty had a small houseboat. First we drove down to Center Point Bar-B-Que and got some food to take with us. Then we drove the seventy or eighty miles up to the lake. When we got to the marina it was almost dark, and Sonny's boat was not tied to the dock. It was tied to a little raft a short distance from the dock, and we had to get someone to take us out in a rowboat. We got on the houseboat and Lefty started it. It ran well, the engine sounded all right, but when we went to untie the boat we couldn't undo the rope. We tried everything, but we couldn't untie that rope, so we stayed right there tied to that little raft all night.

The next morning we headed back down to Nashville. I had my session with Ron Chancey at Woodland Studios. We got there late, of course, because I was with Lefty. I told him, "You must come in with me. I don't know Ron very well and I don't want him mad at me before we even get started."

"You think coming in late with me's gonna help?"

"Yeah, everybody knows you're always late."

Well, it worked. Ron said, "Oh! You're with Lefty. Well, that explains it."

We all had a good laugh and the session went really well. Lefty stayed with us at the studio for awhile.

The morning after the session I went to Ron's office. When I walked in Ron was on the phone and he motioned for me to sit down. After a moment he handed the phone to me and said, "David, talk to this lady, please."

I took the phone, not knowing who it was, and said hello. The lady said, "I'm going to take off all your clothes; then I'm going to take off all of mine; then I'm going to lick your whole body."

"Wa-aait a minute," I interrupted, "you say you're gonna do what?"

Ron had left the office, but I could hear him laughing outside the door.

In a low sexy voice the lady said, "I'll take you in my mouth and…"

I interrupted her again. "Hold on now, don't forget any of

what you're talking about. It's just that I can't talk right now, why don't you call where I'm gonna be later say around eight o'clock?" I gave the lady Lefty's phone number.

That evening I answered the phone and talked to the lady for a moment before saying, "Sonny, there's a young lady on the phone and she wants to talk to you." It took Lefty a few minutes to get into the conversation, but finally he did. I have never witnessed anything as funny in my life as that phone call.

After Lefty left Columbia he credited Gordon Terry with helping him secure a deal. Don Gant signed Lefty to ABC Records and would later become Lefty's producer. Lefty was to cut complete albums and they would release singles from that. Lefty had always recorded singles and albums were put together later, but now he could record songs that fit together. This excited Lefty. He was enthusiastic for the first time in a long while about recording.

A tour of Washington State was put together by booking agent Jack Roberts, for the Frizzell brothers. Lefty would headline, I would emcee, and our younger brother, Allen, would come on in between. First I would come out and do about twenty-five minutes followed by Allen. Then Allen would sing three or four songs and I would come back out and introduce Lefty. I would join Lefty on stage and play guitar, a little harmonica, and sing harmony. That would be the show.

At the time I was working with the Buck Owens group in Bakersfield, California, and flew up to Seattle from there. Lefty, Allen, and Ralph Spicer drove out from Nashville in a motor home. The shows were going fine, and everyone was having a great time.

We pulled into Yakima for a show. I was in Lefty's room when the phone rang. It was the promoter. I told him they had made it to town all right and were looking forward to the show that night. The promoter asked if Lefty wanted to come down to the club and rehearse with the band. I told him that I would check with Lefty.

I turned to Lefty. "Sonny, the promoter wants to know if you want to come down to the club and rehearse with the band."

"What did he say?" I repeated what the promoter had said.

Lefty asked for the phone. "Hello, this is Lefty, what's going on?" The promoter repeated the question to Lefty. "You mean come down there now?"

The promoter said that the band was there, and if Lefty wanted to go over the show, now would be a good time.

"Well, I can come down there now, or I can come down there tonight. I'm only gonna do this once. Which one do you want, now or tonight?" Lefty informed him. There was a slight pause. Then Lefty said, "Okay, I'll see you tonight."

We parked the motor home behind the club. Lefty was having a tough time holding a drink down. He would take a big swig of vodka and throw it right back up. I watched him until it was time for the show to start. I left the motor home hoping that before it was Lefty's turn he would be able to hold one down.

I went on and did my twenty-five minutes and then Allen went next. After I got Allen started, I went back out to the motor home to check on Lefty. He was ready, looking sharp.

After I introduced Lefty, I joined him on stage. Out of the corner of my eye I saw Allen disappear into a side room with a pretty young girl. I didn't think too much about it until a crowd gathered outside of the door. Lefty was still singing, but he motioned for me to go see what was going on. I made my way through the crowd, and when I got to the door the club owner was helping Allen stand up. I could see he had been severely beaten. His face was bleeding and swelling up. The owner and I helped Allen to the office. Someone brought in some wet towels. I told Allen to relax as best he could and that I would be back.

I learned that the young girl was trying to make her boyfriend jealous and she certainly succeeded. When the girl took

Allen into the side room, the boyfriend followed. Somehow the boyfriend caught Allen's little finger between his teeth, and with Allen trying to hold himself up with the other hand, the boyfriend proceeded to smash in Allen's face.

When the show was over Lefty went back to the motor home, and Ralph and I went back inside the club. I asked one of the waitresses who the guy was that busted up Allen. She told me that he was standing right outside the door now. I asked Ralph to watch my back, and I went out the front door. I asked the guy if he was the one that was in the fight inside. He was more than happy to brag.

"It wasn't much of a fight. He was that sissy trying to sing tonight."

When I hit him he fell into a parked car. I hit him again and he hit the ground. "Get up you son-of-a-bitch, and if you whip me I'm gonna personally introduce you to my other brother, Lefty. You may as well have a shot at the whole family." With that said he stayed on the ground. I went back inside, got Brother Allen, and took him to the hospital.

The tour ended in Roy, Washington, and the show that night was special. Lefty had the audience in the palm of his hands. He could do no wrong. Joining us on this last show was famed guitarist Nokie Edwards of The Ventures. I should mention that this was Allen's first major tour, but other than that one episode the rest of the tour was wonderful. This was the last time all three brothers sang together.

Lefty got back to Nashville in time to be inducted into the Songwriters Hall of Fame. Momma and Daddy drove out from California for the event. They stopped by Las Vegas to pick up Betty's daughter, Tina. Allen joined the family at the ceremony.

Lefty recorded his first album for ABC Records on December 14, 15, and 19, 1972. He got most of the songs from Dallas Frazier, Gordon Terry, Eddy Raven, Doodle Owens, Jimmy Buffett, and Whitey Shafer. Lefty recorded the first song written by Whitey and him called "Lucky Arms." A great tune. It would be his fourth single for ABC. Songs recorded on December 14th were "Down By the Railroad Tracks," "Let Me Give Her the Flowers," and "If I Had Half the Sense (A Fool Was Born With)." Songs recorded on December 15th were: "Somebody's Words," "Lucky Arms," "True Love Needs To Be in Touch," and "My House Is Your Honky Tonk." The songs to finish the album on the 19th were: "I Buy the Wine," "If She Just Helps Me Get Over You," "Falling," and "Railroad Lady."

L efty recorded one session for ABC Records on July 17, 1973. With Don Gant at the helm, Lefty recorded only three songs, but they were probably some of the best material Lefty had ever done. "I Can't Get Over You To Save My Life," "I Never Go Around Mirrors (I've Got A Heartache To Hide)," and "That's The Way Love Goes" were all written by Lefty and his new writing partner, Whitey Shafer.

Lefty sang, "I've been throwing horseshoes…" The band really enjoyed playing this song and it was one of his best.

Lefty got his first single release on ABC in September of that year. "I Can't Get Over You To Save My Life" hit the *Billboard* charts on September 22, 1973. It stayed on the charts for thirteen weeks and peaked at number forty-three

In the first part of October 1973, I came to Nashville for the CMA Convention with my best friend, Gary Clawson, from the West Coast. I was with Capitol Records, and I was working with the great Buck Owens and Buck's manager, Jack McFadden, who ran OMAC Artist Agency out of Bakersfield. Gary was excited to finally meet Lefty after listening to me talk about my brother all the time.

We came in my motor home, and we did two jobs in

Texas on our way out—we were beat. We pulled up in front of the Little House, and Lefty came out with no shirt. When I introduced Gary, Lefty grabbed him and gave him a big bear hug, and pulled him into the house. From that moment Gary and Lefty were best friends.

Lefty told us he had to get the gas turned on because it had been turned off while he was out of town. Gary and I sat down while Lefty called the gas company. That conversation went something like this:

"Hello, this is Lefty. I'm calling to see about turning my gas on here at my house in Hendersonville . . . Yeah, I'm a member . . . Well, how long will it take? . . . We can't wait that long. Maybe I'll just turn it on . . . What ya you mean its against the law? All I've got to do is just cut that little wire off and...You'll have me arrested? You've got to be kidding. I've got to get the heat on; there's no hot water. I've got kids here, I can't be without...Well, all right, send them out here as soon as possible."

Lefty looked over at Gary and me. "Where did you two come in from?" It was as if nothing had just happened.

Gary often talks about his visit to Nashville and meeting Lefty. "If someone asked me to try to tell Lefty's fans what he was like, I would have to say, the only way to really know about him was to have known him. I consider myself one of the lucky ones, because I did know him. There is no way to describe him, his character, the way he thought, or the way he phrased his words. The man was unique, to say the least. In October 1973, David and I visited Lefty in Nashville. While we were there, Lefty and I went into town one night to a small bar where a good friend of his named Abe Mulkey was playing. After a few pushes and shoves, Lefty decided to sit and sing most every hit he had. I'll never forget that evening.

"Lefty had a home in Hendersonville, and David and I stayed there while we were visiting. I took a picture of David and Lefty standing in the front yard. One afternoon, while we were there, Lefty said, 'Let's take a ride up to Dallas Frazier's cabin.' It was a one-room cabin on top of a hill where Dallas, Whitey Shafer, and Lefty went to write songs. Whitey, David, Lefty, and I jumped in the car and headed out. We spent half a day singing and playing music. They had just finished writing "That's the Way Love Goes," a great song.

"When we were driving away from the cabin," Gary related, "Lefty asked me who my favorite female singer was, and I said Jeannie Seeley. Shelly West was too young then. Much to my surprise Whitey slammed on the brakes and started to back up, up, and up! Then he put it in forward and we went up a long driveway to a two-story house that sat all by itself in the middle of the acreage. When we stopped we were within inches of the front door. I asked, 'What's going on and who lives here?' Lefty told me to open the door and go inside and find out. When we were all inside, I was introduced to Jeannie Seeley and her husband, Hank Cochran. They were great people and I was really impressed. I remember Jeannie had to give an award or something on one of the shows, The CMA television award show, in town and was in a quandary over not being able to find her blonde wig. She had only a short time left before she would be late. All of a sudden Lefty stood up from the couch and said, 'Oh, is this what you're looking for?' He had been sitting on it all the time. Jeannie made it to her commitment in time and all was well. The rest of us spent the evening and well into the night listening to tapes that Hank had. I could easily write a book about the conversations we had that night.

"I spent a month with David on that trip," Gary said. "I left him in Spokane, Washington, where he was playing another gig. His life was too hard and fast for me. The life of an entertainer is as tough as any lifestyle I have ever seen. I was on my way home to go back to work and relax. Thank God for this trip and the memories I now have of Lefty Frizzell. I think that all country music lovers can be thankful that we still have David Frizzell and his brother, Allen, to carry on the family name with two of the finest voices I have ever heard."

Gary Clawson now lives in Oregon and owns several restaurants up and down the coast.

Lefty's debut album for ABC was released in August 1973. It was titled *The Legendary Lefty Frizzell*. Lefty was so proud of this album he cried when he heard it for the first time. It was no doubt a Frizzell masterpiece. The songs that comprised the album were as good as any Lefty had ever recorded. The songs "That's the Way Love Goes" and "I Never Go Around Mirrors" are in every way equal to such Lefty classics as, "I Love You a Thousand Ways" and "I Want To Be with You Always."

CHAPTER SIXTEEN

THE LAST SESSION

Bill Mack was, and still is, one of the most popular disc jockeys in the music business and a dear friend of Lefty. Bill was with WBAP radio in Ft. Worth for many years, and he has interviewed just about every star in country music. One of Bill's best interviews was when Merle Haggard was his guest and they called Lefty at home. The interview is classic:

"Bad weather, you know," said Lefty.

"Yeah," Bill agreed.

"And . . . ah . . . of course, today I . . . ah . . . had to record from two to five, you know . . . ah . . . so we got . . . ah . . . one and a half numbers . . . ah . . . so we're happy, you know."

Bill and Merle laughed. Bill joked, "One and a half, why don't you send me that half record, I'd like to hear it."

Lefty rattled on, "We got some crazy weather here either; sometimes your body can't adjust to it. Whitey, Whitey Shafer and I, we've been getting on writing a few songs."

"I tell you what, Whitey and you can get together and write some pretty doggone good songs, 'That's the Way Loves Goes.'"

"Well, like Abe Mulkey said we . . . ah . . . ah . . . lucked out a little bit."

"Say Abe's got a good record going on down here."

"Oh, has Abe got a good'n going on?" Lefty asked.

"He sure does."

Lefty laughed. "Is it the one that's got Bill Mack in it?"

Bill and Merle laughed.

Lefty murmured, "I'll be doggone."

"Yeah, it says, 'I sent Bill Mack my latest record.' I like that," Bill said.

"You know I told 'em, I said . . . ah . . . you're gonna make a lot of friends with all them jockeys, you know. He said, 'I don't go to the horse races no way.'"

"Hey, Lefty, how long's it been since you've been interviewed by Merle Haggard."

Lefty thought. "Hey . . . ah . . . oh, it's been a long time."

"I'm gonna put him on and let him interview you for a second."

"Ah, I'll tell you what, he's got it on me . . . ah . . . ah . . . Bill, because see I tried to sleep for a hour or so, but I couldn't and . . . ah . . . Shafer come by and looked and seen the light in my room up there. You know, Alice had me locked in my room for awhile."

Merle asked, "Alice had you locked in your room?"

"But I picked the lock. I said, 'Hey, Whitey, don't come in. I'll come ou . . . u . . . u . . . ut."

Bill and Merle laughed again.

Merle asked, "You'll do what?"

Lefty repeated, "I'll come ou . . . u . . . u . . . ut."

Merle imitated Lefty. "You'll come ou . . . u . . . u . . . ut."

"Yeah, o u out, out you know. It'll be the first, Bill . . . ah . . . Merle, ah . . . what's his last name?"

Bill answered, "Haggard."

"Did what?"

Bill repeated himself. "Haggard."

Merle said, "He's ah up and coming singer."

"Yeah, I heard him. I heard him on radio today."

Both Bill and Merle laughed.

"I thought it was Charlie Walker. Charlie is a friend of mine, you know. This will be the very first, Bill."

Bill told Lefty, "We've been talking about you all night. I told 'em awhile ago. I said, 'It's Merle Haggard night and we're saluting Lefty Frizzell. Merle said, 'Play me a Lefty record.'"

"I wish I was there with you guys."

Merle agreed. "Boy, I sure do, too."

"Hey, I just heard . . . ah . . . this is Merle. Hey I just heard..." Lefty interrupted, "Would you repeat that please?"

"Let me hear you yodel one time," Merle requested.

Lefty complied. "Yodel-de-a lay-e-hee."

Lefty told Merle that the next time he was in California he was planning to stop by.

Lefty loved being with his friends at the Little House, drinking and writing songs. He hated when his friends would go home; he didn't like being alone. Brother Allen was living in Nashville during this time and tells of Lefty calling him at work and talking to him for hours and asking him to come over all the time.

One morning, while Allen was staying at Lefty's house, Lefty came into the room where Allen was sleeping. He started rummaging around, making a lot of noise, and saying, "...you can't find nothing when you want to." Allen believed he was just trying to wake him up.

Allen asked, "What's going on?"

"Oh, I'm trying to find something. Hey, Allen, what if you got up, walked to the bathroom, washed your face, and when you looked into the mirror you looked just like Buck Owens. Boy, I'll bet that would scare the hell right out of you."

"With that," Allen said, "Sonny just turned around and walked out."

When Lefty had a friend, he was loyal through the good times and the bad, and he often contributed to both.

Yvonne, who is still a friend of our family, recalls her long friendship with Lefty:

"Lefty Frizzell was my friend. I met him in 1951, at the VFW Hall in Clinton, Oklahoma. Everyone stood at the stage and just listened instead of dancing. He must have sung a song that my little brother liked. (He was drowned in the Clinton flood a few weeks before.) Tears started falling. I turned away from the crowd. When Lefty took a break, he sent a band member to tell me to come backstage. He asked if he had done something to make me cry. I explained why I was crying and he said, 'Please try not to cry and I'll try not to sing any sad songs.' He had a way of making everything all right. He had me laughing before I left him. For twenty-four years we had a wonderful friendship. When he met my husband, Buddy Tatum, they created the same friendship. What one couldn't come up with the other one could.

"A few years later Lefty was at the Trianon Ballroom in Oklahoma City. Buddy went to see him and brought him to our home. All the way home Lefty kept asking why I didn't come to see him. Buddy finally told him I wasn't feeling well. Lefty came straight to my bedroom and wanted to know what was wrong with me. About that time Buddy brought a tray of medicine and juice to me. That really had Lefty upset. So, I took his hand and laid it on my stomach. Then he knew, and he was really excited. He wanted to name my baby if it was a boy. I told him I already had a name, Martin Shane. No, that wouldn't do. It had to be Aaron Shane. Lefty must have really liked the name Aaron. He told us he didn't get to name his boys, so he had to name mine, which we did, on September 14, 1963. On Christmas of that year we received a package with a beautiful red velvet suit for my little boy. I still have it.

"When I would cook a steak for Buddy and Lefty, it would absolutely take Lefty three hours to eat it. He was too busy laughing and carrying on. He would eat a whole tomato like eating an apple.

"Lefty and David played the Trianon Ballroom on several occasions during that time period. David got to know the owners pretty well and one night the owner was really excited about booking Ricky Nelson for the Ballroom. He told David, 'I just booked Ricky Nelson for $10,000.' David thought, *Ten thousand dollars, wow!*

"Buddy and I have enjoyed many times with him, traveling around and having too much fun. Buddy was always the driver, of course, and I was always there to see that Lefty made it to the stage, that took some doing.I have so many stories it would take a week of Sundays to tell them."

She continued. "We stopped at a little old service station somewhere in Texas. I thought they would never come out. When they came out they were running as hard as they could, Lefty telling Buddy to get out of there quick. The man had a coon in a cage and Lefty just had to let it have several drinks of his orange drink which was quite strong. The coon was pretty tipsy, having a fit in the cage. They were laughing so hard they couldn't even tell me until later what they had done. We did get away.

"Lefty, Buddy, my friend Jean, and I went to the Trianon Ballroom. After Lefty had finished his performance, we were walking to the car and Buddy said something to me that really made me angry . . . so . . . I walked home, right down Broadway in high heel shoes. It was nineteen blocks to my apartment, yeah, nineteen blocks. They drove around town but could not find me, not dreaming I would really walk home. When they came in, Buddy and I continued to argue about something. I went to the bedroom; Buddy came in and shot two holes in my wall under the window beside the bed where I was lying. Here came

Lefty. He just knew Buddy had shot me. The gun was a Python .357 magnum, so it was loud. When the police came in the front door Lefty was standing in the living room twirling the gun like a cowboy movie star. He and Buddy were laughing and carrying on like nothing was happening. At the sight of the officer Lefty dropped the gun to the floor and started trying to explain that it wasn't him, and it had all been done while Buddy was cleaning the gun. Yeah! Cleaning a gun at two o'clock in the morning and it going off not once but twice. Needless to say, Buddy went to jail. Lefty would not leave until we got Buddy out the next morning. Buddy had never been in jail before, so he was really upset until he and Lefty started joking and carrying on again. Nobody could stay upset or mad around Lefty, he kept you laughing.

"Buddy drove a truck for TransCon Freight Lines about fourteen years. When he went to Los Angeles Lefty would pick him up and take him to his home. One morning Lefty couldn't find him. He just happened to look out the upstairs window and there was Buddy washing his Cadillac. Lefty thought that was really something and had to call me and tell me about it.

"Buddy and Lefty were more than just friends. If Lefty was a little short on cash, Buddy would help. Buddy died on March 4, 1970. My mother called Lefty to tell him; she had to leave word with Alice. In about an hour or less I was called to the phone. Lefty said, 'E-vonne, what is wrong? I know something is wrong because I got a message to call Mrs. Buddy Tatum.' Lefty was in the hospital in Nashville with high blood pressure problems and couldn't come to the funeral. The day I buried Buddy, Lefty called me saying he hated to bother me, because he knew I had a lot of people, but he had to talk to me. After telling him that I was alone with my two babies, he was very upset. He called me every night for the next few months, begging me to come to live with him and Alice and that he had me a job. I didn't go but Lefty sent me about $900 all together within the next few months. Even with me telling him all the time I didn't need it.

"I didn't see Lefty [again] until the fall of 1974. I had re-married and my husband and I, with my son that Lefty named Aaron and my daughter Dana, saw Lefty at Waxahachie, Texas. Red Sovine, Webb Pierce, and George Morgan were also there. I went backstage to see Lefty and handed him the $900 he had sent to me and it upset him so bad. He said, 'E-vonne, I did not make you a loan. That was my gift to you for the wonderful years of good times and very special friendship we shared.'

"Lefty gave me a pair of boots in about 1959, which I treasured. You see, he was my rock. Anytime I was sad or wor-ried about anything I would always call him. We would talk for hours, and he would always have a new song he and Whitey had just written that he would sing to me.

"I'll never forget the first time Lefty called me to the stage to sing with him. I was a shaking wreck. We had sung in the car going to shows for years, but to sing on stage was totally different. We got it done. If I remember, it was the Bamboo Club in Enid, Oklahoma. Lefty always stayed backstage and didn't ever want anyone else to come back, just Buddy and I. I was always saying 'Lefty, don't drink.' When he went to Japan he sent a postcard. At the end he wrote, DON'T DRINK, DON'T DRINK, DON'T DRINK. We got a kick out of that."

Yvonne tells of another bit of mischief which they en-gaged in. "We were all at one of Lefty's performances. Because we were late getting there, as usual, we didn't have time to eat. They gave us money to buy pizza. We spent it all. Needless to say, we had pizza the next morning for breakfast. Have you ever had cold pizza, especially for breakfast? Oh! We ask to buy one of the dried pepper shakers, but they said no. We decided to take it any-way, having spent so much on pizza. I still have that shaker. Lefty really had us going, saying the law would be after us. He lived to joke and carry on with us."

Yvonne tells of one of the times when Lefty had over-stressed his voice. "Lefty showed up with a sore throat. Buddy took him to a chiropractor who worked on his vocal cords. It helped enough that he could talk, but not sing. He called the man in Texas where he was to be that night and tried to explain his situation. The man would not take no [for an answer]. He said just showing up would be alright; maybe his voice would be better when he arrived. Lefty, hating to disappoint his fans, finally decided to go. Well, we didn't have time to drive, so we took him to the Downtown Airpark in Oklahoma City and he chartered a plane. I was extremely scared to fly so he went alone. We picked him up at the airpark about four o'clock in the morning. He was livid. The man refused to pay him. After talking to the man on the phone, he knew Lefty's voice was not in good shape at all. We finally got Lefty calmed down by daylight. "

Yvonne described her first meeting with me. "Lefty knocked on my door one day. When I opened it there stood a handsome young man with him, who was his little brother, David. Lefty jokingly said he needed a baby sitter. David was too young to go with him where he was performing and would I mind keeping him with me until he got back. When Buddy came in the next day, we decided to take David to the NCO Club at Tinker Field in Oklahoma City. He talked the band into letting David sing with them. Since he was Lefty Frizzell's brother, it was no problem. He brought the house down with his rock and roll song and dance. He looked like Elvis on stage. In fact, I have the pictures to prove it.

"I met Aaron Conner in 1989; we were getting ready to go to Nashville with L. D. Allen [a friend of Yvonne's] for Aaron to do his first recording session. Something was wrong with his boots. I went to my closet and handed Aaron a pair of boots, saying, 'You can wear these boots to do your recording.' He looked at me real strange and said, 'I can't wear these boots.' I finally got him to put them on and they fit. Later I took an album of Lefty's to him and ask if anything looked familiar. At first he said no then he saw the boots. We still have them."

Yvonne added, "I took my best friend, Jean, to a dance in Enid, Oklahoma, one night to see Lefty. Danged if he didn't take her to California with him. She came back to Oklahoma a few years later. Every time I would see him, he would always ask 'have you seen this friend of mine.'"

Lefty was playing the Bamboo Club in Enid, Oklahoma, in the summer of 1954. Yvonne Conner's (neé Baskett) uncle drove her and her friend, Jean Armitage, up from Oklahoma City to see Lefty. Jean was living in Winnsboro, Texas, at the time. When Lefty met Jean he thought he had never seen anyone as beautiful. By the time the last song was sung and the car was packed, Lefty and Jean were on their way to California. Yvonne said she didn't see her friend again for the next year and a half.

Jean had a sister living in Montebello, California, just south of Los Angeles, so that is where Lefty took her. Earlier that year Lefty had sold his home in Beaumont, Texas, and had moved his family to Granada Hills, California.

By the time I joined Lefty in 1956, Jean had already moved back to Oklahoma, but Lefty sometimes would talk about his beautiful friend, Jean. One evening, while on tour throughout Texas and Oklahoma, we drove by Jean's house. Lefty was right, she was one of the most beautiful and nicest ladies that I have ever met.

Recently I asked Jean why she left California. She told me, "It took me awhile, but I finally realized that Lefty loved his kids, and I didn't want to have any part in that kind of a breakup, so I knew I had to leave."

While touring in Vietnam in 1969, Lefty sent a postcard to Buddy and Yvonne saying, "Say hello to the family and someone, I guess I'll always love her."

Yvonne saw Lefty for the last time in October 1974. The last thing he said to her was, "Have you talked to our friend lately?"

Lefty and Alice fought for any reason or no reason at all. Doodle Owens recalls: "Lefty and Alice would call each other and each would try to hang up on the other first. Lefty would hate it if Alice got the best of him and hung up first. Finally, when, or if, Alice answered the phone and heard Lefty's voice, she'd just hang up right then and there. Lefty would be so mad. One time Lefty begged me to call Alice and try to get her to at least talk to him. It took a lot of talking, but finally she gave in and told me to have Lefty call and she would listen to what he had to say. Lefty called Alice and before she said much more then hello Lefty hung up on her. I didn't want to have any more to do with that."

One evening I was at our Momma and Daddy's house in Tipton, California, a few miles north of Bakersfield, when Sonny called. "I got a call last night," he said, "around eight, Alice and the two boys were gone, some guy says, 'Lefty, you don't know me, but I wanted to tell you where your two boys are, and I believe they could be in danger.' Then he said, 'In that old park over by the lake behind your house is a bunch of people, and they're all on drugs, and they've got your two boys.'

"I asked him who he was, but he wouldn't tell me, so I asked him how many people are over there and he said he didn't know for sure, but there was at least fifteen to twenty cars.

"I thanked the guy and went and got my .22 rifle. I got in the car and drove around the lake toward the park. I stopped at Whitey's house on the way, but he couldn't go. I went on around to the park. When I drove up it was all dark except for my head-lights. I stopped, and then all of a sudden, headlights came on all around me. I got out of the car and I couldn't see anyone. All I could see was lights, then I saw a few shadows moving in and around the lights. I just said out loud, 'I'm here to get my boys!' There was not a sound, so I showed my gun, and I said a little louder, 'I'm here to get my boys!' Someone threw a rock and it hit me in the head, almost knocked me out. I just started firing that gun in all directions. I must of fired five or six times when I heard a voice say, 'Here's your boys!' I got 'em in the car and drove back to Whitey's house and they helped me clean the blood from my head."

Sometime later Whitey told me about this incident. "Lefty came by the house one night. Rickey and Marlon were in that old park across the creek there, Saunders Ferry Park. That was before they fixed it up. He wanted me to go down there with him, said he was gonna go over there and get 'em. I . . . I wasn't feeling good . . . actually, I didn't want to get mixed up in family business, you know. When he came back his forehead was bleeding. He said, 'One of 'em hit me with a damn brick.' There was a gang of kids and one of them threw a brick and hit him in the head. He said, 'I sure appreciate you going with me.' I always felt bad about that."

L efty came out to California in early April and was at our folk's house in Tipton. Our nephew, Jimmy Frizzell, came over and Lefty showed him the television guide on which he had written an idea for a song.

"Jimmy, what do you think of this idea?" Jimmy looked at what Lefty had written: "We're so happy, darling, in my wishing room."

Jimmy said he thought it was great. Lefty and Whitey finished the song and Lefty recorded it at the end of the month.

That evening I came over to visit. While I was there a call came in from Merle Haggard. After Lefty and Merle talked for awhile, plans were made to go to Merle's house in Bakersfield the next day.

Everyone got into my motor home including Momma, Daddy and a whole slew of Frizzells; Allen, Jimmy, and Dennis Knutson, a friend of mine who wrote songs for Buck Owens. The little bus was packed. When we got to Merle's and everyone started piling out of the motor home, Merle probably thought he had never seen so many Frizzells in his life. Invite one, you get 'em all. Merle didn't seem to mind, and at least Lefty was in this crowd somewhere.

Everyone had a wonderful time. Merle gave a tour of his house, and he showed the little train that went through every room. Then everyone settled down, and Merle played a tape of some of Lefty's songs he had recorded. Merle said that he really tried to capture Lefty's original sound. He recorded it in Dallas and it was important to him to make it as close to Lefty's sound as he could.

Lefty listened and said, "I don't know why you went to all that trouble; I could've gave you my old records they sound just alike." Everyone laughed, and then Lefty said, "Merle, they're great."

Merle got one of his guitars and played a song that he had just written called "Here in Frisco." Everyone loved it and then Jimmy sang a Jimmie Rodgers song, "All Around the Water Tank." After spending the afternoon with Merle and Bonnie, his wife, it felt like the Frizzells had just added two more to the family.

L efty went back to the studio on April 30, 1974, to record his second album for ABC. Of the three songs recorded, two were written by Lefty and Whitey, "She Found the Key" and "My Wishing Room." The third song was "I Wonder Who's Building the Bridge" written by Doodle Owens and Roger Burch.

Lefty's health was getting worse. His continual drinking, not eating right, and especially not taking his high blood pressure pills were taking their toll.

Whitey recalls taking Lefty to the doctor one day. "Lefty came out after seeing the doctor and told me the doctor said, 'If you're not going to take your medicine, get out of my office, 'cause I don't want you dying around here.' Lefty would laugh and we'd go on back to the house and Lefty would have another drink."

Whitey remembers going out on the road with Lefty. "There was this one night I went up and played piano with Lefty and there was just magic. I was playing anything I wanted to, hitting the right chords and everything. I'm not that good a player, but that night I could do anything. I couldn't do that again to save my life; there was just some kind of magic that night."

Of Lefty's joke telling, Whitey said, "Lefty had this one joke about keeping an eye out for you. It was kind of dirty, but the punch line wasn't what was funny when he told a joke, 'cause he would take fifteen minutes to tell one. He'd make every line in it funny, so by the time he got to the punch line it didn't matter."

Whitey told me that one day in 1972, he went over to the Little House in Hendersonville to see Lefty. Lefty was cooking a steak and had some tomatoes and onions sliced. He said Lefty would take the steak out of the oven, cut himself a bite, and then put the steak back in the oven. He watched Lefty do this all afternoon. In between they would have a drink and just carry on.

Whitey describes a songwriting session with Lefty. "I told Lefty, 'Llisten, I've got a few lines of an idea for a song. I've been working on it, and maybe you can jump in here.' Lefty said, 'I'm just the guy to do the jumping, what is it?' So, I sang, 'I've been throwing horseshoes over my left shoulder, I've spent most all my life searching for that four leaf clover, yet you run with me chasing my rainbow.' Then Lefty chimed in with, 'hum, hum, I love you, too, that's the way love goes.' We wrote that song right then. Later Johnny Rodriguez heard and recorded the song, and it went to number one in 1972. Lefty recorded it on July, 17, 1973.

"We met at the studio that day. Lefty was recording three of our songs, "I Can't Get Over You To Save My Life," "I Never Go Around Mirrors," and "That's the Way Love Goes." As we walked into the studio, Lefty was carrying his briefcase. We said hello to everyone, set down his briefcase, and opened it. Everyone thought he had the song lyrics and maybe some demo tapes inside, but all Lefty had in his briefcase was a bottle of vodka, a small shaker of salt, and one lemon."

Whitey and I laughed about these memories. I said, "In all my life I've never met anyone like him. Everything he did was not like anyone else. "

"That's because there wasn't anyone." Whitey thought for a minute and then added, "I never knew how this would all end; I just knew it wasn't going to be good."

Lefty's next single for ABC was "I Never Go Around Mirrors." It hit the *Billboard* charts February 16, 1974, and after spending twelve weeks it climbed to number twenty-five. Lefty was making a strong comeback thanks to incredible material and a record label that was excited enough about him to promote his records. In December 1972, Lefty recorded a song written by Jimmy Buffett, "Railroad Lady," which would be his next single. Everyone that ever heard this song liked it, at least a little, but Lefty didn't like it a whole lot. He never once sang it on a show or anywhere else. He was probably glad that it never got out of the top fifties on the charts. The next single was one of Lefty's favorites, though, a song written by him and Whitey called "Lucky Arms." This song also was recorded in December, 1972, and was released in September 1974, and stayed on the charts for fourteen weeks. It peaked at number twenty-one.

Lefty was enjoying his studio work, although he had to work at keeping his voice in shape. Even though he didn't want to, he still had to go on the road and do shows. The fact was he dreaded going out on the road. He had done everything out there that he wanted to do, now he just wanted to stay home, write songs with his buddies, go to the studio and make great records, and drink.

Lefty told Doodle, "I'm coming off the road. I can't stand it anymore. I wanna be home!"

Three songs were picked for Lefty's next session. The first song, "Yesterday Just Passed My Way Again," was written by Whitey—Lefty pulled all the emotions out of this great song. Next was a Merle Haggard song, "Life's Like Poetry," and again Lefty didn't hold anything back.

This session, recorded on October 22, 1974, was the last session of Lefty's life.

CHAPTER SEVENTEEN

FOREVER AND ALWAYS

Lefty started 1975, with a new single, "Life's Like Poetry." It was released in February, but was hardly noticed. Billboard held on to it for only seven weeks and it made a showing of sixty-seven on the charts, such a bad showing for such a good song. Lefty was excited, though, about his next album project. He had wanted to record a gospel album for years;, not a remake of all the old songs, but new songs that he wanted to write with all his buddies.

Lefty and Alice hadn't gotten along in years. People who knew them well couldn't figure out what kept them together. They should have gone their separate ways a long time ago. Alice had every reason in the world to divorce Lefty, and Lefty may have had a reason or two of his own, or at least he thought so.

Lefty and Alice separated in January 1975. She filed for divorce on April 30, 1975; charging cruel and inhuman treatment. She wanted alimony, of course, and their 1970 Oldsmobile, a vacant lot in Winnsboro, Texas, a sixty-eight acre piece of undeveloped land in Collinwood, Tennessee, and a trailer house to put on the property. Last, she wanted the big house to be sold and the money to be applied to the Collinwood acres. Whether Alice meant to go through with the divorce, or just wanted something to hold over Lefty's head to try and help him straighten up, we'll never know. Lefty, for his part, was trying to straighten up, starting with recording a gospel album, and he wanted to get off the road completely. That just wasn't happening. Someone had to work to bring in money to live on.

Lefty somehow managed to hold on. Shorty Hall and Bill Phillips drove him to a show in Indianapolis. "Lefty lay in the backseat and talked about not being able to do the show," Shorty remembered, "but he did great and even got a standing ovation."

ABC Records released "Falling" written by Whitey Shafer and Doodle Owens, and sung by Lefty, as a single on July 5, 1975. It was a fine song and well produced; however, it stayed on the charts for eleven weeks and peaked at number fifty.

Lefty was booked at the Delaware State Fair for July 19th, and a few days earlier Lefty was with Doodle Owens and Shorty Hall. He talked about the new gospel album, and told them how excited he was about writing songs for it.

"We can all write songs," he said, "and we'll just take the best ones."

Shorty said, "Suddenly, Lefty grabbed his head, you know right above his eyes. He had felt a terrific pain. Lefty went into the bathroom and stayed there a long time. Finally, I went in to check on him and he was having a real bad time. I took him home and made sure he had something to eat. Then I went on home myself."

On July 18th, Lefty was packing his clothes, getting ready to leave, to go to Delaware. He and Shorty had a redeye flight at three o'clock the next morning. When Alice and Lois came by to see him, they said he looked awful, and it was apparent he didn't want to go. Lois said he was saying that he had done everything in his life and there wasn't anything else he wanted to do. He didn't want to go out there anymore.

"I've done more than I ever wanted to do and I'm so tired I can't hardly stand it."

Shorty came by later and brought an eight pack of Miller ponies. He left saying he had to go and get ready for the flight. Now came the part Lefty hated the most, he was alone.

Lefty went to bed early, but woke up just after midnight lying on the floor next to the bed. He had thrown up on himself. He tried to get up, but couldn't. Then he tried to put a shirt on, but he couldn't do that either. He knew what had happened. He struggled to grasp the phone and call Alice; he told her he'd had a stroke. Alice called an ambulance and hurried over to the Little House. Lefty asked her to help him up; he didn't want anyone to see him like that lying on the floor. Alice calmed him, saying that he should lie still and everything would be all right. When the ambulance got there they couldn't help Lefty any more than Alice could. They were community volunteers, not trained paramedics. They put Lefty in the ambulance and headed to the hospital. Lefty had a massive cerebral hemorrhage on the way. He was in a coma by the time they reached the hospital.

Alice called Lois early the next morning and told her to get to the hospital as quickly as possible. Marlon and Rickey were camping out down on the Collinwood property, so the sheriff's department sent a patrolman out to tell them. Momma and Daddy were notified around ten o'clock, Pacific time, on the morning of the nineteenth. Bill was at home in Bakersfield when he got the call from Daddy. Betty was living in Las Vegas and was at home when Momma called her. Betty told Momma she should get on a plane and that she would fly out and meet her. Momma said she was too scared to fly, that they were going to drive.

Mae was contacted by Momma, who told her the same thing. It was agreed Daddy and Momma would drive through Bakersfield to pick up Bill and then drive over to Betty's in Las Vegas. In the meantime, Mae would fly into Vegas, Betty would pick her up, and together they would wait for the others. Momma, Daddy, Bill, Mae, and Betty would drive to Nashville together. Either Alice or Lois called Allen and Jimmy, who were in Yuma,

Arizona, and told them that Lefty had suffered a stroke and that they would be kept informed.

I was in Puyallup, Washington, playing a fair with Red Simpson, Buddy Allen, and the Canadian Sweethearts. Dennis Knutson, my songwriting friend, was standing with me when the promoter came up and told me that I had an emergency call. On my last show that evening I told the audience that Lefty was in the hospital due to a stroke.

Johnnie Lee was called; she was still living in Sulphur Springs, Texas, and she immediately made plans to leave for Nashville. Lesley was living and working in Houston when he heard the news that afternoon. All the Frizzell family had been notified. The family was in motion, each one making plans from different locations around the country. We all knew this was not a normal visit to the hospital; we knew this was a lot more serious.

Betty picked Mae up at McCarren Airport in Vegas at 2:00 P.M., and they waited for Daddy, Momma, and Bill to get in from California. They arrived at around 5:00 P.M. Daddy came in the house and immediately called and talked to Alice.

"Alice, we've made it to Betty's and everyone is packed and ready to go. How's Sonny?"

"Well, the doctors are keeping a close watch on him and with all the prayers going on here he's just got to pull through."

Daddy sighed. "Keep up those prayers; we're on our way. Betty, Mae, and Bill are coming with us to help drive and look after AD. We have to stop every so often because her asthma is so bad. She has to use her breathing machine a lot and we have to plug it in, but I'll call you as often as we can."

Alice's voice sounded tired and weak when they said goodbye. The last words Daddy heard Alice say as she hung up were, "Drive safe and please hurry."

Betty and Mae helped our mother into the back seat of the Cadillac. Betty hugged her daughter, Tina, and told her she would keep in touch. Daddy slid in behind the wheel and Bill got in the on passenger side. The Frizzell Cadillac pulled out of Las Vegas at 6:00 P.M., Saturday, July 19, 1975, heading for Nashville. Momma had a washcloth and a small ice chest on the floor of the car. She would dip the cloth into the ice water and wash her face whenever she felt faint. No one felt much like talking, each person was deep in his or her own thoughts. They all heard and felt the deep sorrow in Momma when she softly cried, "I should have flown; oh my God, I should have flown."

Allen and our nephew, Jimmy, Mae's son, were playing music in Yuma, Arizona. They had been there a week and were being held over for two more weeks. About 11:30 P.M. the manager walked up to the bandstand and motioned for Allen. Allen leaned down and the manager told him that he had an emergency phone call. Allen asked Jimmy to keep the music going. He put down his guitar and walked off the bandstand and down the hall to the little office. Jimmy played two more songs and took a break. He set down his bass and went to find Allen. Allen was sitting on a stool, leaning against an old desk, and his head was cradled in his arms. He was staring at the pool of tears at his feet.

Jimmy said, "Allen, I don't care if we do have another set to play. I can't do it, man, I'm through. I've had it, there's no more music left in me."

Allen lifted his head. "Look, Jimmy, I won't blame you if you don't. If you want to go back to the room, I'll get someone to take you but, as for me, I'm gonna play. I believe in my heart Sonny would've wanted us to finish out the night, to play the music and not quit until it's over. We'll be going to Nashville in the morning but tonight I'm playing my music. Make up your mind, are you staying or going?"

Jimmy was silent for a long while, head bent looking at the ground. Finally, he said, "Okay, but I'm not gonna sing."

Jeanette, my wife at the time, was staying at my Momma and Daddy's house in Tipton, California. She had said goodbye to them earlier that day. She promised that she would stay by the phone and relay all information to me in Washington.

The Frizzell Cadillac, with our Momma, Daddy, Brother Bill and two sisters, had left Las Vegas around six that afternoon. The next stop was Williams, Arizona. Daddy pulled into a truck stop and took Momma's breathing machine inside to plug it in. While Momma was using the machine, Daddy fueled the car. Bill and Mae got out and went inside. Betty walked over to a pay phone and called the hospital in Nashville. She talked to the nurse in the intensive care unit.

"How's my brother?"

"Well, he's still with us."

"I hope you don't mind, I may be calling a lot. I'm traveling across country with Lefty's mom and dad and we just need to know how he's doing."

"Don't worry. You can call anytime you want to."

Betty told Momma that Sonny was doing all right. "Momma, you know how strong Sonny is. He's not gonna let something like this get him down. He always says you've got to have a strong will and you know he's got lots of that."

Sunday morning, July 20th, the big Cadillac rolled into Amarillo, Texas. Daddy drove the car to a gas pump, and everyone got out. While Daddy pumped the gas, Bill and Mae went inside the station and came back out after a few minutes. Daddy, after filling the car, pulled over to the side of the station. Daddy went in to pay for the gas and then walked over to Betty. Betty had once again made the call to the hospital. She asked for the intensive care unit and told the nurse who she was. "I'm calling to see how my brother is."

The nurse hesitated. "I'm sorry. He didn't make it through the night."

If the nurse said anything more we'll never know, because, all of a sudden, the phone seemed very hot and Betty dropped it. She turned and looked at Daddy. She didn't have to say a word, he knew.

Bill and Mae were walking around by the car. Momma was sitting in it on the driver's side with the door open. They all saw Daddy and Betty at the same time. Not a word passed between them. They didn't go or reach out to each other; no one comforted the other; each was dealing with the news of this tragic event in their own, separate way.

Momma collapsed against the steering wheel; Bill was bent over by the hood; Mae was crying at the back of the car; Daddy was standing close by Momma. Betty was standing on the passenger side of the car half out of her mind with grief. Once the first wave of sadness passed, Betty looked around and noticed that all the other people at the station were staring at them. Somewhere in a part of her mind she wondered, *Why is everyone staring at us?*

On Saturday evening, July 19, 1975, Lefty had passed on. Alice called Jeanette in California. Now she had to deliver the news to me.

Jeanette, after talking to me, called Lesley. He, in turn, dialed Johnnie Lee in Sulphur Springs, and told her the news. He made arrangements to pick her up early the next morning and together they would drive to Nashville.

I had talked to Jeanette several times that day, and everything had pretty much stayed the same with Lefty's condition. I did my shows and went back to the motel to wait for any news of what was going on. Even though I knew the situation was bad, I just couldn't believe anything like death could take my brother. In my mind, Lefty just wouldn't put up with dying. He was only forty-seven years old, and he was way too tough to die young.

Dennis Knutson and the Canadian Sweethearts had

stayed with me to keep me company and to be there for me if anything happened that night. We were all sitting around the motel lounge when the call came in around eleven o'clock.

The wall phone rang. I picked it up. "Hello, this is me." Everyone held their breath. I dropped the phone. My knees buckled and I sank to the floor. All my friends were at my side immediately. Dennis tried to pick me up, and with help from the others, he got me to my room.

I sat down on the bed for a moment, tears were flowing from my eyes. Dennis was standing by the bed and he was crying, too. I got up and walked into the bathroom. Fully clothed, I stepped into the shower and turned on the cold water.

My brother, Sonny, was gone.

The great Lefty Frizzell . . . Gone.

Lesley left Houston early Sunday morning and drove to Sulphur Springs to pick up Johnnie Lee. They headed toward Nashville. Sulphur Springs to Nashville is normally a twelve-hour drive, but Lesley cut that time down considerably.

Reservations for me to fly out of the Seattle-Tacoma airport were made for Sunday morning. Dennis later said that when he drove me to the airport and watched me board the plane, he thought he had never seen anyone so sad. He hoped I wouldn't miss my connecting flight in Dallas because I seemed to be in a daze, and seemed unaware of my surroundings.

Allen and Jimmy were dropped off at the Phoenix airport late Sunday morning. They purchased tickets to Nashville with a stop over in Dallas. Neither had slept much and they had eaten nothing, but their minds were not on themselves that day.

Sunday morning Russell, Betty's husband, woke up their daughter, Tina, and gave her a plane ticket to Nashville. He had talked to Alice earlier and found out that Lefty was gone, but didn't tell Tina. He simply said, "I think you need to be there with your mother and family." Tina got ready and Russell drove her to the Las Vegas airport.

I got off the plane in Dallas and after asking where my departure gate was, I started walking in that direction. It's a good thing I had an hour between flights because I was walking very slowly with my head down. I met Allen and Jimmy, who were looking for the same plane to Nashville. Actually, I walked right into Allen.

"Excuse me, I..." I looked up and saw Allen, then I saw Jimmy. Confused I said, "Where in the hell am I, and where did you guys come from?"

We flew to Nashville together, I rented a car, and we drove to Hendersonville. Cole and Garrett Funeral Home is on the main drag on the east side of town, and across the street was a little hamburger stand. I parked the car in front of the hamburger place. We got out and ordered a drink. We stood there looking at the funeral home across the street. It took us a while before we got back in the car and drove across the street. I got out and went inside. After a minute I came out and told Jimmy and Allen that we were at the wrong place. There was a sigh of relief as we headed for Goodlettsville, only a few miles away.

When we walked into the funeral home, Alice, Lois, Marlon, and Rickey were in the parlor. They welcomed the first Frizzell arrivals. After several attempts I made my way up to my brother, Sonny. Allen and Jimmy followed me.

When Tina's plane arrived in Nashville, Marlon was at the airport to pick her up. He told her that his dad had passed away. She had never felt such grief as she did on the ride back to the funeral home.

As Tina made her way up to Lefty's side, she thought about something he once said to her: "You are like a rosebud; so young and beautiful, yet so fragile, and one of these days you are going to bloom into a beautiful lady." Tina went to Alice and asked if it would be all right to put a rose in the casket with him, and Alice told her that it would be fine. Tina went out and bought a fully bloomed rose, and ever so gently, laid it beside Lefty.

Lesley and Johnnie Lee arrived late that evening at the funeral home. They joined the rest of the rest of the family inside.

The Frizzell car was heading east on Interstate 40. All the occupants were so deep in their own misery that they hardly knew where they were, much less paying any attention to the fact that Daddy had pulled out into the oncoming lane to pass a truck. He didn't seem to be in a hurry to go around. If he noticed the oncoming truck, he wasn't doing anything to avoid it. No one else said anything about the approaching truck either.

Betty, however, who was sitting directly behind Daddy, saw the truck. She thought, *Well, it looks like we're all gonna die… Who cares?*

Daddy must have finally realized how close the approaching truck was, because he threw on the brakes and swerved back behind the truck he was trying to pass, right in the nick of time. Still, no one spoke immediately.

After a minute or two Bill said very calmly, "Daddy, why don't you pull over and I'll take it awhile."

Bill had been driving for an hour or so when Daddy muttered to himself, "I knew it, I felt it last night. A feeling came over me and I knew it. I didn't want to say anything, but I knew it."

On the afternoon of July 21st, the Frizzell Cadillac pulled up to the funeral home.

The morning of July 22, 1975, the family gathered at the big house before going to the funeral services. Johnny Cash had sent over enough barbeque and fix'ns to feed the town of Hendersonville. Alice was about ready to leave when the phone rang. She answered it. I was standing there when she answered it. "Hello." She stood listening for a moment, then she handed me the phone. "David, can you take care of this for me?" I took the phone and looked at her. I saw tears in her eyes.

"Hello, who is this?"

A man's voice said, "I want to come by and pick up one of Lefty's show suits and a pair of boots. He told me I could have one, so I thought I'd come by and get it now."

"Which suit and boots did you say he gave you?" I asked.

"Well, he didn't say any specific one. I guess he was gonna let me just pick one out."

"Wow, what a guy! I tell you what, I'll pick you one out and you can meet me behind the funeral home in a couple of hours. I'll give it to you then. What do ya say?"

"All right, I'll see you there."

I told all my brothers, especially Lesley, to be on the look out for anyone coming to pick up any clothing, but no one showed. For Alice's sake I notified the Hendersonville police and they put a policeman at both houses.

Flowers completely covered the viewing room from floor to ceiling. It took seven vans to take them out to the gravesite. The pallbearers were Abe Mulkey, Tommy Smith, Dallas Frazier, Rusty Adams, Doodle Owens, and Whitey Shafer. Alice had arranged for the first limo to carry our parents, out of respect for them.

The two and a half mile drive from the funeral home to the gravesite was lined with people on both sides of the road. Some were crying, others were waving goodbye. They were all there, fans of Lefty's and fans of country music, all saying a final goodbye to a legend.

The most beautiful flowers in the world were placed around the gravesite. One in particular was sent by Merle Haggard with a card reading: "Life's Like Poetry and thank yous are Always Late; we'll miss you Forever and Always."

EPILOGUE

When Lefty died, the impact was awesome, like the world was coming to an end.

I remember saying, "I can't believe it; you're not going to tell me he's dead! Sonny would not put up with it. He's too strong! You're lying to me."

Even today, I still can't believe it. I thought no stroke in the world could get this guy! He was too mean. He was too strong. In my dreams, after he passed away, he and I would be dodging bullets, and he never got hit. He never died. For years, every night, Sonny and I would be doing this or that, then all of a sudden, people would be trying to hurt him. I would try to help him, and I would get hurt trying to make sure people didn't bother him.

Then one night, I had a different dream. This one was more real than any other dream I have ever had; it was so clear that it was like I was really there. It was almost like a press conference. My dad, Sonny, and I were standing together and in the background were Willie and Merle. They were both there talking to people, like at a press conference, and while they were talking Sonny turned to our dad and said, "I was only joking. I never did die. I never really was hurt that bad."

I got mad! For the first time in my life I took hold of his shoulder and I shook him as hard as I could and I said, "Don't you ever, ever play like that again!"

Since then I have not dreamed of Sonny. I have tried to figure out that dream and the only thing I can come up with is that during those years I felt inferior. I felt like I had never and would never accomplish anything like Sonny had.

I kept telling myself, "Hey, Sonny is the best and you'll always be second." But at that time, in that dream, I felt that I was equal to him. For the first time in my life I stood up to him. It was only in my dream, but now, in my mind, we are the same—brothers.

A few months after Lefty passed away, Willie played the Golden Nugget in Las Vegas. Tina went down to the show and ended up backstage. Willie asked Tina to call her mother, Betty, and invite her to the show. Betty declined, saying she just wasn't in the mood to go out.

The next afternoon Connie, Willie's wife, called Betty and asked her to join them for the show that evening. She said that Willie wanted to talk to her. She added that Willie's mother would be there, too. That evening Betty joined Connie, Willie's mother, and actor Dennis Hopper. After the show Connie took Betty backstage. Willie told Betty that sometime back he had recorded a tribute album to Lefty. He had stopped the release of it after Lefty passed away and was not going to release it until a more appropriate time. He wanted her to tell the family, and then he asked for our mom and dad's address because he wanted to send them a copy of it. Betty also received a copy of the album.

Once, when Mae was really young, Sonny asked her, "Who am I to you?"

"You're Santa Claus; you're magic."

When we were kids, Sonny would tell us, "Your world is small, but find a dream and never let go. When you have achieved your dream, your world will be as big as you want it to be."

Lefty was inducted into the Country Music Hall of Fame in October 1982.

SONG CREDITS

The following songs are used by permission of Peer International Corporation.
"In The Jailhouse Now" by Jimmie Rodgers
"Pistol Packin' Papa" by Waldo O'Neal and Jimmie Rodgers
"I'm Lonely And Blue" by Elsie McWilliams and Jimmie Rodgers
"I Know You're Lonesome While Waiting For Me"
    by Lefty Frizzell
"Blue Yodel #4" by Jimmie Rodgers
"Blue Yodel #8" by Jimmie Rodgers
"If You've Got the Money, I've Got The Time"
    by James A. Beck and Lefty Frizzell
"Mom and Dad's Waltz" by Lefty Frizzell
"Forever and Always" by Lefty Frizzell and Lessie Lyle
"I'm An Old, Old Man Trying To Live While I Can"
    by Lefty Frizzell
"We Crucified Our Jesus" by Lefty Frizzell
"That's The Way Love Goes" by Lefty Frizzell and Sanger Shafer
"My Rough and Rowdy Ways"
    by Elsie McWilliams and Jimmie Rodgers

The following song is used by the permission of Peer International Corporation
and Sure Fire Music.
"I Love You a Thousand Ways" by Lefty Frizzell

The following song has never been published.
"Please Be Mine, Dear Blue Eyes" by Lefty Frizzell

DISCOGRAPHY

CHART POSITION AND WEEKS ON CHARTS

DATE	PEAK (WKS.)	WEEKS ON CHART	SONG
10/28/50	1 (3)	22	If You've Got the Money, I've Got the Time
11/4/50	1 (3)	32	I Love You a Thousand Ways
3/3/51	4	12	Look What Thoughts Will Do
3/10/51	7	2	Shine, Shave, Shower (It's Saturday)
4/14/51	1 (11)	27	I Want To Be with You Always
		B Side	My Baby's Just Like Money
8/4/51	1 (12)	28	Always Late (With Your Kisses)
8/8/51	2 (8)	29	Mom and Dad's Waltz
10/13/51	6	9	Travelin' Blues
		B Side	Blue Yodel No. 6
12/22/51	1 (3)	21	Give Me More, More, More (Of Your Kisses)
1/12/52	7	5	How Long Will It Take (To Stop Loving You)
4/12/52	2 (1)	12	Don't Stay Away (Til Love Grows Cold)
		B Side	You're Here, So Everything's All Right
9/27/52	6	5	Forever (And Always)
		B Side	I Know You're Lonesome While Waiting for Me
12/6/52	3	9	I'm an Old, Old Man (Tryin' To Live While I Can)
		B Side	You're Just Mine (Only in My Dreams)
5/23/53	8	1	(Honey, Baby, Hurry!) Bring Your Sweet Self Back to Me
		B Side	Time Changes Things
2/20/54	8	2	Run 'Em Off
		B Side	The Darkest Moment

DATE	PEAK (WKS.)	WEEKS ON CHART	SONG
1/15/55	11	4	I Love You Mostly
		B Side	Mama
11/24/58	13	11	Cigarettes and Coffee Blues (written by Marty Robbins)
		B Side	You're Humbuggin' Me
6/8/59	6	15	The Long Black Veil
		B Side	Knock Again, True Love
4/27/63	23	2	Forbidden Lovers
		B Side	A Few Steps Away
11/9/63	30	1	Don't Let Her See Me Cry
		B Side	James River
1/11/64	1 (4)	26	Saginaw, Michigan
		B Side	The Rider
8/8/64	28	11	The Nester
		B Side	The Rider
1/16/65	50	2	'Gator Hollow
		B Side	Make That One for the Road a Cup of Coffee
5/1/65	12	15	She's Gone, Gone, Gone
		B Side	Confused
10/16/65	36	5	A Little Unfair
11/13/65	41	4	Love Looks Good on You
10/15/66	51	6	I Just Couldn't See The Forest (For the Trees)
		B Side	Everything Keeps Coming Back (But You)
3/25/67	49	10	You Gotta Be Puttin' Me On
		B Side	A Song from a Lonely Heart
9/2/67	63	4	Get This Stranger Out of Me
		B Side	Hobo's Pride
8/10/68	59	3	The Marriage Bit
		B Side	When the Grass Grows Green Again
3/22/69	64	4	An Article from Life
		B Side	Only Way To Fly

DATE	PEAK (WKS.)	WEEKS ON CHART	SONG
8/22/70	49	10	Watermelon Time in Georgia
		B Side	Out of You
8/12/72	59	10	You, Babe
		B Side	When It Rains the Blues
9/22/73	43	13	I Can't Get Over You To Save My Life
		B Side	Somebody's Words
2/16/74	25	12	I Never Go Around Mirrors
		B Side	That's the Way Love Goes
6/15/74	52	9	Railroad Lady
		B Side	If I Had Half the Sense (A Fool Was Born With)
9/21/74	21	14	Lucky Arms
		B Side	If She Just Helps Me Get Over You
2/22/75	67	7	Life's Like Poetry
		B Side	Sittin' and Thinkin'
7/5/75	50	11	Falling
		B Side	I Love You a Thousand Ways

INDEX

SONG TITLES